DUARTE

DUARTE
MY STORY

José Napoleón Duarte
with Diana Page

with a preface by
The Reverend Theodore M. Hesburgh, C.S.C.,
of the University of Notre Dame

G. P. Putnam's Sons
New York

G. P. Putnam's Sons
Publishers Since 1838
200 Madison Avenue
New York, NY 10016

Typeset by Fisher Composition, Inc.

Library of Congress Cataloging-in-Publication Data

Duarte, José Napoleón.
Duarte: my story.

1. Duarte, José Napoleón.
2. El Salvador—Politics and government—1979–   .
3. El Salvador—Presidents—Biography.   I. Title.
F1488.42.D83A3   1986   972.84'053'0924   [B]   86-16983
ISBN 0-399-13202-3

Printed in the United States of America
1   2   3   4   5   6   7   8   9   10

To the youth of the world, especially the Scout movement, to my own children and to the Salvadoran people:

Above all, I believe that we must have convictions and principles in order to serve our fellow citizens, in order to leave this world a better place than we found it.

I want to dedicate this book to my wife, Ney, who has not only inspired me, but also renewed my determination to live according to my principles through her own total dedication to the needy.

Contents

Preface

I began this preface with the sure knowledge, born of many years of experience, that there will be not a few readers who will severely criticize me for doing so. They will read this book, not to attempt to understand José Napoleón Duarte, but as a means of finding old or new chinks in his armor.

All of us have chinks in our armor. The only way to avoid criticism is to sit on the fence and do nothing, except maybe to criticize others who are trying to create a better and more just world. I have received dozens of letters from critics who wrote them safely from comfortable quarters far from the fray. I am sure President Duarte has received many more, because he has been sitting, by his own choice, in the middle of the target, the most critical spot of all.

He is attempting to change a situation that has existed for over a half century, in a "culture of violence," to use his own words. Neither he nor his programs of action are perfect. But at least he is and has been trying to ameliorate a situation he has inherited. Either the Right or the Left could kill him at any time. God knows, both have tried often enough. No matter how hard he tries, there is no assurance whatever of either success or survival, for himself or his family. I know that Napo, as I have called him for over forty years, is an honest man, vowed to justice and a better life for his people. He tells his story in an honest and straightforward way. While he shares his dreams, he also admits to his mistakes.

When he asked me to write a preface to this autobiography, I was happy to do so, even while acknowledging the risks involved. One does not do less for one's friends, and Napo has been my friend from the day in 1945 when I threatened to toss him out of the first class I taught at Notre Dame, Christian Virtues, because he was talking Spanish to a countryman sitting next to him in the front row. More of that later, in his own account.

All I would ask of the honest reader is to try to understand, in the pages that follow, how one man has tried and is trying to make a difference, despite the heavy odds against him. More than all-knowing criticism from afar, he needs prayers.

This is a book about a man who started out to become a civil engineer and ended up—partly at my urging—a social engineer, and one, I might add, who has found justice a lot more difficult to construct than public housing. It also is the story of his small, anguished country, bent by poverty, violence and political corruption.

And it is yet another affirmation of his dream for his land, an affirmation not stitched together from old campaign oratory, but rooted in deed. Whatever one might think of José Napoleón Duarte's ideas, they come earned in suffering. Time and again, his convictions have been put to stern tests, from being beaten near to death in the wake of a stolen election, through seven years of exile, to the despicable 1985 kidnapping of his daughter by Salvadoran guerrillas.

Duarte's political philosophy is not a complex, nuanced one. It is as simple and as straightforward as the Boy Scout oath that so impressed him as a boy. It began, as he relates, when he joined a Catholic study group in San Salvador in 1960. There, he found inspiration in the social teachings of Pope Leo XIII as refined by others, including the great French philosopher Jacques Maritain, and Chilean President Eduardo Frei, who set them in contrast to the atheistic determinism of Karl Marx. "Christians must reject class warfare and materialism," Duarte notes early on in this autobiography. "Christian Democrats believe in a new social order built not on materialist values, but on solidarity among human beings," a solidarity resting on the dignity each has as a child of God.

Duarte began to seek that new social order in 1964, shortly after founding the Christian Democratic Party in El Salvador. He ran for mayor of the country's capital only to find himself speaking to streets emptied by the fear of the ruling military. He is still seeking it more than two decades later as the first freely elected president of El Salvador in more than half a century. And, while no one has to cower inside out of fear for one's life anymore, democracy has not made life easy for the citizens of this Central American country. The continuing problem is described by Duarte as the lack of "political space." The political space he refers to is in the middle, between the Right of the old oligarchy–military coalition and the Left, whose guerrillas want to wrest power violently by civil war rather than try to win it peacefully by vote.

The two other major players in El Salvador's drama are the Catholic Church, exercising a newly articulated "option for the poor" in distancing itself from the former ruling classes with whom it has been historically associated, and the United States, continuing the search for a coherent Latin-American policy that signals hope to the oppressed while denying any advantage to Communism, which always fishes in troubled waters.

The contradictions in American foreign policy, such as democracy at home and support of totalitarian regimes in Latin America, concerned Duarte very early in his political career. In his lifetime he has seen American attitudes go from complete indifference toward human-rights abuses in Latin America to periodic certification of human-rights progress as a requisite to aid. Duarte asserts that President Kennedy's Alliance for Progress "only put a new face on old regimes." He notes on more than one occasion that, at crucial junctures in the life of his country, the United States was distracted by events much further from its backyard— hostages in Iran, a war in the Falkland Islands. And the view from the North was not always infallible. "There was always a difference between what the United States thought could be done in El Salvador and the results when Washington applied its formulas," he observes. Since Duarte openly acknowledges that he owes his life to American intervention after his arrest by Salvadoran military leaders in 1972, and he frequently expresses gratitude for U.S. help, his is the important criticism of a friend.

My own personal criticism of the often prevailing U.S. policy for Central America is that it tends to put too much emphasis on military solutions. One cannot be naïve or unmindful of the military morass that is Central America today, on the Left and on the Right. However, it is my deepest conviction that there really is no ultimate military solution to the basic problem, which is the historical cancer of social injustice, the crass denial of human rights, the shattered economy, the wanton and cruel killings on both sides, the almost total lack of the most basic human aspirations for dignity and personal development. Violence is not eliminated by more violence, injustice by more injustice.

While one military scheme for total victory—and presumably for peace—follows on the heels of each preceding military disaster, one should be able to envision a different use of the billions of dollars and thousands of lives that past military strategies have cost. We have seen in recent years the utter bankruptcy of military regimes in South America, including the one in Chile under Pinochet, the only surviving one.

Why not seize the initiative in Central America and declare that military solutions are obsolete and that the wave of the future is economic development and a total restoration of social justice for all the people, whatever that would entail. It would certainly cost less than all the military solutions that have been tried successively and have failed, causing an incredible loss of lives and money.

I realize that this would involve a twin solution for El Salvador and Nicaragua, but their futures are inevitably tied together, as are all those of the other small nations in the region. In fact, all of Central America could prosper together, rather than suffer together and add to each country's afflictions. It would be comical, were it not so tragic—the guerrillas will not talk with the government in El Salvador except to discuss the sharing of power, whereas the government will not talk to the Contras in Nicaragua because they don't want to share the power they have grabbed.

In my opinion, a unitary solution for the region makes more sense than individual ad hoc solutions for so many small nations with common problems and conflicting answers. But all of this gets me too far afield. Let us return to Duarte's account of his special problems in El Salvador.

Regarding the Church, Duarte sees its social objectives in Latin America as being squarely in line with his own. He devotes a whole chapter to the notorious 1980 murder of three sisters and a laywoman missionary, for which five Salvadoran Guardsmen were convicted four long years later. The incident strained Duarte's relationship with some Church people (as well as with some Congressmen), and his detailed account will probably not convince those who believe that military higher-ups ordered the killings and are still free. What the chapter does show clearly is a country where justice is shackled by inept law, uncooperative security forces (five independent agencies), incompetent investigative personnel, witnesses lacking courage, judges lacking integrity, and a protective old-boy network. Duarte rightly calls the women "martyrs, perhaps saints" to "a mentality created by years of repressive violence, by the fear of revolutionary violence and by the corruption of a legal system that permits atrocities to take place without any control."

The Salvadoran military looms large in Duarte's story. Early in his career, he taught topography and ballistics at El Salvador's Military Academy. "The formation of military officers at the Academy probably has more influence on the nation's politics than any other institution," he notes. "I could have used this opportunity, but my mind was on engineering, not on politics." As it happened, Duarte was to have many opportunities to make up for this missed one. His early impressions of El Salvador's repressive military regimes, which occasionally sugarcoated a coup with talk of social change and blatantly stole what elections they allowed, were confirmed in his 1972 detainment, beating and forced exile to Venezuela. In 1979, he balked at a Christian Democratic pact with a postcoup military junta, believing it would compromise the party. He was uncomfortable with the military mind. "One of the problems with analyzing the military is that officers do not fit neatly into political categories. They change. Because they lack an ideological formation, the military decide questions on a case-by-case basis, often influenced by whoever spoke to them most recently." Nonetheless, he soon found himself on a ruling junta with the military, a move he made only because he saw it as a stepping-stone to a legitimate democratic election, but a decision his critics still cite today to "prove" he is a pawn for the military, despite the fact that he did get the elections and the first legitimate government in decades. Slowly, Duarte was able to gain the confidence of the military, primarily by suggesting alternative tactics to its knee-jerk repression, tactics that proved successful. Eventually, the ideological flexibility of the military mind proved an asset in gaining its support for the Christian Democratic reform agenda, and Duarte today claims that great change has taken place in the Salvadoran military. He credits them with protecting the last (March 1985) of the four elections in four years that have led to a Christian Democratic majority in the country's National Assembly. "The rapprochement between the people and the armed forces is essential to bringing peace to our country. The armed forces have learned that this war cannot be won with guns and helicopters alone," he writes.

As an official U.S. observer of the first election leading to the presidency for Duarte—the March 1982 election of a sixty-member constituent assembly—I could see the new role of the military. Instead of being in charge of making sure the election was fixed for its candidate, the job of the Army was instead to ensure honest balloting. March 28, 1985, was a day that renewed one's faith in democracy. Voting with their feet, more than a million people defied guerrilla intimidation to cast ballots, some standing in lines that stretched miles over the dirt roads between villages. A helicopter ferried our inspection team from village to village, often in guerrilla-controlled provinces, and everywhere people tired of bloodshed were lined up to vote for an alternative. In one stop, I came across a funeral cortege. A mother grieved for her young son, a victim of the civil war. There was no priest with the burial party, so I blessed the mutilated body of a young soldier who was defending the right of the people to vote and did what I could to comfort the mother. This was the pain and tragedy people were longing to be free of.

In his last chapter, Duarte says he wants to write a sequel when he finishes his presidency. "I would," he says, "like to write how we made peace. . . . how the structure of the economy changed. . . . how the political structures became vibrantly democratic; how the social structure became multifaceted, representing everyone with dignity. . . . how our values changed. . . . This is my dream." He goes on to describe the continuing goals of his social revolution as humanization, pacification, democratization, individual participation and economic revitalization. He is not sanguine that the guerrillas can be brought into this dream. The surge of optimism that accompanied the La Palma peace meeting with rebel leaders has gone, but Duarte still seeks a common ground that can end the killing and destruction. He seeks power-sharing through the electoral process rather than out of the barrel of a gun, but this is not popular in a world of violence. Whatever the political implications, I think he is right.

May I conclude where I began. In a world of violence, injustice and strong ideological convictions, Duarte can seem compromised by his own deeply held convictions. I am always remembering the familiar Mexican saying, "So far from God and so close to the United States." This may be part of Duarte's problem—although I doubt he is ever far from God, he is close and almost totally dependent on the United States. He must always walk a narrow line, but I am convinced that he will be true to himself and his own deepest convictions. It is not an easy path to walk. Yet I hearken back to those days at Notre Dame when I tried my best to convince him that "Christian Virtues" were worth studying, worth contemplating, worth living by. I am prepared to testify that he has walked this difficult path with more risk than I, and with at least equal integrity. For that, I salute him and wish him well. I have read his story and cannot fault him for taking seriously, and at life's risk, all the good virtues I tried to teach him so long ago. When I met him some time ago in the Presidential Palace, he told my companions: "He's responsible for all my troubles. He laid out the path of virtue and I took him seriously. I may not survive him."

I hope and pray that he will. Read his story and pray for him. I do.

—THE REVEREND THEODORE M. HESBURGH, C.S.C.

Prologue

Blessed be the Lord, for he has wondrously shown his steadfast love to me when I was beset as in a besieged city.

I had said in my alarm, "I am driven from thy sight." But thou didst hear my supplications when I cried to thee for help.

—Thirty-first Psalm

THE price of political conviction is high in El Salvador. I learned this the first time I ran for president in 1972.

On the night of March 25, 1972, when the men with rifles shoved their way into the Venezuelan diplomat's home in San Salvador where I had taken refuge, my first reaction was outrage. They threw Gonzalo Espina's diplomatic credentials back in his face and knocked him down when he demanded they respect the right of political asylum. They even hit his wife. After handcuffing me, one of them struck me with his rifle butt.

"Wait. Not here," said the leader. Although they did not wear uniforms, I recognized the leader as a police officer.

They pushed me into the back of their Buick, face down on the floor. I realized then the price I was going to pay for my belief in democracy. A knife blade slashed my shirt. The man used the piece of cloth he cut to blindfold me. They had me under their feet, hammering on my head and back with their rifle butts.

"So you want to be president, you son of a bitch?" a voice growled. "You'll be president after we beat the shit out of you."

Soon we will reach some isolated edge of San Salvador, I thought, and these men are going to kill me. I imagined my wife and children learning the news, and remembered that I had prepared them for this possibility. My oldest son, Alejandro, had my instructions.

How quickly the forty-six years of my life had passed before me! I asked myself, Was it worth this? I could have lived comfortably, working just as an engineer, if I had ignored the hunger and injustice in El Salvador. For forty years, a military dictatorship had protected the interests of a few wealthy families. I had known that any serious attempt to change the structure of Salvadoran society would be countered by tricks, fraud and repression. Yet twelve years earlier I was one of a group that founded the Christian Democratic Party to try to bring peaceful change based on Christian ideology. We believed that we could lead the Salvadoran people to a better life based on democratic principles, without a violent revolution taking them toward Marxist dictatorship. I still believed this.

I thought about the noble people who had worked with me for a just, democratic society. Perhaps my sacrifice would be vindicated by those who eventually reached our goal. I knew in my heart, as I awaited death, that I would not change any of the choices I had made in my life.

These thoughts probably took only a few seconds. The effect was like an injection of tranquilizers as I prayed to God to forgive my sins. Ever since that moment, when I feel danger and despair closing in around me, I have repeated the same thoughts.

The car stopped somewhere and I was dragged out. The pain overcame my power to think as the men took turns beating me until I was unconscious.

When I became conscious again, I painfully realized that I must still be alive. They were taking my fingerprints. A smock was placed over me, and even though my eyes wouldn't focus I felt a shock of pain when a flash camera went off. I was dragged into another room, where there was a typewriter. The interrogation began.

I was so groggy I cannot remember most of the questions or my answers. Then they took me to another room, sat me in a chair, tightened the handcuffs and told me not to move. I sat there until I fell onto the floor from pain. There was no way I could move my fingers any longer, and my arms had lost feeling. I lay there all night.

The reveille brought me back to my senses, telling me that I must be in a barracks. I heard a guard come into the room. He lifted me back onto the chair and said, "I'm going to take the handcuffs and blindfold off. You can eat now, but if you turn around and look at me, you'll regret it." In front of me was a tortilla with a few beans and a cup of black coffee. I ate, and was tied up again.

The day went by, the same ritual of eating repeated before I was taken to another room. Someone said, "The prosecutor is coming." Whoever he was, his style of interrogation was one of alternating threats and questions. His main purpose was to learn who had financed my presidential campaign.

They seemed to think that some foreign power was behind my effort to defeat the military government at the polls. General Fidel Sánchez Hernández had picked his presidential successor, Arturo Molina, then expected the official party to take this colonel through the formal ritual of being elected. My Christian Democratic Party sought an alliance with other parties to unify the opposition to the ruling elite. We ended up with only two small leftist parties in our coalition. I had agreed to run for president without expecting to win. We hoped that my presidential campaign could generate enough popular enthusiasm to win a substantial number of seats in the National Legislative Assembly. Our goal was to generate such momentum that the military government would be forced to take the people's desire for a democracy into account.

We were more successful than we had dreamed. Our own tallies showed that I had won a plurality of the votes for President. But the military-supported ruling party declared themselves the winner. Arrest and torture were my rewards for victory at the polls.

"Did your campaign money come from the gringos at the embassy? We know the State Department gave you funds, but we want to know how many millions you spent on the campaign," the officer said, sneering.

The idea was so far from the truth that it was hard to take his question seriously. But I realized the officer did not understand anything about our campaign.

"Look, the campaign didn't cost millions. It cost exactly two hundred thousand colones and I have the receipts!" I answered. "We didn't get money from the Americans or any other foreign country. Most of our work was done by volunteers. We don't have to pay people the way the government party does. And what money we had came from the Salvadoran people!"

The interrogator wanted the names of people who had contributed. He pressed me until I said, "Look, it's no secret who my friends are, but because of our friendship I can't name them." He kept insisting, so I began to name people high up in the government. This shocked him. He could not use this information without getting into trouble. He changed his line of questioning. Next he claimed the Catholic Church must be financing the Christian Democrats.

"Did any priest make contributions to your campaign?"

"Yes."

"Who?"

"My brother."

My answers disconcerted the prosecutor, but he began to relax a little. The tone of voice changed. I was allowed to have a drink of water and a cigarette.

Next the interrogator questioned me about why I took part in the attempted coup after the election fraud. I told him the truth. I did not know anything about the coup until I heard the fighting in the city. Afterward, I received a telephone call from the leader of the military officers who had decided it was wrong to deny the will of the majority. They rebelled against the regime, but the government troops outnumbered the rebels, and heavy fire on rebel positions cost dozens of lives. Colonel Benjamín Mejía asked me to make a radio appeal to the population, warning them of the dangers. This was my only role in the coup. I called on the people to evacuate areas where a battle was expected and to build barricades in the streets. When the colonel advised me later that he was surrendering, I sought political asylum from the Venezuelan government.

When I finished my explanation, the prosecutor asked how I had been treated. It must have been obvious how badly I was beaten. I told him what his men had done, that my wallet had been stolen as well and I had been left blindfolded and handcuffed to sleep on the floor. Was this government procedure?

When I was taken back to a cell, the officer ordered a cot to be installed, the blindfold removed and the handcuffs taken away. I could move, I could see. From the structure of the building and the height of the room, I guessed that it was either the telecommunications building or the police headquarters. My mind immediately started looking for a way to escape.

Left alone, I found I could see through a nail hole in the boarded-up window, six feet off the floor. What I saw was a man's shoes, disappearing upward from the sidewalk. I recognized where I was. I was looking at a bus stop from the basement of the National Police headquarters!

My greatest worry was how to let my family know where I was. I pried a nail out of the wood and enlarged my hole a bit. Next I got a tiny metal piece from the cot and found some cardboard scraps under the mattress. With the nail I scrawled, "Duarte prisoner here—send word."

I pulled one of the window boards loose enough to insert my sign behind it, pushing the cardboard up against the window screen and bars. Whenever I saw someone's feet at the bus stop, I would try to get their attention by making little noises, but trying at the same time not to attract the attention of the guards. I never succeeded in getting anyone's help.

The next day I noticed that the guard who brought me food spoke with more civility in his tone. I appealed to him to let my family know I was alive. He did not respond.

In the afternoon they searched my cell. I nearly panicked at the thought of their finding my nail, my piece of metal, some pork fat I had saved as grease, or my bit of cardboard. But nothing was found. A man came in with papers he said were my statement, and forced me to sign without reading them.

Finally a guard entered to handcuff and blindfold me again. It seemed more ceremonial this time. I was given a clean shirt to put on, then cotton was taped over my eyes. They led me out of the prison cell. When I found myself being forced to lie on the floor of a large car, I thought of other times in El Salvador's history when a body has appeared in a field, handcuffed and blindfolded.

As the car drove away, I counted the seconds, concentrating on which direction we must be turning. East. A while later, we stopped at a guardpost, because I heard the order to let us pass. There was the noise of airplane motors. They took me out of the car and walked me up the steps of a small plane, still blindfolded. We must have flown for about half an hour before I felt the plane coming down. After the landing, everyone got out, leaving me alone in the plane for another half hour.

Then I heard the door open and a voice with a Guatemalan accent.

"Bring him out now," the voice said. "Take off the handcuffs and blinders."

"You take off the blindfold after we've gone," my guard replied.

When it was removed, I was sitting in a room in Guatemala's airport, being observed by the chief immigration officer, someone later told me that he was the head of Guatemala's death squad, the "White Hand." The police chief and an army officer were with him. I was offered a cup of coffee. They had orders to take me in the direction of Chimaltenango, a town in the mountains to the west. Given that I looked like a beggar, unbathed and with only rags to wear, I asked if I could go first to Guatemala City, to the home of my old friend Oscar Echeverría, to change. The immigration officer politely agreed, calling the Echeverrías to say they were bringing me over.

When Dorita Echeverría opened the door, she burst out crying.

"Oh my God, you're alive. We thought they were bringing your body here." She took me away from the guards, saying I must bathe and then leading me to the phone in the bedroom so that I could call home secretly. My wife, Inés, could not believe I was alive until she heard my voice.

The last time we had seen each other was when I drove her to her father's home before I went to seek political asylum. Our four daughters went with her, but my sons Alejandro and Napoleón had been sent to Mexico a few days earlier. Alejandro, who dropped out of the university to work on my campaign, had been the target of assassination attempts, so we had sent the boys out of the country for a while.

In Mexico, unaware of what was happening, Alejandro had picked up the morning paper. His eyes jumped down to the headline "Duarte Assassinated in El Salvador." He tried not to let anyone see that he was crying.

Ironically, we all had planned to meet in Guatemala for a postelection vacation during Easter week. In less than a week I had ended up in Guatemala, but my life and my family's had been changed forever.

My friends the Echeverrías wanted to take care of me, but the Guatemalan government was vacillating over my fate. Once I had had a bath and changed clothes, my armed Guatemalan escort drove me out of the city, then another police car caught up and ordered us back. There had been a change of plans. The Foreign Ministry decided I could have asylum in Guatemala if I abstained from all political contacts. The Echeverrías welcomed me again, and this time they were able to get medical treatment for me. The doctors were most worried about my eyesight, which was partially gone from the blows. But I eventually recovered my vision.

Although I needed time to heal, I had to make some decision about my future quickly. The options were limited. The only money I had was what my brother could wire immediately, although later I received many touching contributions. Even the poor market women of San Salvador took up a collection, a peddler sent me one colón, and a child sent me five cents. I put aside those contributions, saving them for the time when I could use them to help the people in El Salvador.

My family and friends urged me to leave Guatemala as soon as possible. They were afraid the arm of Sánchez Hernández could reach across the border. There might be an assassination attempt. The Guatemalan guards around the Echeverrías' house were suddenly withdrawn, a sign that the government was no longer responsible for me. I had to find a safe country. Mexico, for reasons that were never explained, refused to give me asylum. The U.S. ambassador was helpful, providing me with a tourist visa only. But I will never forget how generous Venezuela's Christian Democratic government was. Venezuela offered to provide me and my family with whatever we needed.

A German working for the Konrad Adenauer Foundation also came to my rescue. He arranged for my ticket to Caracas, and personally went to El Salvador to bring my wife and daughters out. I call him "Federico," because pronouncing Wolfgang Braille was too much for me. Whenever I go to Germany, we get together. I will always be grateful to the Christian Democrats in various countries who did so much for me when I seemed to have no political future at all.

President Rafael Caldera made me feel welcome and safe in Venezuela. I was met at the Caracas airport and taken to a hotel with bodyguards for protection. A few hours after I had been left to rest in my hotel room, there was a knock on the door. It was my son Alejandro. One phone call to Mexico from my brother telling him that I was headed for Venezuela, and Alejandro had boarded the next plane without even waiting for his mother. When he asked about me at the airport, the alert Venezuelan policemen held him for questioning. He finally convinced them that he was indeed my son, but he had trouble getting into the hotel until he saw Luis Herrera Campins, a Christian Democrat who would later become president of Venezuela.

"It's me, Alejandro Duarte," he called out to the astonished

Herrera, who was walking through the lobby and did not recognize him. Herrera brought him directly up to me.

That night, as Alejandro rubbed some cream on my wounds to relieve the pain, he said, "So this is how we've ended up."

"No," I told him. "This is where we begin."

1

Growing Up

IN the beginning, as a young man, I never dreamed of becoming president of El Salvador. Unlike the United States, where someone takes up politics as another takes up medicine, in my country the historical route to the presidency seemed to start at the Military Academy. Power derived from guns and those rich enough to pay for the defense of the existing system. For fifty years, the wealthy families left the bloody business of governing by force to military regimes which safeguarded the economic privileges of less than one percent of the population. To oppose the oligarchy and their guardians meant risking life, liberty and property. My parents had learned this from bitter experience.

My father had become involved in a tragic attempt to change El Salvador in the 1930s.

One of my earliest memories is my father arriving at night in the mountain village of Tejutla with the presidential candidate he was supporting, Arturo Araujo. Their campaign caravan rolled into the town in Chalatenango province, where I was staying with my aunts. It was 1931 and I was only five, but I can still remember the flickering lights of candles and kerosene lamps as people crowded into the street to welcome the presidential candidate. The next morning, my father let me ride a short way in the Dodge convertible with Araujo, and I waved a flag just as I had seen others wave them. My father had joined Araujo's campaign to improve conditions for the workingman because he himself headed an organization of Salvadoran craftsmen.

My parents both began life with nothing, depending only on their hard work and determination to get ahead. My mother's family came from that province of Chalatenango. Amelia Fuentes was one of more than forty children fathered by a rancher of Spanish origin named Bartolo Alvarado. My blue eyes come from my mother's side of the family. Orphaned at seven, my mother was raised by her aunts, who remained close long after she was sent to San Salvador to begin working as a maid, later as a seamstress.

In their humble beginnings, my family was no different from the vast majority of Salvadorans. My father's ethnic origins are typically Central American. His surname stems from an adventurer named Duarte who followed Columbus to the New World, settling in what would become the Dominican Republic. His descendants spread through the Caribbean basin. My father's maternal relatives were Mayan Indians from an area near Chiquimula, in Guatemala. My great-grandmother moved from Guatemala to the town of Santa Ana in western El Salvador, where she and her children retained their Indian dress and customs, rather than adopt the Spanish ways. To support her family, my grandmother sold punch in the marketplace, mixing milk and eggs in a caldron over fire, adding a taste of liquor.

My father was born there in 1893, the oldest of her twenty-two children by several common-law husbands. In our country, illegitimacy has been more common than legitimate births; a 1935 demographic study showed that sixty out of every one hundred babies in El Salvador were born outside the institution of marriage. All we know about my grandfather is that he was a traveling Italian engineer named Salvestrucci, who had families in San Salvador and Honduras as well.

My father, José Jesús Duarte, became a tailor's apprentice. At sixteen he left home for the capital city, San Salvador, where he eventually opened his own tailoring shop, the World of Elegance. His reputation was solidly established among the local gentry by the time he came to know my mother, Amelia, a seamstress who sewed for the wives of his customers. He already had two children by another woman, but he was unmarried and maintained his bachelor quarters in his tailor shop. After he fell in love with my mother, he still divided his time between living in the shop and living with her.

My brother Rolando was born in 1924. I followed fourteen months later, on November 23, 1925. My birth certificate says 1926, but that's because my father did not bother to register me until a year later, and rather than pay the fine imposed for late registrations he simply changed the date. In 1927, his third son, Alejandro, was born. My father loved history, which he read avidly and which became the source of the names he chose for his three sons: Rolando, Napoleón and Alejandro. It is sad that he never lived to see his son become president of his nation.

My parents did not formally marry until Alejandro wanted to enter the seminary school to become a priest; unless they did so, he could not be accepted. My mother had been trying to convince my father to wed her ever since Rolando was born. She was tenacious, a trait I inherited from her. When my parents finally exchanged vows, their union had already lasted a dozen years and endured the misfortunes that struck my father because of his commitment to political change in the early 1930s.

Just as the Depression swept over the world, a rare opportunity arose in El Salvador: a presidential election without a prearranged winner. The incumbent representative of the oligarchy, angry because none of his political heirs showed the proper deference to his wishes, capriciously opted for clean elections. Of the five aristocrats who ran, only one, Araujo, was sensitive to the needs of his countrymen. After studying engineering at the University of London and gaining practical experience at a factory in Liverpool, Araujo came home with the idea that El Salvador needed a party modeled on Britain's Labour Party. He found inspiration in Alberto Masferrer, a Salvadoran who wrote about the need for a "vital minimum," the necessities for a decent life: sufficient food, housing, health care, hygienic conditions, jobs, free time, education and justice. Araujo said the government ought to guarantee the vital minimum. For the first time, the issue of land reform in El Salvador was raised, reflecting the influence of the Mexican Revolution, which was then in its final stages.

Araujo asked my father to support his campaign. Besides managing his thriving tailor shop, my father was president of the Salvadoran Workers' Society, a place where skilled craftsmen played billiards and dominoes more than they talked politics. The billiard tables are still there today. My father agreed to work for Araujo, but members of the Workers' Society responded to calls from other candidates. At that time, politics relied on personal loyalties. There were few organizations or ideological concepts to support them, which added to everyone's amazement when Araujo launched his reformist program. He asked my father to speak in the campaign. My father had a good memory, and by rote he recited three speeches on workers' rights that were written for him by Masferrer.

Araujo was victorious in the 1931 election. As the newly elected president, he asked my father to head the labor ministry he was creating. "Thank you for the honor," my father replied, "but I'm a tailor, and you need a lawyer for that job. I could serve you better by taking charge of the production of army uniforms. That's what I know how to do." The President granted him that position, overseeing the provision of uniforms.

Araujo became the first fairly elected president of El Salvador at the worst possible moment in the country's economic history, in the midst of a world depression. The price of coffee had fallen so low that the cost of harvesting the beans was more than their market value. Landowners left the crop to rot. Coffee pickers earned nothing. Mobs formed outside the Presidential Palace demanding that Araujo fulfill his promises of agrarian reform. When he arranged for a few plots of land to be distributed, there were one hundred applicants for each plot. As conditions worsened, the disappointment in Araujo's government grew and the success of Communist organizers increased.

The Communist leader was a young lawyer named Agustín Farabundo Martí, in whose name leftist guerrillas fight today. He planned an uprising, organizing among the small pockets of remaining pure-blood Indians in the western region of the country. Farabundo Martí had traveled throughout North and Central America and had tried to fight alongside General Augusto César Sandino against the U.S. Marines in Nicaragua. Ironically, Sandino, who rejected Farabundo Martí and his Communist ideology, has become the symbol of the Marxist revolutionaries governing Nicaragua today.

As the strength of the Communists became evident among students, workers and Indian peasants, the military officers decided that Araujo was too weak and had to be deposed. The economic situation had left the government unable to meet its payroll. By not making an exception to pay the military officers, Araujo probably lost whatever support he had in the army ranks. The military acted before the Communists did. In December, they forced Araujo to flee overland to Guatemala while General Maximiliano Hernández Martínez, his vice-president, took over as president.

Although I was only six, I can still remember this moment in history because I connect it with seasickness. My mother, as Mrs. Araujo's seamstress, had become her close friend. With me by the hand, my mother accompanied the President's wife and daughter as they left for exile on a ship anchored in the harbor of La Libertad. The Pacific Ocean swells tossing around the launch that took us out to the ship made me miserably sick. Ever since that day I have been unable to board a boat without feeling seasick.

General Hernández Martínez knew that the Communist-inspired revolt was coming, but he made no move beforehand. He planned to permit the uprising to begin, then to wipe out every rebel. He captured Farabundo Martí and the other leaders on the eve of the rebellion, then waited.

On January 22, 1932, as the Izalco volcano lit the skies, the Communist Indians Organizations, with machetes and guns, attacked several towns and plantations, killing without mercy anyone serving or connected with the local well-to-do families.

The general struck back, retaliating with a brutality that exceeded many times the bloodshed of the revolt. Both sides killed tens of thousands of innocent people. Women and children who got in the way were killed as well. No records were kept of the massacre. Hernández Martínez sent soldiers into villages to kill everyone who had a machete, or who had strong Indian features. Whatever government documents did exist in this period disappeared, but Salvadorans believe somewhere from fifteen thousand to thirty thousand people died in the slaughter. Although the rebellion took place in the countryside, hundreds of people suspected of being Communists were arrested in the city. My father was among them.

Because he had taken a prominent role in Araujo's campaign and spoken in favor of reforms, my father was thrown into jail with Farabundo Martí and the Communists. Nine times he was taken from the penitentiary at dawn to the paupers' cemetery, where the firing squad carried out executions. Nine times the guns were aimed at someone else, and he found himself alive, never knowing why he was spared or when his turn would come.

My mother anguished over the fate of my father. She went to his friends, pleading with them to help save his life. She asked the wealthy men who were his tailoring clients to intervene on his behalf, but no one wanted to get involved. Only one man, José María Durán, risked going to the police to ask about my father. Durán, who ran a construction business, belonged to the same Workers' Society as my father, and they were close friends. My father was with Durán when his first child, Inés, was born. She would one day become my wife. When Durán tried to intercede for my father, the police questioned him suspiciously, charging that he had also been involved in the workers' organization. He barely escaped arrest himself.

Weeks went by and my mother despaired. One night she heard a noise in the front room, the sewing room facing the street. It was nearly dawn and she was sleeping with the children in the only other room, in back. She rose quietly and peered into the shop. No one was there, but lying on the chair was a picture of the Holy Child of Atocha. The sacred image comes from Spain, but represents the Jesus of the New World, holding a Mexican gourd. A chill went through her. There was no rational explanation for the appearance of the holy image, but she told herself, "This is a good sign, a sign of life." She knelt and prayed that my father would be saved.

That day he was freed by the police. My mother gave the holy picture to help my wife when I was jailed. We had lent the image to relatives, but when my daughter Inés Guadalupe was kidnapped I brought it back into our home to aid us.

Being freed was not the end of my father's problems. When policemen were stationed in front of his tailor shop, his clients fearfully stayed away. Bankrupt, he sold off a small piece of land bought earlier as an investment, paid his debts and started over. He began baking and selling candy. My mother continued sewing, her income sustaining us through the difficult days.

Fortunately, her burden had been lightened a little, since she had to care only for my younger brother and me. My older brother, Rolando, had gone to live with the Funes family, our neighbors, who owned a print shop and lived comfortably. The Funeses' attachment to Rolando began because the daughters liked to play with little Rolando, mothering him as if he were their live doll. The family became so fond of him they wanted him to stay. Rolando enjoyed being at their house, where he could eat as much as he liked, where he was fussed over. My mother had more than enough work, so Rolando stayed on with the Funeses. They took over his education, and by sending him to the best schools they set a precedent for me to follow.

When the Funeses enrolled Rolando in the Liceo Salvadoreño, one of the best private schools, run by the Marist brothers, my mother went to the rector and asked for a scholarship for her two younger sons. Determined that all her sons receive the best possible education, she convinced the brother in charge of the Liceo to grant me a half scholarship and Alejandro a full scholarship.

As a child I gained a reputation for too much energy and a

talent for mischief. On the first day of school one year, my friend
Matheu and I bounded into the classroom, jumping from one desk
to another until we landed in our preferred seats in the back. The
teacher ordered us to march up to the front. "You two crazies
sit here," the brother said, pointing to the first row. From
that day, our nicknames were Loco Matheu y Loco Duarte,
Crazy Matheu and Crazy Duarte. My political adversaries still
use that name, probably unaware that I have grown accustomed
to the nickname. All social reformers in my country have been
called crazy.

The economic limitations I felt as a child caused no resentment
in me. I always believed I could overcome any obstacle if I tried
hard enough. My mother made sure we never lacked the essen-
tials, but I was aware of how hard she worked. I learned not to ask
for too much. Like any child, I wanted certain toys, particularly a
model airplane one Christmas. I talked about the airplane,
dreamed about it and cried about it. My mother managed to
scrimp enough to give me a tiny airplane. When I took my little
plane down the block to the store window where the larger model
hung, I stood and stared at it. At that moment, I realized I would
have to work even harder than my mother if some of my dreams
were to materialize.

From the age of seven, I was a Cub Scout. Father Juanito, the
Scoutmaster, had his favorites in the troop, and I, the scrappy,
rambunctious kid, was not one of them. It was clear that certain
other boys got all the merit badges. I was determined to match
them, doing everything possible to be the best Scout, but Father
Juanito forced me to work harder than anyone else to get a badge.
He was unfair, but that helped to build my determination to stick
to whatever I had to do until I showed everyone I could accomplish it.

My scholastic record was not outstanding, but I had the intelligence to get by without much effort. My reputation as a star athlete pleased me much more. Sports became the area where I excelled, particularly when there was a personal challenge. One of the Liceo's older students started a junior soccer club called the Porvenir. My brother Alejandro and my best friend, Matheu, were both accepted, but the coach rejected me, saying I was too unruly. From that moment on, I knew I must get on that soccer team and become the best player. I practiced, I watched them practice. I was always hanging around the field, asking the coach to let me try out again. Finally, one day, after one more plea, he nodded, saying only the Salvadoran phrase for "Okay," "*Vaya pues.*" It had taken me two years, but I had won him over. Today my former soccer coach, Ricardo Romero, is part of my team in the government.

In addition to being persistent, I was a scrappy kid. I got into fights easily. Every Wednesday night at the Liceo, cartoons were shown to the honor students as an inducement for good scholarship and proper behavior. To make the weekly honor roll, one needed a grade of ten in every area. My other grades were good, but I never got better than a seven or an eight in deportment. Basketball practice ended just before the chosen scholars went in to see the Mickey Mouse movies. My failure to make the grade was rubbed in to me each week by one of the older boys. When he provoked a fight, I would beat him up, every Wednesday. I never saw the cartoons, but I came away with a great sense of satisfaction. Although I was short, I was strong and agile, protecting even my older brother in fights. This impulse to settle arguments by fighting physically was a defect I overcame only at the university. If I had not learned to control myself, I could never have stood the insults of my political enemies. With Major Roberto d'Aubuisson, a fistfight would probably have ended with him pulling out a gun. And I have never owned a gun.

My first political activities seemed to be leading me toward confrontation as well. During my last year of high school, the thirteen-year-old dictatorship of General Hernández Martínez began to collapse. A coup was attempted in April 1944, and though it failed, workers and students stepped up their protests. One student killed in demonstrations May 7 was José Wright, the American-born son of a wealthy landowner. I remember how significant the death of an American seemed to the people. We students told each other how José's death would actually free us from the dictatorship. We earnestly believed the United States would send in the Marines to avenge him. At that time, the United States was supposed to be able to change governments in Central America at will. We could not understand how a country that practiced democracy at home would support dictatorships abroad, particularly if they killed Americans. The contradictions of American policy toward Latin America have concerned me ever since my earliest political awareness.

To the horror of my parents, who knew the danger involved in political opposition, I became directly involved in the student movement against General Hernández Martínez. University students planning a general strike to paralyze the country came to my high school and asked us to send representatives to the strike-coordinating group. I was named a delegate and attended some of the meetings that were broken up by police. To escape once, I raced down into a ravine, leaped a fence and landed on spiny thorns, tearing my clothes and skin. When I returned home, my parents had only to look at me to know I was in serious trouble. The day of the general strike, our committee set out to create a disturbance at the Liceo to force the suspension of classes. We stole some sulfuric acid from chemistry lab to make stink bombs, then threw stones to break school windows and lob in our home-made bombs. The strike was successful. No one went to school that day, but I was nearly expelled. The teachers and the parents convinced the principal to give us only a thirty-day suspension.

The dictator resigned, but the calls for democratic elections were frustrated by another coup, another military dictatorship. At this point, I was so angry that I was ready to join a rebel army to end the hated regime. The leader of the rebels, exiled in Guatemala, was our family doctor, Arturo Romero. He was only one of several plotters against Hernández Martínez, but, after an inspiring radio broadcast during the attempted coup, he had become the real leader to most Salvadorans.

Dr. Romero so eloquently laid out the need for democracy that for the next twenty years people looked to him as the keeper of our aspirations. Twice I was caught by guards while trying to slip across the border to Guatemala to join Romero's band. Worried by my determination to fight against the dictatorship, my parents decided to send me away immediately to the United States. Their plan was to enroll me in Notre Dame University, where my brother Rolando was studying his first year of economics. Two years earlier, my father had won a modest fortune in the national lottery. His good luck enabled me to gain a university education I could never have afforded. My parents were thinking about my future, but I was thinking only about joining the army of Arturo Romero.

The road north to South Bend, Indiana, led through Guatemala. Along with Edgardo Córdova, another classmate who was headed there, I landed in Guatemala City and went straight to the Palace Hotel, where Dr. Romero had his headquarters. The doctor listened to my story—how I wanted to fight with him for democracy instead of going to Notre Dame.

"No, Napo, I have another mission I need you to carry out," he said, explaining that he needed someone to take crucial letters to the United States. He handed me a small package with instructions to buy stamps and mail it as soon as I crossed the border. This task filled me with delusions of importance. Picturing myself as the courier of the revolution, I proceeded to Notre Dame by bus. In his wisdom, Romero knew I could do more for the country by preparing myself at that university than by dying for him in the hills.

In St. Louis we stopped at a bar to have a beer, and someone asked where we were going. Edgardo, whose English was better than my useless schoolbook phrases, said, "We're going to Notre Dame." One of the men laughed. "Looks like Notre Dame's importing Latin-American football players to beat Army and Navy," he said. I was surprised that Americans would think of a university in terms of a sports team. When I arrived at South Bend, I went to try out for this famous football team, woefully ignorant of what the American sport involved. I realized how little I knew when I was flattened seconds after someone tossed me the ball. There was a lot I had to learn in the States, but principally how to speak English.

One of my first classes at Notre Dame, Christian Virtues, was taught by a young priest beginning his teaching career, Father Theodore Hesburgh. I listened but could not understand a word he was saying about philosophy and ethics. I leaned toward my friend Córdova's desk, asking in Spanish what was being said. My whispers annoyed the nervous professor, who pointed at me.

"What's your name?"

"Napoleón Duarte."

"Well, Nappy, if you continue talking in class, I'm going to throw you out the window," Father Hesburgh said. After class, he motioned for me to stay. "Why were you talking in class?" he asked.

In my best English, acquired mainly during that week, I replied, "To understand what you say I need help."

Father Hesburgh's countenance changed. He smiled. "Well, there's a better way. You stay after class and I'll give you an outline in Italian of what I've talked about." Italian was close enough to Spanish for our communication, and these sessions helped me get started at Notre Dame. Father Hesburgh would guide and rescue me at other critical times in my life.

Learning English wasn't my only hurdle. I also needed money to live on. My college days began at 5 A.M., when I got up to work in the cafeteria as a dishwasher. I worked in the laundry, I washed windows, I worked in an ice factory, at a brewery. Notre Dame was on a three-term system during World War II, and I worked and studied straight through the summers. But I also had time for sports, particularly basketball and soccer. When I completed my degree in civil engineering, I received a few offers from the job recruiters who came to interview on the campus, but they couldn't tempt me. I had one immediate objective: to return to El Salvador to marry Inés Durán.

We grew up together, Inés and I. There was no one closer to my family than the family of José María Durán, who had tried to help my father in the darkest hours of 1932. Inés was two years younger than I, the same age as my brother Alejandro. We always played together. I pulled her hair, I teased her. I excluded her from games because she was a girl, making her angry. But when I got into trouble, Inés would defend me. About the time she was fifteen, I think she had a crush on me, but to this day she denies it.

I was a local basketball star, flirting with all the girls. My friends and I would go to the horse races, and Inés would be there, too. When she saw me paying attention to the girls, she felt ignored, but I thought of her as my sister. Even so, she remembers my jealousy, my telling her not to flirt with the boys because I was going to marry her someday. My sudden departure for

Notre Dame left us both feeling bereaved, having each lost our best friend. I wrote to her, and the following year when Inés came to the United States to study at a women's college in Paterson, New Jersey, her mother brought her to Notre Dame to visit my brother and me. It was at that moment, when I saw her coming toward me in South Bend, that I knew she was the one woman for me. We ran into each other's arms. Without a single word, we had said everything to each other. From that moment on, my mind was set on two things: getting my engineering degree and marrying Inés.

Twice I went to New York to see Inés before she returned to El Salvador the following year. Ours was a romance by mail, four years of letters. When I came back to San Salvador with my degree, I began working for Inés' father, in his construction company. We were formally engaged for a year while I saved my money. During this time, we bought our furniture for the small apartment my father-in-law was building for us. We were married in the seminary chapel in San Miguelito, August 14, 1949.

Our first child, Inés Guadalupe, was born the next year; our son Alejandro the following year. The third child was also a boy, Napoleón. The next three children were our daughters María Eugenia, María Elena and Ana Lorena.

That decade of my life, the 1950s, was filled with my family, my career and private community service. I had come back from Notre Dame ready to build the highest buildings, the wonders of concrete and steel, banks and hospitals. I saw myself purely as an engineer and wanted to build bridges and roads in my country. When I was asked to teach a course at the National University, I was flattered and agreed, not realizing how different my Notre Dame experience had been from a Salvadoran university. I was shocked to find that Salvadoran students never did their homework. They considered being a student at the university, and the status that went with it, more important than learning. All they wanted was a passing grade on the final exams so that they would receive their diplomas. Frustrated, I gave up on teaching, excusing myself because the construction business with my father-in-law was expanding. We had several contracts for projects outside the capital, and I had to travel.

Even the topography and ballistics courses that I had been teaching at the Military Academy could not fit into my schedule. The formation of military officers at the Academy probably has more influence on the nation's politics than any other institution. I could have used this opportunity, but my mind was on engineering, not on politics. My activities were all apolitical, like Scouting. I coached the basketball team that would become the Latin-American champions. I served on the board of the Red Cross, helped set up an Anti-Tuberculosis Society, and the Twenty-Thirty clubs, a group like the Rotary or the Kiwanis for men in that age bracket. I later realized that all the effort I put into these community causes was a warm-up for my work in the Christian Democratic Party.

During the 1950s, I shunned politics. I felt disdain for those who joined the political parties of the day. They were only serving their own personal ambitions, along with those of the military. My only ambition was to be the best civil engineer in El Salvador. I was helping to develop my country through building projects and making a comfortable living for my wife and six children. With my volunteer activities, I could take on small social projects without really confronting the tyrannical political and economic system. But in 1960 the moment came when I was forced to look at my country in a different light.

On the evening of October 29, 1960, my brother Rolando and I were relaxing at our sports club when a radio broadcast by the leaders of the latest coup began. We listened with a sense of apprehension. The political winds were shifting throughout the Americas.

Fidel Castro's revolution in Cuba had raised both hopes and fears. He had overthrown a brutal dictatorship, but where was he taking his country? In the United States, the election campaign was winding up after the debates between Richard M. Nixon and John F. Kennedy. How would the great democracy of the North react to Castro's challenge? Meanwhile, El Salvador was suffering a deep recession due to a decline in the coffee prices that traditionally governed our economy.

Only recently, the dictator on duty, Colonel José María Lemus, had lashed out with new brutality at university students daring to hold a rally in praise of Castro. Lemus' fellow officers decided he was losing his grip, and a coup ousted him. To my surprise, the junta that emerged that October contained three civilians from the intellectual community. The junta called for elections, legalized the April-May Revolutionary Party (PRAM) that served as a front for the Communists, and generally shocked the more conservative military officers with its democratic mentality. The United States frowned on these developments, withholding recognition from the junta for fear of leftist influence.

When the new junta announced its plan to hold free elections, I was surprised. I remember commenting to my brother in dismay, "Look, these men want us to have a democracy, but the only organized political forces in the country are the Marxists and the PRUD." The PRUD was the party the military used to impose their candidates on the country.

Besides the PRUD and the Marxist PRAM, there was one old standby opposition party, the PAR (Renovative Action Party). There were no natural leaders, no clear programs. Who, and what, were the people supposed to choose in a free election?

"There isn't any independent, democratic party to offer an

alternative to the country," I complained to Rolando. "Why don't we go and talk this over with some of our friends?"

That night we met with several people who shared our frustration. The next morning, I received a phone call from a close friend, Salvador Choussy, an architect who had worked with me on building projects. He asked if I would be interested in attending a discussion group.

"Napoleón, a group of us have been meeting to study the Christian social philosophy," Choussy said. "We've been reading Jacques Maritain and other Catholic thinkers. The talk is going to be on the meaning of human dignity, at the Novoa house this Friday."

These intellectual Catholic study groups had been meeting for some time. They found inspiration in the papal encyclical of Pope Leo XIII, *Rerum novarum* (1891), calling on Christians to improve society, particularly the condition of workers, while rejecting the Marxist doctrine. Christians must reject class warfare and materialism, but draw on their spiritual values to stop exploitation of the poor, according to the Church.

Pope John XXIII reinforced this Social Christian doctrine, and the works of the French philosopher Jacques Maritain influenced his Salvadoran readers just as he had postwar Europeans. Maritain urged Christians to defend their values against Fascism and Communism through active participation in the democratic political process. The followers of Marx or the free-market ideologists believe that the economic system determines the social welfare, while Christian Democrats view the economic mechanisms as simply instruments of man's free will to be used for the common good. These instruments are not absolutes, but are subject to adjustment and change.

The Christian Democrats believe in a new social order built not on materialist values, but on solidarity among human beings. The common good is achieved by participation from every member of the community. Recognizing the rights of each human being in a democratic society is the essence of Christian Democracy. The Christian Democratic parties embodied these values, first in Europe, and then in Latin America, most successfully in Chile and Venezuela. I learned that some of my Salvadoran friends were well versed in the philosophy and familiar with the work of the Christian Democrat Eduardo Frei, who preceded the Marxist Salvador Allende as president of Chile, and of Rafael Caldera, who became president of Venezuela.

The first time I realized that such a movement existed was when I joined the people crowding into the Novoa family home. Two respected law professors, Roberto Lara Velado and Abraham Rodríguez, spoke to us that night on the Catholic doctrine of human dignity and social justice. What they said coincided in many ways with what I had been thinking, particularly with the ideas implanted in me by Father Hesburgh. By then president of Notre Dame University, my teacher and friend had spoken to me a few months before, during his visit to alumni in Central America.

Father Hesburgh was appalled at the conditions of the poor in El Salvador. He insisted to me that every Notre Dame graduate had a moral responsibility to his society. "Just building bridges and roads isn't enough," he told me. "You have a greater commitment, ethically, morally and historically." Remembering Father Hesburgh's words, I was ready to speak out at the Novoa meeting.

A high-school principal said we needed to offer the country an alternative by starting "a party with an ideology, any ideology." This phrase struck me as outrageously empty, after our discussion of Christian principles. I asked to speak.

"I expected moral concepts from an educator," I began. "This confirms one of the problems of our society. Our youth grow up to be egotists, professionals and businessmen using whatever ideology serves their own interests. In the history of our country, three sectors, the Army, the Church and the oligarchy, have influenced the structure of our society. But the intellectuals, the middle class, the workers and the peasants have been powerless, because they were disorganized, self-centered or afraid of the dictatorship.

"Today we're here to analyze not only the political but the social and economic situation. We're aware of our responsibility as the new generation. We've stood by with our arms crossed for too long, doing nothing about the hunger, the misery and the brutality our brothers have suffered. The time has come when we can no longer stand by. If we continue to watch with our arms crossed, the destiny of our people will be tragic. We must extend our arms, help the people in need, show them the ideological path toward a democratic society with Christian justice in our country."

Later that same night, the group decided to immediately begin the organization of a Christian Democratic Party for El Salvador. My "arms crossed" speech must have made an impression, because even though I was a newcomer I became one of the eight elected to the organizing committee.

The one committee member whom I knew fairly well was Julio Adolfo Rey Prendes. I had not realized he was active in these discussion groups, but we had worked together in the Boy Scouts. For years, my old Scoutmaster, Father Juanito, had been in charge of Scouting in El Salvador. The aging Father neglected troops outside of the elite private schools, making no effort to spread Scouting to underprivileged boys as Rey Prendes and I hoped to do. When a Central American jamboree was held in the mountain village of La Palma, the Salvadoran troops proved helpless as campers. The troops from neighboring countries were far better prepared, and our national pride was stung. That was the moment Rey Prendes and I got ourselves elected to lead the Scouts, and Father Juan retired. When our political partnership began, I could not imagine that we two scoutmasters would found a political party and eventually govern the country. Today Rey Prendes is my minister of communications.

The other six members of the Christian Democratic Party organizing committee included the professors Rodríguez and Lara Velado, plus León Cuellar, Juan Ricardo Ramírez, Italo Giammattei and the senior Guillermo Ungo. His son Guillermo Ungo, Jr., had expected to be named to the committee, but the group assumed that the elder Ungo would be better able to generate support for the new party. Rather than work with his father, the younger Guillermo Ungo went off to form another party. The party he eventually led, the National Revolutionary Movement (MNR), was once our ally, but he would finally join the leftist guerrillas.

Within a few weeks, we drafted the Christian Democratic Party manifesto and the organizational structure. But before we convoked an open meeting, a representative of the new junta contacted us. The spokesman said that the junta, with the exception of one member who was sympathetic to the Communists, welcomed the formation of our new party. It was clear that the Left wanted no competition and already eyed us as a threat.

From the beginning, everyone in our party was suspicious of everyone else's intentions. The task assigned to me by the committee was organizing, so I launched into that with all my energy. I invited a group of professionals to meet with me one night, but the entire Christian Democratic committee turned up, angry. They were convinced I was trying to take over the party. They stayed after the meeting until four in the morning, when I had finally allayed their distrust.

By the time of our first open meeting, at the Hotel Internacional on November 25, 1960, a split had already developed. The purists, generally the younger members, wanted the party to be free from any links to the past. They wanted to break out of the mold of pragmatic parties and uphold the principles of Social Christianity.

Other members wanted to use the party for personal power. They had served other parties and were more interested in gaining government positions than in following ideological principles. The party had attracted conservatives who saw Christian Democracy as an antidote for Communism, but they were not truly committed to real reforms in El Salvador's social structure.

Our initial organization, called the Committee of Eight, heard rumors that a military coup was coming against the junta. Officers began contacting us to sound out our position. After considerable discussion, we decided that our incipient party could too easily, and prematurely, become identified with a particular leader or the government itself. We needed time to be recognized for our ideology. Each of us on the committee made a pact that we would oppose participation in a government installed by force. We would only work for a constitutional democracy.

I had to leave for the United States to prepare a bid for the contract to build an Esso refinery. So I was not in El Salvador when the coup took place January 25, 1961.

The military officers selected their junta members—this time they called the governing body a "directorate"—and declared their firm anti-Communist principles. That was all they needed for recognition from the United States, where John F. Kennedy had just moved into the White House. The officers went to one of the committee, Abraham Rodríguez, to ask him to join the directorate and bring our party members into the Cabinet. Rodríguez stuck to our pact and refused. The three civilians who did take part in the directorate, however, were men involved in some of the formative meetings of the Christian Democrats. My own brother Rolando became economy minister, but he resigned three months later in opposition to the directorate's nationalization of the Central Bank.

The directorate promised elections, but the way they prepared for them left no doubt that they planned to stay in power. They saw social reform merely as a platform for winning votes. One of the directorate told me, "We have a farmworkers' welfare plan, a rent control law and labor laws that are going to screw the rich." This same man, Antonio Rodríguez Porth, later went on to become the mastermind of the rightist groups.

I thought their policies sounded opportunistic. Their only ideology was a belief in their right to power. Without a commitment to social change based on the right of all citizens to participate in the political and economic process, any reforms dispensed could easily be reversed. (They were all eventually revoked or nullified after the electoral period.)

Some of our Christian Democrats, however, argued we should join with the new government in order to promote social change, even if it meant sacrificing some principles. The Committee of Eight's boycott of military governments was becoming unpopular with some of our members. They said we would be able to carry out our plans if we had influence inside the government. Power on easy terms always tempts personal ambitions. In fact, one of the Committee of Eight, Giammattei, kept in contact with those in the government all along. Open contacts took place between various Christian Democrats and the directorate, as the two colonels and two civilians looked for political scaffolds to support their presidential aspirations. Colonel Aníbal Portillo invited me to the Presidential Palace to offer the Christian Democrats all the Cabinet and legislative posts if we would back his presidential candidacy. Colonel Julio Rivera, his fellow officer on the directorate, came to my house to make a similar offer to the party officials. Rivera warned that either the Communists or the reactionaries would win the elections unless we backed his presidential candidacy. He thought he had a right to our support because only he could guarantee that a reformist government would continue to exist. We responded that he knew better than anyone else that the Communists were too weak to win, and that the reactionaries had no electoral appeal. The best guarantee of a new, reformist government, we insisted, would be to convince the armed forces to allow a true democracy. We rejected his proposal.

These attempts by the military rulers to negotiate with us divided the party. By the time of our first convention, in May 1961, two factions vied for leadership—those who wanted to collaborate with the military government, and the purists. My instinct was not to get involved in a power struggle. There I was, a novice in politics, talking to party members like myself, who identified with the ideological purists but wanted to avoid a divisive struggle. What if the convention reached a deadlock? One person suggested I should be nominated. I agreed if that would help keep the party intact.

When neither of the other candidates had the two-thirds majority necessary, my name was proposed. A recess allowed the purists time to reassure themselves that I basically shared their concerns. I was elected the first secretary general of the Christian Democratic Party, and the purists then won most of the seats on the national committee.

The faction that lost revealed their true motives. Since they could not take control of the Christian Democratic Party, they formed another new party as the official standard-bearer for Colonel Rivera. Their National Conciliation Party (PCN) was no sooner unveiled than the directorate announced elections for a constituent assembly, to prepare for presidential elections. Rivera left the government to head the PCN. From then on, the PCN took over as the party of the military candidates.

There had never been any intention to hold fair elections, we were convinced. The Christian Democrats called a public meeting in the Plaza Libertad, where I read our manifesto denouncing the PCN, a party formed only to maintain those governing in power. This speech, called "Betrayal of the Salvadoran People," was my debut as a public speaker.

The Christian Democrats' electoral debut, in the race for seats in the Constituent Assembly, was a disaster. The PCN won every single seat. Because our own organization was not yet strong enough to win on its own, we had entered into an alliance with the other parties against the new official party. This ill-conceived alliance taught me a painful lesson. We had no alternative program to present when everyone in the alliance disagreed. The coalition of bankrupt rightist parties and inexperienced Christian Democrats sounded totally incoherent. Our opponents in the government cleverly claimed to be the party of reform, waving the banners underwritten by Kennedy's Alliance for Progress.

The Alliance for Progress was a good idea. But the U.S. aid program, meant to cure the ills that led to leftist revolutions, only put a new face on old regimes. The Alliance promoted land reform, fair wages, education and health programs as well as private investment and economic integration. While its rhetoric gave political legitimacy to terms like "social justice," the results never matched the goals. The idealistic intentions of the Alliance could not be carried out by undemocratic governments.

Under the auspices of the Alliance, representatives of the Salvadoran government and the political parties were invited to meet and discuss the economic situation. As secretary general of the Christian Democrats, I was designated to represent our concerns. As an engineer, I felt unprepared for the fine points of economic argument, so I gathered all the statistics I could find. I searched the libraries and spent hours poring over books on trade, agricultural production, health and education. I made graphs based on yearly reports going back to the colonial period. I showed the number of schools, teachers and students, the incidence of disease, the distribution of land.

My own figures shocked me. I had no idea that conditions in my country were so bad. The government ministers certainly did not present these figures. After they spoke, I questioned them. I went to the board in the conference room and put up my graphs. The ministers could not refute my statistics. At least three ministers lost their posts shortly thereafter.

While the Christian Democratic Party was still learning about politics, Colonel Rivera's government grew more confident due to the economic upswing in the early 1960s. The Alliance for Progress and the formation of a Central American Common Market provided the momentum. Colonel Rivera had won the presidency, but he lacked a legitimate popular mandate, since all the opposition parties had boycotted the 1962 presidential election, knowing that it would not be fair. The only candidate standing against Rivera was the donkey nominated by university students.

As the economy began to expand, Rivera grew more cocky. He decided that the PCN could stand a little competition from other parties, if only to refurbish the facade of democracy. As the 1964 elections for the National Legislative Assembly and for municipal offices approached, the Christian Democrats felt we had a chance to gain a political foothold. I was ready for my first political campaign.

2

San Salvador's
Mayor

M Y first campaign, in the election of March 1964, played
to an empty house—or empty streets, to be exact. I was
running for mayor of San Salvador.

We did not expect to win, but it was a way of getting our
Christian Democratic message to the people. We hoped to get
enough votes to at least carry some of our candidates into the
National Assembly. We did not have much of an organization, so
I began by driving around the city in a pickup truck with loudspeakers, accompanied by a party activist to introduce me. Our
arrival in a neighborhood of San Salvador would clear the streets;
the people were so afraid of the military regime that no one
wanted to be seen with us.

One young man who began his political career riding that truck
with me was Fidel Chávez Mena. After graduating from law
school, he had decided to study politics in Chile, where the Christian Democratic Party was strong, working toward Eduardo Frei's

eventual presidential victory. Chávez Mena returned to El Salvador full of enthusiasm and found himself standing on the back of the truck, introducing his candidate for mayor to a void of dusty walls. The two of us learned public speaking without an audience.

"You don't have to come out to this truck, just listen to us from inside your houses," we blared out. Then we explained the Christian Democratic option for San Salvador, hoping someone had heard.

We said the country needed an elected Christian Democratic mayor because the city was the base of the community, the place to start a real democracy. Our plans called for community action—to bring people into the political process to resolve social problems. I outlined the municipal reforms we wanted: modern administration with moral principles, a sound financial base, better marketplaces, sanitation, streetlights, parks and cemeteries, adult education and recreation. The theme was democratic participation: our slogan was "Your vote is your weapon. Use it well. Vote green." The party color was green and we chose the fish as our symbol, as had the early Christians.

When our sound truck made its second round of the neighborhoods, a few people started coming out to listen. By the third round, there was more of a crowd.

Two weeks before the election, I spoke to the women of the municipal marketplace about my plans for helping them. The importance of the market women can easily be overlooked. Their share of the national product may be minuscule, but they develop a sharp business sense no politician can fool. The talk of the marketplace is quite literally the talk of the town, and we were encouraged by the market women's enthusiastic response. In fact, our final campaign rally attracted tens of thousands.

I won the election by a small margin over the government's

man and the traditional opposition candidate. The Christian Democrats won fourteen seats in the National Assembly and elected thirty-six other mayors. With the 1964 election, the Christian Democrats became the opposition to be reckoned with by the overconfident military-backed government.

When I assumed the mayor's office, the problem facing me was where to start. I had very limited powers and few resources. The first thing we had to resolve was the city's finances. San Salvador was broke. The city owed money everywhere, had not collected on its own debts, and could not levy taxes without a law passed by the National Assembly. In the past, when the mayor had been a political crony of the President, the government subsidized the municipal deficit and ran the city itself. This was the first time an opposition party controlled the mayor's office. Colonel Rivera cut the city loose, hoping we would sink.

There had to be a way around Rivera to finance the city government. Going over the records, we found large outstanding debts for water bills and garbage collection fees under the names associated with the "Fourteen Families" said to rule El Salvador. There are actually many more than that among the wealthy oligarchy, but the popular phrase correctly expressed how very few actually lived in the splendor sustained by mass misery. Certain names will always appear on anyone's list of the Fourteen: Escalón, Regalado, Quiñónez, Dueñas, etc. I began collecting from them the back taxes owed the city for more than twenty years. Sometimes I presented the bills to them myself. They resisted, calling me a Communist, but they finally paid up, making the city solvent.

Although the national government worked against us, tax reform became one of our causes. Even the most basic ideas, such as lighting the streets, were blocked by the government and its allies. The government, the banks and the Canadian-owned electric company all refused to help us provide streetlights for the people. The city owed a large debt to the electric company and I offered to pay if they would join in the streetlights project. They refused, saying they did not believe that my revenue-generating scheme was economically feasible.

We looked for international financing instead, but the World Bank and others required national-government guarantees which we could not get. General Electric and Westinghouse were interested in helping with credit lines if the Central Bank would stand behind the city. The president of the Central Bank would not even give me an appointment. I chose a date and told the press I would present the street-lighting project to the Central Bank personally. In front of the television cameras, I walked into the bank, where the only person who would receive the plan was the janitor. Publicizing this absurd scene intimidated the bank president, who finally agreed to help.

The government allowed the project to go through only because they felt it would backfire. They thought our increase in electricity rates would make us unpopular. When it looked as though I would get the streetlights, the Canadian president of the electric company came to San Salvador to negotiate. I told him that his problem was the company's local manager, who, as a member of the oligarchy, had no sympathy for my project. After I explained the city's plan, with new revenues and credits for the electric company, the Canadian agreed to join in.

The night the streetlights were turned on throughout San Salvador there was dancing and singing in many neighborhoods. When the government saw this success, they launched their own streetlight program throughout the country to try to win political support.

In 1965, San Salvador was shaken by earth tremors, sometimes as many as ten a day. Hammock Valley (Valle de las Hamacas) was living up to its name. It did not take a geologist to realize that a major earthquake was likely. I asked President Rivera to organize an emergency plan. He appointed a committee, but it diddled.

From the mayor's office, we asked neighborhoods to organize civil-defense committees to work with the Red Cross on first aid, potable water and food supplies, rescue and demolition teams, information and communications centers. We also asked the Archbishop of San Salvador to join our efforts, organizing a procession and a Mass to pray to God for His help. The act of faith calmed people and inspired greater participation in our emergency committees.

At dawn on May 3, the quake came. It threw San Salvador back and forth. Furniture crashed, crockery broke, reinforced concrete groaned, walls collapsed. My wife and I were in bed as our children came running in. We all hugged each other. I was confident our house would hold because I knew the degree of resistance I had built into the concrete walls. After the first shock subsided, I told my family to stay in the safest part of the house, in case a second, stronger shock came.

I headed for my office, making a quick survey of the initial damage throughout the city. Our preparations had worked. A system of two-way radios enabled us to communicate with mobile units and to coordinate rescue efforts. There were thousands of people in the streets, afraid to reenter their damaged houses. To make matters worse, the rainy season chose this moment to begin. I ordered my employees to buy all the plastic cloth in the city to improvise shelters. When we ran out, we sent to Guatemala for more. We asked the United States to send field tents, and they quickly cooperated.

The 1965 quake took over one hundred lives and left forty thousand people homeless. The President called a meeting of officials to discuss disaster relief and announced that the United

States would provide several million dollars for reconstruction. I proposed that we use the money for a public-housing plan, providing land and construction materials for the poor in planned zones with water, sanitation and public services. These communities would replace the precarious shantytowns that had grown around the city, then collapsed in the quake.

"It would be too dangerous to concentrate all the poor in an area like that, because the Communists would use it as a base of operations," President Rivera said. The U.S. money was wasted on other projects that resolved nothing.

In 1966 and 1968 I was reelected mayor of San Salvador, each time by a larger margin, each time with growing resentment from the official PCN. I was unaware of the political violence that was to come, but we still knew moments of fear. In 1966 I experienced the first threat to one of my children. During the mayoral campaign, my sons had seen the party activists pasting up flyers and painting little fish, the party symbol, on the streets and the walls. They wanted to take part. We agreed to let them work on the corner of our street, accompanied by our maid. The third night, while they were repasting posters that had been painted over by the PCN, two carloads of PCN men pulled up and started chasing the boys. They caught little Napoleón, then thirteen, knocked down the maid, who was holding on to him, and drove off with the boy. Alejandro had escaped into a neighbor's home.

As soon as I was called, I informed the party, then phoned the President, the Defense Minister and Francisco (Chachi) Guerrero, secretary general of the PCN.

"Chachi," I told Guerrero, "I'm calling to tell you that one of my sons has just been kidnapped. I want to warn you that if he isn't returned to me immediately, this situation could get out of control. If anything happens to my son, I will not be responsible for any desperate action I take," I said.

At that moment, I felt a violence in me I had never known

before. It was the same reaction that would drive people to take up arms and go to the hills after members of their families were killed by official agents of violence in this country. All my non-violent principles were being torn apart as I thought of what could have happened to my son.

Angry Christian Democrats encircled the PCN headquarters, demanding my son be released. Not long afterward, he was dropped off at the corner near the house, shaken but unharmed. The groups who started out as bullies, shock forces of the PCN, later would develop into paramilitary forces and death squads. The Right was beginning to use force even outside the military structure.

Meanwhile I was trying to organize groups to attack social problems and help their communities. The community-action program expanded until we had more than eighty organizations bringing neighbors together to work on building projects such as schools, retaining walls, paths and parks. Adult-education courses were organized, and each community-action group lobbied for its concerns with the city government. Local self-help organizations may have been common in other countries, but they were new to El Salvador. The government feared them, suspecting that they were only meant to serve our political purposes. The government believed this because that is what their own motivation would have been. They lacked the Christian Democratic ideology that promoted participatory democracy and decentralization.

Experience quickly showed how well the community organizations served the nation, first in the earthquake disaster, again during our unfortunate war with Honduras.

In retrospect, the way El Salvador went to war with Honduras showed me how politicians and even military officers can be forced into a collective psychosis. The grievances between Honduras and El Salvador festered in the hills between them, where no exact borderline had ever been agreed on. These regions fell between the reach of either government, making them a haven for outlaws. Hunger and misery knew no boundaries, but there were Salvadorans who thought they would have more opportunity in Honduras. The Salvadorans had first been drawn to Honduras by the good wages paid by the American banana companies. Afterward they stayed on, squatting on available land or opening small businesses.

In 1967, El Salvador's National Guard surrounded the farm of a notorious smuggler in the disputed area and arrested him on charges of murder. The outlaw happened to be a close friend of the general then ruling Honduras, who angrily charged El Salvador with invading his country to make the arrest. A few days later, two Salvadoran army officers led a heavily armed patrol into the Honduran town of Nueva Ocotepeque, where they were captured. The officers claimed to have gotten lost. The most likely explanation is that they were lured into helping a Honduran coup plot that never materialized. The Honduran government howled against the Salvadorans, building up the tension until President Lyndon Johnson was due to arrive for a Central American summit. To stop the squabbling, the United States leaned on Honduras and El Salvador to exchange prisoners—the Salvadoran officers for the Honduran smuggler. This raised the tension even higher.

For Honduras, the nationalist, anti-Salvadoran sentiment served to distract its people from the failings of their own government. The pressure then building for land reform could be channeled into a take-from-the-Salvadoran-squatters, give-to-our-own-people feeling. The aggressive Salvadoran entrepreneurs had practically taken over the Honduran market, pushing out local small businesses and creating unemployment. Resentment erupted into violence. Unhampered or perhaps even abetted by the Honduran

authorities, vigilante groups attacked Salvadorans, causing a panic
that drove terrorized families to flee back home. Those returning to
El Salvador brought stories of persecution and brutality against our
innocent countrymen.

In June 1969, the soccer matches to decide which country would
be represented at the World Cup games took place. The world
press would later label the war to come the "Soccer War," mocking its real causes. In Honduras, the Salvadoran soccer team was
harassed, kept awake the night before the game. The Salvadorans
retaliated. The night before the rematch in San Salvador, I drove
home from the countryside to find the street facing the Honduran
team's hotel filled with a mob making raucous music. I recognized
Colonel José Medrano, head of the Salvadoran National Guard,
overseeing the musical assault. The next day the Hondurans lost
the game, and mobs in their capital, Tegucigalpa, smashed the
fronts of Salvadoran-owned businesses. The Honduran government turned a blind eye to the violence.

Meanwhile, the Salvadoran press played up horror stories
throughout the month of June. These tales of rape, mutilation
and murder were exaggerated. I sent a group of doctors from the
Christian Democratic Party to the frontier to treat the refugees.
The doctors went through the hospitals without finding any such
cases. The Salvadoran people, however, were seized by a collective
psychosis. There was not a Salvadoran family without some relative in Honduras who had been mistreated. Salvadoran business
was heavily involved in the Honduran economy, and our investment was being destroyed.

I wrote a letter to General Sánchez Hernández, the military
man who had become El Salvador's president in 1967, requesting
a meeting of all political and government leaders to consider the
grave situation. We met two days later, June 21, for a discussion
that revealed an unprecedented unity. There was agreement that

we had to stop the persecution of Salvadorans in Honduras. I suggested an ultimatum giving the Honduran government three days to take action to protect our citizens. We notified the Organization of American States that if no action was taken to safeguard Salvadoran interests, all pacific means of resolving the question would be exhausted.

The only objection came from the Economy Minister, Alfonso Rochac, who warned that any action we took might destroy the Central American Common Market. "It's already gone," someone responded. Sánchez Hernández, thinking as a general, said we wouldn't be able to back up any threat unless El Salvador got more arms. Other nations would not supply us openly for this cause. "It's going to cost some fifty million dollars on the black market," Sánchez Hernández worried.

One of our legislative leaders, Lara Velado, usually as antimilitary as anyone I know, turned to the general and said, "Declare war now and I'll get you that fifty million dollars from the legislature."

There was one group opposing the war, the Communists. They called a pacifist rally, only to find themselves completely alone.

What finally pushed Sánchez Hernández into a surprise attack on Honduras was his fellow officers. The people were saying that the military were cowards, that they couldn't even defend the country. The officers reacted, confident about going to war. They had been impressed by Israel's recent success in the Six-Day War and thought they could match General Moshe Dayan. A few days before the attack, Sánchez Hernández called me to his office and told me to plan for sufficient food and water in the city in case of war. On July 14, the President summoned me at 5:45 P.M. to say that our planes were already flying toward Honduras.

By the second day of the war, we had no planes left. Two crashed into each other on the runway, others were shot down or broke down. Honduran planes bombed San Salvador's airport, and the oil storage tanks at our ports went up in flames. An army invasion thrust up the two main roads linking El Salvador and Honduras, but the farther they went, the more troops were left along the way to protect the supply lines. The second day, still far from the Honduran cities, the invading army had reached the end of its tether.

"We can't go farther, or we won't be able to defend ourselves," Sánchez Hernández told me.

"If you allow me to call up volunteers here in the city, I can organize a ten-thousand-man civil-defense force to guarantee your logistical support and free more soldiers for combat," I offered. "Give me some retired officers to train and lead them."

The military chiefs liked the plan, but some officers objected. It meant assigning me a military command. We might be united during the war, but afterward I would still be a politician they considered subversive to their way of life. "If this man is dangerous as a politician," one officer said, "what's going to stop him if we give him a military command?"

Instead, they named me "coordinator" of civil defense, assigning a colonel to be the head of any forces I could organize. They said our forces must be unarmed and stay off the streets. That night, the duty officer of the National Guard called to say they had received information that Honduran paratroopers were being dropped into the San Salvador area. The colonel wanted me to call out my patrols into the streets. The city was blacked out. I suggested we would do better to turn on the lights and use the radio network to mobilize my organization calmly, to avoid causing panic.

"Negative, you must use other means," the officer replied. We did have an alternative, a pyramidal telephone network. Within ten minutes we alerted the local leaders, and within half an hour twenty thousand men armed with old rifles, machetes, sticks and shovels were patrolling the streets.

We proved the value of our organization when a Honduran who was living in San Salvador threw a bomb from a passing car at the Air Force headquarters. The Chiefs of Staff asked for our help, giving us only a description of the Volkswagen used. We alerted our neighborhood patrols, telling them not to detain the Volkswagen at any checkpoint, just to radio its location. We picked up the trail and tracked the car to a house behind the university. The Army surrounded the house and surprised the group inside, capturing their arms and radio transmitters. Gradually, the armed forces began to trust my ability to safeguard the city.

By the fourth day, a cease-fire imposed by the Organization of American States was to go into effect. But there was resistance within the military. What Sánchez Hernández had negotiated, the front-line military officers were not about to surrender. To save face for the military, I sent my lawyers into Honduras—Fidel Chávez Mena to San Marcos, and Antonio Morales Erlich to Ocotepeque. The Salvadoran officers thus could hand control over to their own civilian leaders, who would then carry out the truce arrangements with Honduran officers and OAS observers.

We had committed El Salvador to peace before the OAS and the world, but our troops in Honduras were mutinous. Sánchez Hernández was afraid they wouldn't obey his orders to march home to El Salvador.

"I'll get them out," I told him. "We'll organize a triumphant welcome, a parade and a tribute to our nation's heroes at the National Stadium."

The commanders of the troops were reluctant at first. Their men were too dirty, they said, and didn't know how to march properly for a parade. Besides, how could we lodge and feed them all? But we organized the reception anyway, with a publicity campaign to revive everyone's spirits. Our "victory" parade served the purpose. The Army came home to a grateful people, and one avenue leading to the stadium was renamed "Boulevard of the Heroes."

My objective was not to soothe the military egos, but to salvage our national pride from a feeling of defeat and the guilt being imposed on us. War is hell, but hell is also the world's indifference to the persecuted. If the diplomatic community, the OAS human-rights commission, or the United Nations had been able to enforce protection for the Salvadoran people in Honduras, this war between two brother nations would have been unnecessary.

The war, however, served another purpose for General Sánchez Hernández. He tried to turn the pride of the nation into capital for his PCN. Riding the wave of nationalist slogans, he ignored the nation's social inequalities, the hunger, the unemployment, the overpopulation, that caused the emigration to Honduras and led to the hatred exploited in the war. The government rode the patriotic sentiment into an election victory in the 1970 legislative elections. The Christian Democrats lost three seats in the assembly, and the number of Christian Democratic mayors was reduced from seventy-eight to eight. Fortunately, we did not lose San Salvador, even though the government ran one of the heroes of the war, Colonel Mario Velásquez, against my successor, Carlos Herrera Rebollo.

I had decided not to run for a fourth term as mayor. Six years as mayor had made me restless. I had started most of the programs I envisioned, and others could carry out their administration better than I. My family needed more of my time. I wanted to start my own engineering firm.

Another reason was the tension within the party. A younger group in the Christian Democrats was becoming more radical. The election setback in 1970 forced a reexamination of where the

Christian Democrats were going. Those of us who had thought Sánchez Hernández would allow more democratization had been proven wrong. He had moved backward, allowing less freedom because he feared that his government would be seen as weak. The party youth saw us as compromisers, tainted by contacts with the military government. Abraham Rodríguez, who had the vision that only by working within the armed forces would we ever be able to establish a democracy, resigned from the party when his counsel was rejected. I worried that the radicalization within the party carried the seeds of violence. Our youth were angry. They would push harder on agrarian reform, and some were preparing for armed revolution.

This was not my way, but nonviolence was out of style as the 1970s began. The time had come for me to resign as secretary general of the party. Pablo Mauricio Alvergue succeeded me and guided the party through this difficult period. The new leadership of the party began talking with other opposition groups, concluding that the best hope for the future was a broad political alliance against the military government. The strategy for the 1972 elections was to unite all the opposition behind one slate, led by the Christian Democrats.

Members of the party began approaching me about the presidential candidacy. I discouraged them. We already had had one bad experience with a coalition in 1961. I was pessimistic about the outcome even if we could unite everyone against the government. There would be fraud and violence used by the official party.

The two splinter rightist parties backed away from the coalition and supported their leaders as candidates. This left the Christian Democrats allied with two small leftist parties, one of them a front for the illegal Communist Party. I did not like the alliance with the Communists, since our philosophies were totally opposed. I did not want to become president, if there were even a chance, owing the Communists a place in the government.

Then some of my party colleagues came to convince me to run for president, on the assumption I could not win. They argued that our objective in 1972 should be to gain as many seats as possible in the legislature for the opposition parties. By leading the opposition, I could inspire more votes, adding to our proportion in the assembly even if I did not win the presidency. With enough seats to counter the PCN in the assembly, we could make the government more democratic. On these terms, I could consider becoming a pawn in the election game. The alliance with the Communists was tolerable because I believed they had a right to representation in the assembly. This was the same analysis made in 1963 when I ran for mayor of San Salvador, and no one thought I could win but I did. Now they wanted me to run for president to help the legislative ticket. They still did not know me and my ability to run for office. Before agreeing to run, however, I asked for time to talk it over with my family.

The family conference included my wife, my children, my mother, my brothers, all the in-laws and their children. Everyone, young and old, was asked what he or she thought about my running for president. Only one person said, "I don't like the idea at all." All the others, in turn, said they would support whatever decision I made.

I knew how hard this was for my family. My teenage sons Napoleón and Alejandro needed me now because I had spent so much time away from them while I was mayor, but they understood my duty to my country. My wife, Inés, was afraid for me. So was my mother. Both women had vivid memories of the violence that political involvement had brought into their lives. The father of Inés' closest friend had been shot after the coup attempt in 1944. Her own father had been arrested then because a rebel took refuge in the Duráns house. When I had decided to run for mayor in 1964, Inés could not understand why I should take the risk.

"Our country is in danger," I told her then. "It is going to end up in the hands of the Communists, because they will be the only alternative to the military. Do you want your children and grand-children to grow up in a Communist country? We have to make democracy work."

Reluctantly, Inés went along. Her instinct about the danger proved to be correct.

3

The 1972 Race

GENERAL Sánchez Hernández picked Colonel Arturo Molina to be his successor as president. The PCN duly endorsed the choice, despite some grumbling among the Army and the oligarchy about Molina's qualifications. The government's political campaign ignored the rightist opposition factions and concentrated its guns on the coalition of the Christian Democrats and the leftists, under the banner of the United National Opposition (UNO).

The local military commanders outside the capital saw any campaigning by UNO in their dominions as a challenge to their authority. At first, they limited their action to throwing itching powder into our cars or intimidating local Christian Democrats with threats. Later, there were attempts on my life and attacks on my son Alejandro, who worked as my campaign factotum.

On the morning of December 31, 1971, tired from the previous day's campaign tour, I was squeezing in an extra hour at a friend's house. Our campaign workers went on ahead to try to stir up enthusiasm for the rallies planned in Intipucá and other villages up the road. Miguel Angel Barrera, my driver, was taking the lead car, a pickup truck with loudspeakers mounted on the back. Alejandro followed in the caravan's rear car.

They were just beyond Intipucá when Alejandro heard shots, then saw people yelling at him to turn back. Miguel Angel, wounded in the chest, fell over the wheel, but his companion managed to keep the pickup from going straight off a steep embankment. The gunman, dressed in white, looked down from the rocks above the dusty road. The men in the pickup decided to drive on to the hospital in the next town. Meanwhile, Alejandro quickly headed back to tell me what had happened.

When we reached the hospital, we learned Miguel Angel had died on the operating table. The National Guard had arrested not the killer, but the men who had driven with Miguel Angel to the hospital. The Guard commander sent a message to me. If we intended to use the campaign rally that night to denounce anyone for killing Miguel Angel, we would never see our captured friends again.

We decided to go ahead with the rally as planned. I asked the other speakers not to mention the shooting. I took that responsibility myself. When my turn came, I told the crowd what had happened, cautioning them that I could not say for sure who had killed Miguel Angel.

"But the people of Intipucá identified the man they saw fire the shots," I said, naming the man, omitting only that he belonged to the National Guard. "Why, then, has the National Guard arrested the campaign workers who took Miguel Angel to the hospital?" I asked. "The Guard must be responsible for the safety of those men from now on."

The maneuver worked. My party workers were freed, but some

of them were beaten and sustained permanent injuries. However, no charges were ever brought against the killer of Miguel Angel. The murderer continued his military career. No one expected an investigation, because the concept of holding a military man responsible for a crime did not then exist in El Salvador. The military forces used the law as their instrument, never as their judge. For this reason, it has been very hard, even when the Christian Democrats were in the government a decade later, to bring to justice the killers of so many Salvadorans, even of American citizens.

No one could be held responsible the second time someone tried to kill me. We were driving on the Pan-American Highway late at night, returning from a rally, with Alejandro at the wheel. A bullet pierced the windshield, ricocheting into the roof. Alejandro floored the accelerator, sending the car careening around the curve ahead and racing on for miles to the nearest lights, a gasoline station at San Vicente.

This was no high-level plot to kill me. The climate of violence, the immunity of the military class, and the hatred whipped up by the government spawned these spontaneous attempts at assassination. The Guardsman who killed Miguel Angel probably acted on his own initiative, as did my would-be murderer. He knew that his action would be condoned by the government, if not rewarded. This attitude generated more random violence and abuses of authority over the next decade, but when the foreign press began looking into crimes here they always assumed there had to be higher-ranking officers who gave the orders.

The mentality of the local commanders in 1972 was epitomized for me by the sergeant in San Alejo who laid an ambush for my campaign group in the outskirts of that hamlet in the eastern mountains. The townspeople knew and warned us, walking protectively beside our cars to the edge of town. The sergeant had apparently seen one too many Westerns. He stood in front of his roadblock, posing like a sheriff confronting the outlaws.

"Go ahead and shoot me, you sons of whores," he yelled. "You might kill me, but not one of you will leave this town alive."

"Sergeant, calm down. What's the problem?" I said, trying to soothe him. But he closed in, ordering his men to tie up my companions and to shoot if we made any sudden moves. To frighten away the villagers who were interceding, he fired his machine pistol over their heads. He was determined to take his prisoners to military headquarters in San Miguel, the largest town in eastern El Salvador. He loaded the men into the back of our pickup truck. I climbed into the cab beside the sergeant. One local woman squeezed in, too, insisting she would go along to protect me.

As the sergeant drove, I tried to talk to him, but he would not listen.

"You're the enemy," he growled. His logic was simple. We opposed the government, therefore we were attacking the armed forces. He was a soldier who thought he was defending his comrades and the patriotic institution that guarded the country. He also intuitively knew that any change in the power structure would mean an end to his comfortable status as the village bully.

At the barracks in San Miguel, we waited under guard until the commander ambled out. He wore a PCN vest and complained about being tired from so many campaign duties. Then the commander recognized me. He smiled, not at a political opponent, but at his former teacher.

"Professor, remember me?"

He had been one of my students at the Military Academy when I taught an engineering course. The commander took me to one side. "Look, I know you're a good man," he explained. "I like you, I respect you. But you're keeping company with the Communists. Therefore you must be a Communist. I have no choice but to treat you as one. You can be thankful I've been your student, otherwise this could have been much worse." He detained us until word came from San Salvador to release us.

The military officers always suspected anyone advocating change of being a Communist. To them, Franklin D. Roosevelt or Mahatma Gandhi would have been a Communist. They could not distinguish between Communists, Socialists, Democrats or any group critical of the status quo. It has always been an irony that I am called a Communist by the Right, when all my life I have opposed the Communist philosophy and presented a democratic alternative. But the Right takes glee in recalling who ran on the ticket with me in 1972.

With only two other parties in the coalition, we had to agree on a vice-presidential candidate from one of them. I ruled out anyone linked to the Communists. That left the leader of the tiny Nationalist Revolutionary Movement (MNR), Guillermo Ungo. He was the son of one of the eight organizers of the Christian Democratic Party, but his party, the MNR, at that time was closer to the Social Democratic parties of Europe.

I agreed to run with Ungo because I knew him as a good man, intellectual, stubborn, but neither decisive nor charismatic. During the campaign, Ungo preferred to stick close to my side, because when he led a rally on his own no one would show up. To this day, the photos of Ungo and me together are used by the Right as evidence that I am secretly allied with the Marxist revolutionaries. Ungo chose that road in 1980, taking up the leadership of the Revolutionary Democratic Front (FDR), the political alliance that supports the Farabundo Martí National Liberation Front guerrillas.

Just before election day, the secretary general of the Communist Party, Shafik Handal, came to talk to me.

"Napoleón, I think you really have a chance to win this election," Handal said, "but to actually be allowed to become president you've got to denounce the Communist Party. I've come to tell you we believe you must do this. Attack us, say you want nothing to do with us. We will understand that it's necessary for this election and we will attack you."

"Shafik, I'm going to stick by the pact we made," I told him. "I said you might gain some seats in the legislature by working with us, but I would never give you any posts in a government. All I promised was your right to participate in the democratic process. I assumed you would respect the rules. You have done so, and I'm going to stand by my word."

Although I knew the Handal family, Palestinians who had settled in Usulatán, I had never met Shafik before the campaign. I remember a few years earlier his mother came out to my car when I picked up one of his brothers, who was going to Honduras as part of our Twenty-Thirty service club activities. Mrs. Handal asked me to take good care of her son. A decade later, her sons would be fighting as guerrillas and Shafik would be one of the FMLN leaders.

On election day, February 20, 1972, there was a large voter turnout in the city despite the fact that the only buses allowed to circulate were those contracted by the PCN. Once the polls closed, the radio and television began providing official results, which the Central Election Council passed on only from those places where the government was winning. By 2 A.M. they could not find any results which didn't favor UNO. The broadcasts faded off the airways.

General Sánchez Hernández had underestimated the number of false votes his candidate would need. The official party bosses received some 200,000 fake identification cards to use for double vote casting, but they had not used them enough. At 5 A.M., our party announced the final results obtained from reports sent by our delegates at the polling places: UNO had 327,000 votes against the government's 318,000. As soon as the government candidate heard this, Molina claimed he'd gotten 370,000 votes. The official election council went the other way, taking 30,000 votes away from UNO but maintaining the government votes at 318,000.

The confusion lasted until the government could rearrange enough ballot boxes to extract its false victory.

We decided to expose the fraud with proof that the results from La Unión province were falsified. Alejandro drove out to pick up the official copies of the original count, done before all party observers at the polls. The government controlled the newspapers, but the night foreman at one paper was a Christian Democrat. He stopped the presses to insert in the final edition our information exposing the fraud. He lost his job in the process. My son Alejandro, for his part, became the target of gunmen shooting from a passing car as he walked out of our campaign headquarters. Fortunately, they missed.

In the official recount, the results changed by several thousand votes in five different provinces. It gave Molina 334,000 votes and reduced ours to 324,000. Half an hour after the official recount ended on February 25, pro-government legislators rushed into an illegal session of the assembly to declare Molina the president-elect. The assembly vote was necessary because, even with the fraud, the two minor rightist candidates had claimed enough votes to deny Molina a 51 percent majority.

As the news spread, an angry crowd gathered in the Plaza Libertad, shouting slogans against the government fraud. Again, Shafik Handal came to see me.

"Our theory is that now is the time to take to the streets," the

Communist leader said. "The people must defend the election victory. It's time to play all our confrontation cards."

"I don't think people are prepared for that," I warned. "We couldn't even organize a successful general strike, because the union structure is too weak! For the past ten years, we've been preparing people to use their vote. We've fought with words and taught them to participate at the polls. But if you take the people into something they're not prepared for, it's going to be a massacre."

I didn't need to say "Remember 1932." None of us has forgotten. Those too young to remember the events know the stories of La Matanza, the Massacre, when as many as thirty thousand were killed as the military put down the Communist-led revolt. Not until the 1980s would El Salvador again count its dead in numbers that numb the meaning of death.

But in 1972 bloodshed did not seem inevitable. I believed there were still ways to use the electoral process to eventually thwart the military rulers.

The legislative elections were two weeks away. The original goal for the presidential campaign had been to unite the people into a coalition that could win a majority in the assembly. The government split the election into two separate dates to try to discourage us, but I still thought we could win the second election. The danger again was fraud, but there had to be a point where the military government would be afraid to deny the will of the majority. The strategy I hoped to sell to the people gathering in the Plaza Libertad was to show our strength in the next stage of elections, for legislators and mayors.

First I wanted to make sure my own house was prepared for whatever could happen. Again I summoned the whole family to a meeting. My brothers, my in-laws, parents and children, nieces and nephews listened to my explanation of the political situation and what I wanted to do. I told the family we would try to avoid violence. "We're going to tell people to make a legal effort, but at this moment they're ready for anything, and you never know what might happen."

Then I asked my son Alejandro, who was impatiently waiting to leave for the plaza, to step into my room alone. He would not be accompanying me this time, I said. He must stay with his mother. He was too shocked to argue. We made an agreement about his responsibility should anything happen to me.

I called Inés in to reassure her. "I'm a man who doesn't believe in arms or violence, so don't worry, Inés. I don't want to be the cause of the death of any of my people. I'm going to show them the peaceful way out."

Explaining to the average voter the way to confront the government's election tricks was not going to be easy. The government's Central Election Council rejected most of the names on our list of candidates for the assembly. Only their candidates would appear on most ballots. In the capital, we had to explain to our supporters to vote for UNO's candidate for mayor, then to deface the ballot for legislators so that it would be nullified. We had found an obscure clause in the electoral law requiring a new election to be held if the null votes outnumbered the valid votes.

The people understood. On March 12, Salvadorans went back to the polls. The city election council of San Salvador found that the null votes had a majority and annulled the election. The national government overruled them, ignored the law and changed the results.

Public disgust was so great that it permeated even the military ranks. A few officers, who sensed the danger of mocking democracy and frustrating the hopes of the majority, rebelled. At dawn on March 25, 1972, a military uprising began in San Salvador.

In the darkness, spurts from machine guns and the motor of an Air Force plane passing again and again to the north signaled that a rift had developed in the armed forces. Awakened by the gunfire, I was up on the flat porch roof of my house, overlooking San Salvador from the side of San Benito Mountain, trying to figure out who was fighting whom. It was 5 A.M. when Abraham Rodríguez drove up in his Volkswagen to see if I knew anything. We decided to drive down into the city. At the National Palace, the old government office building in the center of town, I jumped out of the car to ask the officer in charge who was behind this coup, but Rodríguez pulled me back in as the officer angrily waved us off.

The gunfire was too heavy to approach San Carlos barracks. We turned back and went to pick up another of our colleagues, Fidel Chávez Mena, before returning to my house, where Christian Democratic Party leaders had gathered. The phone rang. A voice said he was Colonel Benjamín Mejía, the leader of the coup. He said they had seized President Sánchez Hernández, but still needed to establish complete military control. He would call back then to discuss with me the restoration of democracy.

"Don't do anything rash, Napoleón," Rodríguez warned me. "There's no need to commit yourself. If the coup succeeds, they're bound to come to you anyway. If it fails, you must not be compromised by any involvement."

That made sense, but after Rodríguez and Chávez left, another phone call came asking for my help. Mejía believed I could save lives by making an appeal on the radio, explaining what was happening and advising people how to protect themselves. I decided to do it.

My friends have criticized me for broadcasting the radio appeal and thus taking an active role in a military coup—a failing one at that. How could I, as a democrat, join a military coup? I felt a certain responsibility for what might happen after Mejía's request for help. I had been preaching democracy for the last ten years. Perhaps this group of young officers had risked their lives because they had been drawn to my ideals. Even if I had not influenced them, their intervention on the side of democracy united us. To do nothing for them seemed hypocritical.

I could have waited cautiously for events to unfold. The coup might succeed without my help. But once they had won without my help, the military leaders might be dissuaded from allowing a democratic process to be instituted. And because I had been unwilling to run their risks, I would have absolutely no influence over them. On the other hand, the coup might fail, with or without me. Would I be able to live with my conscience, not knowing whether my action would have made a difference? I concluded that the only way I could live with myself was by taking the side of those fighting for a better form of government.

A truckload of rebel soldiers came to take me to the radio station. They offered me a revolver, which I accepted without saying that I could not shoot. As we drove into the city, shots suddenly exploded around us. The soldiers returned the fire as an automatic reflex, and I held my gun with the awkward realization that I had no idea how to use it. I have never learned, and have yet to fire a gun.

We escaped unharmed, reaching the radio station. On the air, I warned those living near the National Guard headquarters to evacuate before rebel artillery opened fire. I called for the people to erect barricades in the streets to stop loyalist reinforcements from coming into the city.

Afterward we headed for El Zapote, the fortress on the hill adjacent to the Presidential Palace at the southern edge of San Salvador. Mejía and other officers were there. A negotiating team led by the Papal Nuncio was trying to prevent more bloodshed between the rebel officers and Sánchez Hernández' men.

The Air Force, loyal to the government, was threatening to bomb El Zapote and to rally the other military forces in the outlying areas. Nicaraguan dictator Anastasio Somoza also offered his help to the loyalists, and according to his own account he spoke by radio to different officers throughout El Salvador to organize the counterattack.

At San Carlos army barracks, where the rest of the coup supporters were entrenched, things looked bleak. Colonel Manuel Antonio Nuñez warned me, "We've intercepted their radio communications. They're looking for you. Try to get asylum in an embassy and don't forget us. We'll be prisoners, and your influence on the outside might help us." I promised. Nuñez was imprisoned and cashiered from the armed forces after the coup. When I became president, a decade later, I restored him to his rightful place as an officer in a command post.

My colleague Rodríguez was distraught when he had heard my voice over his car radio, allying myself with the rebels. Convinced that the coup was a lost cause, he picked up the keys to the Gonzalo Espina home and took them to my wife. He told her I should take refuge there, because the home of that friendly Venezuelan diplomat would be less closely watched than the embassy itself. As the coup crumbled, I followed Rodríguez' suggestion.

We underestimated the vengeful fury of the government. The thugs whom Sánchez Hernández sent to find me were unconcerned about diplomatic repercussions when they dragged me away. The military government might have disposed of me before the world took notice if my family and my friends had not reacted with such determination to save me.

My wife was waiting at her parents' home. I had given Inés all the passports and financial papers to enable her to leave the country once I received asylum. Before I left the house, I asked my father-in-law to take care of her for me, whatever happened. Hours later, the phone call came from Gonzalo Espina, who had to tell my family how the armed men had broken into his home and taken me. No one in the family wanted to say it aloud, but they all came to the same conclusion: if a diplomat was treated that badly, then surely I would be killed.

Inés would not allow her fears to overcome her. She forced herself to pick up the telephone and make calls. She called the American ambassador, who said he would notify other ambassadors and see what he could do.

Her next thought was to have my brother Rolando reach my former professor, Father Theodore Hesburgh, the president of Notre Dame University, to get his help in mobilizing international pressure to demand my safety. It was Sunday night when Father Hesburgh heard Rolando's voice on the other end of the phone.

"Padrecito, they've put Napo in jail and they're going to give him a quick trial and shoot him at dawn. You've got to save him."

"How am I going to save him when I'm fifteen hundred miles away and it's Sunday night? You want a miracle," replied Father Hesburgh. He then spent the night on the phone trying to work that miracle. He could not convince the State Department to connect him with Secretary of State Henry Kissinger, so he sent him a cable. The only response he received was a letter from Kissinger three weeks later. But Hesburgh's calls did get through to the presidents of Panama and Venezuela, who quickly expressed their concern to Sánchez Hernández. Hesburgh also alerted Vatican officials. The Pope himself asked Sánchez Hernández to ensure my safety.

I am sure the United States intervened to save me, because only U.S. pressure could have kept the military from eliminating me.

The hatred of me among the ruling officers was so great that after the court-martial cleared me of treason each of the judges who acquitted me saw his military career ruined.

After I went to live in exile in Venezuela, Anastasio Somoza boasted that he had saved my life. The Nicaraguan dictator claimed that he had advised the Salvadoran armed forces not to make a martyr out of me, only bring me to trial for treason. Years later, General Somoza sent his cousin Noel Pallais Debayle to collect on the debt of gratitude he claimed I owed him. He wanted me to come to Nicaragua to meet with the opposition politicians, to convince them they would be wiser to work out a deal with Somoza. Pallais called at my house in Caracas at three o'clock one morning to present this plan. He expected me to leave with him immediately for Managua.

My refusal to feel any such obligation to my supposed benefactor outraged Pallais. "They wanted to shoot you, they were all worked up about it, and Tachito persuaded them not to kill you. You owe your life to him."

Regardless of what Somoza may or may not have done for me, I despised everything he stood for. I told Pallais he would someday regret having served his cousin rather than his country.

"I know Tachito does many things wrong," Pallais replied. "But he's my cousin and I'm going to stand by him." And he stood there until the Sandinistas overthrew Somoza in 1979.

That same year the military ruler of El Salvador would be overthrown by officers trying to prevent a civil war. But the violence only mounted. The events of 1972 laid the trap that was to close on El Salvador and bleed her.

4

Exile

EXILES tend to live in the past or in the future. I chose the future.

During the seven years I lived outside El Salvador, in Venezuela, my thoughts, my plans, my concerns, all centered on how the situation was evolving back in my country. I couldn't sleep some nights, waiting for the telephone call that would tell me that the time had come for me to return. I would dream that democratically inclined military officers would rebel and create the right conditions for free elections.

The dreams continued, but reality grew harsher. Every phone conversation, every visitor from El Salvador, brought grimmer news. The military government was squelching all chances of political expression. The violence increased and the society became more polarized as I bore the years of exile. The more I worried about my country, the harder it was to get through the days in Venezuela.

This does not mean I waited idly. On the contrary, I had to keep busy or risk going crazy. When I first arrived in Venezuela, the government assigned me to an office without any work to do. After two weeks I couldn't stand the idleness. I went back to my profession—being an engineer. There were more than enough engineering projects—public and private—to keep me busy. Often I took on several at one time, preferring to work overtime. The public sector occupied me with waste disposal systems, public housing and recreation centers, but I also worked for several private Venezuelan companies. A major construction firm assigned me to a grain storage project in the Acarigua region.

There, while building the silos, I suffered the accident that took three fingers from my left hand. Some people believe I lost these fingers when I was tortured after the 1972 presidential elections. The truth is more banal. A cement mixer had jammed. I was pointing out exactly where the problem was when the mechanic leaned over to see, knocking the switch that set the machine in motion. My hand was crushed between the two pieces. I was flown back to Caracas for medical care.

Besides earning my living as an engineer, I spent my time in Venezuela studying and reflecting on the Christian Democratic movement. The exile years served to build a deeper foundation for my ideology, because my ideas matured in interchanges with other leaders. I was a student, then a teacher, at the Institute for Latin American Christian Democratic Leadership. I wrote a book summing up my philosophy on recreating society through each community structure, the application of Christian Democratic principles. There were many opportunities in Venezuela to meet with other Christian Democrats and political leaders from the Americas and Europe, but I also traveled constantly. I met with Salvadoran Christian Democrats in other Central American countries so that we could plan what to do next.

El Salvador's elections for mayors and the assembly were to be held in March 1974. Our party had internal problems. There was division over who should be the candidate for mayor of San Salvador, but we settled on Antonio Morales Erlich. While I was mayor, Morales had served as a lawyer for the city. He became my defense lawyer when the military charged me with treason for my role in the attempted coup after the 1972 election fraud. The court-martial, carried out after I had been forced into exile, found me innocent. Since there were no longer any charges against me to prevent my return, and since I wanted to help with Morales' campaign, this seemed like the right moment to return to El Salvador.

There was little enthusiasm for these elections. Everyone expected the government to fix the ballot boxes as they had done in 1972. I decided to go back fifteen days before the polling date to try to encourage the voters to turn out, to fight the apathy. The party needed my help to stir up our followers, I argued. The truth was that my own need to return to El Salvador was overwhelming me.

President Molina's advisers debated whether or not to allow my return. "Duarte's nobody anymore," one of them was heard to say. "Let him come back. It will prove he's finished politically. No one will pay any attention to him."

They believed that the people had turned against me because all my efforts in the 1972 campaign proved ineffective. Even the coup which I had joined after the election failed. It was true that the Christian Democrats were demoralized and our organization was weaker. Like Molina, I certainly would not have predicted an enthusiastic welcome. But as I made my way from Ilopango Airport into the city, all along the road the factories ground to a halt. The workers left their posts to cheer me. On both sides of the highway were solid walls of people. Some of the crowd started tearing palm branches from trees, waving them. Suddenly it seemed the whole route was lined by green palm branches, an awesome tribute recalling Jerusalem on Palm Sunday. It took four or five hours to proceed the dozen kilometers to Plaza Libertad, which was filled. The truck's motor gave out along the way, but the crowd pushed us forward. That triumphant procession, defying all the power of the government to deny the popular will, was one of the most gratifying experiences of my life.

But those in power still thought that by manipulating the election machinery they could control the country. Once again, the government rearranged the votes to suit itself. They never even bothered to publish official returns. By these tactics, they kept the opposition to less than a third of the seats in the assembly, although they didn't dare take away the San Salvador mayor's office from our candidate, Morales. In the next election two years later, the opposition parties boycotted the sham entirely.

Despite the discouraging situation in 1974, I intended to stay in El Salvador. After the election, I headed for Caracas to help my wife pack, close the apartment and settle our business affairs. Once these arrangements were completed, I took off for San Salvador, making connections through Central America. As the plane crossed the Gulf of Fonseca, moving from Nicaraguan territory into Salvadoran airspace, the pilot received radio orders to turn back. He was told he would not be allowed to land with me on board. The government had reconsidered their opinion on my political demise, and prescribed a longer period of exile.

When the plane landed in Managua, the airline representative asked me to get off, but the Nicaraguans wouldn't allow it. The Nicaraguan airport officials had contacted President Somoza. "I'm no fool. They can't dump this package on me," he said, ordering the plane to leave at once. The pilot flew east to the nearest Caribbean island, San Andrés, where I was left behind.

Prohibited from making phone calls, I was held on that island three days until another airline agreed to fly me to Barranquilla, Colombia. It took a week to finally get back to Caracas, where my wife was staying with some friends. There was nothing to do but search for a new apartment and start our life in exile all over again.

I now knew it would be a long time before I could expect to return to El Salvador. But I never stopped working toward that day. For the 1977 presidential elections, our opposition coalition tried one last compromise. We had analyzed our problem as the armed forces' basic distrust of Christian Democrats. We felt the military officers might accept our election victory if they had confidence in the candidate. Therefore, he had to be one of their own. The party looked among the military officers for someone compatible with our ideals, settling on a retired colonel, Ernesto Claramount.

While I had doubts about whether Claramount was the right man, the choice of Antonio Morales Erlich for vice-president reassured me. The party sent Mario Zamora to Caracas to ask me for a recorded statement endorsing the ticket of Claramount and Morales. I provided one taped campaign commercial and wrote out another statement for use in the newspapers.

Looking abroad, Jimmy Carter had just been elected president in the United States, and from the sound of his words we thought U.S. influence might finally be turning to favor fair elections in Latin America. A push toward democracy from the United States might convince the Salvadoran government to respect the votes this time, particularly since we had chosen a military man as our presidential candidate. Hoping to focus U.S. attention on the 1977 election, I headed for Washington to lobby for democracy in Central America.

My welcome to the United States has fluctuated over the years in direct ratio to my political fortunes. During the exile years, each time I came through U.S. customs the FBI would question me for hours. Before I could claim my luggage, someone with an FBI badge would come up to me, politely asking that I accompany him to a special room. He would ask why I came, whom I was going to see in the United States, even if I was involved in drugs.

On this particular trip in 1977, the only person I could state with assurance that I was going to see was Senator Edward M. Kennedy. My contact came through a former Peace Corps volunteer, Mark Schneider, who served in El Salvador while I was mayor, then became an aide to Senator Kennedy. The Church-sponsored Washington Office on Latin America tried to set up other meetings for me, but the only congressman who would see me was Tom Harkin, a Democrat from Iowa.

Harkin was cordial and suggested we might try to catch Vice-President Walter Mondale in the halls of the Senate. He guided me through the corridors of the Capitol. This seemed to be my only chance, as an out-of-office politician from a forgotten country, to reach a high-ranking official in the Carter Administration. When Mondale came by, Harkin approached him, explaining quickly who I was. Mondale turned, shook my hand while a flashbulb went off, then disappeared into an elevator. That was the extent of my contact with the Carter government until 1979, when revolts in Central America finally attracted U.S. attention.

As U.S. policy changed over the years, American politicians saw me in terms of how I fit into their policy. Congressman Harkin and I would meet again in 1982 under very different circumstances. He was visiting El Salvador and I was then president of the junta. He asked me if I really had any influence in the government, and suggested he would put me to a test. I asked what he would like.

"I want to visit a prison, a jail in the barracks, but without any advance warning," Harkin said.

"Okay, let's go right now," I answered. "Don't tell me where we're going, let's get into the car and then you name the destination.''

He asked for the National Police headquarters. There was someone with him from a U.S. human-rights organization, who had a hand-drawn map. Apparently it was meant to lead to secret prison cells. When we walked into the police headquarters, with the officials scrambling out in surprise to meet me, Harkin followed the man with the map. They went down the halls, one way, then another, tapping on the walls, seeking a false one. We came to a boarded-up door. "This is it!" Harkin's companion cried.

I ordered the police to get the tools to break down the door. When the door gave way, there was nothing on the other side. Harkin and his guide went charging off in another direction. After we had scoured the building without finding hidden dungeons, Harkin turned to me in front of the police chief, Colonel Reynaldo López Nuila. "I will testify to what I've seen here in the National Police," Harkin said.

"That's all I ask, just tell what you've seen," I said.

As we drove back to drop him at his hotel, Harkin looked out the window, saying, "You know, you've become too isolated from your people. You wouldn't dare walk these streets among them."

"Stop the car right here," I told the driver. We got out in the heart of the city at dusk, in an area near the market where gamblers, prostitutes and riff-raff mingle. I started walking down the street, Harkin at my side, and a crowd gathered around us. There were shouts of "Viva Duarte!" The more people appeared, the more nervous Harkin looked, so I asked if he was ready to go back to the car.

"I'm going to tell about this when I get home," Harkin said, obviously impressed. But he never did. To have said anything in favor of Duarte would not have advanced his political position at home. He was involved in the Democratic Party's opposition to military aid for El Salvador. He went home saying what he had planned to say all along.

But back in 1977 there was hardly an American politician who cared what happened one way or another in Central America. The Salvadoran government could shoot up the university, persecute the Christian Democrats, eliminate peasant leaders and steal elections without any outcry being raised in the United States. There was no television coverage, no inquiring congressional delegations.

When our election was stolen from us in 1972, American attention was on President Nixon's visit to China. During the years I spent in exile, Latin America had almost no priority with the U.S. government. But it was during that period that the coming violence became inevitable. If democracy could not work, then people had to look for other solutions to their problems. When the armed forces threw me out of El Salvador, faith in the electoral process faded away. Many people concluded that the powers ruling El Salvador would never permit votes to defeat them. Change had to come by other means.

The oligarchy controlling the economy, the armed forces running the government, and the United States protecting its interest in stability all worked to maintain the status quo in El Salvador. These powers did not call themselves conservative. In fact, the Salvadoran Right thinks in a way that could only have been understood by the West in the last century. Their ideology would be found in Manchester's nineteenth-century Liberalism. "Liberal" in El Salvador means a capitalist and can be compared to a "mercantilist" who believes that complete freedom of private enterprise should be zealously guarded by the state, without controls, and should be free to act at will.

The Left wants to eliminate this system completely, recognizing that the pillars of the hegemony—the oligarchy, the armed forces and the United States—each stands in the way. Their strategy is to attack the economy, undermine the government, wage guerrilla war against the Army and use their international influence to discredit U.S. policy. If they succeeded, their violent revolution would replace the old rulers with a new minority, governing in the name of the workers.

We Christian Democrats opposed the same forces of the hegemony that the Left attacked, but we planned a different solution. Our ideology was based on a democratic revolution. The changes would be gradual and selective, eliminating the harmful and pernicious aspects of the status quo, while reforming the reactionary elements. The economy would be based on free enterprise and free association, with the government as director and promoter of a more just society for everyone, including workers and peasants. The armed forces must protect national interests, not special groups. And once the United States learned that supporting democracies can serve its own interests, then that great nation to the north would no longer be part of our problem. It could contribute to our solution.

The Right wanted to maintain its hegemony. The Left sought to replace that hegemony. We wanted to weaken the hegemony by changing the structure so that the will of the people would be the basis of a new society. With the participation and solidarity of all sectors, we could confront the social problems facing the nation. But the Left and the Right both prefer political polarization. The Left concentrated on all the injustices of the Right, claiming that violent revolution was the only alternative. The Right used the fear of the violent revolution to maintain its power, knowing it must defeat the Left militarily, because it is weak politically. These two forces preferred violent confrontation, and, in the process, by the end of the 1970s they had decimated the Christian Democrats, eroding away any democratic center ground.

How were we going to have a peaceful revolution, and create a democracy, in the midst of an armed struggle between Left and Right?

The Left had been weak since Farabundo Martí's rebellion was wiped out by the military forces in 1932. For the next forty years, the Communist Party's objective was survival. Ties with other political forces became their strategy, although not without strong dissent among some party members. The Communist Party couldn't overcome its basic weakness among the working class. El Salvador's worker did not respond to the Marxist view. Its unions never had any strength. The Salvadoran worker's mentality is too individualistic. The oligarchy's "liberal" philosophy has been absorbed into the workers' minds. Worse, much of Salvadoran society thinks like the oligarchs. Without any affinity among the workers, the Communists had to work through other political groups during a period of forty years.

After the government destroyed all chances for fair elections, the Communists turned inward. Their dissident underground organizations—the Trotskyites, the Maoists, the Anarchists—gained power among the Left. The Communists' former secretary general, Salvador Cayetano Carpio, had split with the party in 1970. Along with younger members, he founded a guerrilla group, the Farabundo Martí People's Liberation Forces (FPL). After the 1972 election farce, Carpio seemed vindicated. Another guerrilla group, the People's Revolutionary Army (ERP), emerged in 1972 under the leadership of poet Roque Dalton. After Dalton was executed by his own comrades, Joaquín Villalobos took over the ERP. Dalton's supporters then formed their own guerrilla organization, Armed Forces of the National Resistance (FARN).

As the guerrilla groups became well established, alliances were formed with the broad, nonviolent federations of unions and peasant organizations. These mass organizations, the People's Revolutionary Block of the FPL, or the People's United Action Front of the FARN, protested openly. They called strikes, sit-ins and marches, using the tactics of civil disobedience. The mass organizations grew while our party withered.

The guerrillas planned to lead the masses gradually toward an insurrection, strengthening the guerrilla movements but without exposing themselves to any risks. It was important to them to keep the mass organizations and guerrilla groups separate. The mass organizations denied any relation to the military forces of the guerrillas and vice versa. They knew that the Salvadoran people weren't ready or willing to take part in guerrilla warfare. But working through the mass organizations the guerrillas would select judiciously the ones who were ready to take that step.

The university, the Church and the workers could all work together to undermine the existing system of inequities under the banners of the mass organizations. The nonviolent theory, Gandhi's model, appealed to many university students. Christian Democrats, orphaned because so many leaders like myself were forced into exile, gravitated into the nonviolent mass movements. The Jesuits played an important role, strengthening and orienting these organizations, even though they never controlled them. The guerrillas were clever. They were careful not to contaminate this movement—which they knew would turn toward them as soon as the government repressed it.

The Right reacted violently against the protests. The government blundered along with a heavy hand. Molina's first act as president was to close the university, only reopening it a year later under government management. But he failed to tame the students who were provoked into major demonstrations when the government callously decided to spend over a million dollars hosting the Miss Universe Pageant in 1975. At least twelve students died when National Guardsmen opened fire on the demonstrators.

In 1975, a right-wing terrorist group calling itself FALANGE appeared, promising to kill all Communists, including priests. In the village of Aguilares, less than a year after the arrival of some Jesuit priests, the sugar mill workers struck for a raise they had been promised. The Right wouldn't stand for priests who showed peasants how to demand their rights. Father Rutilio Grande of Aguilares was murdered by the White Warrior Union in March 1977. Two months later, leftist terrorists assassinated the Foreign Minister; then the right-wing terrorists killed another priest. All through the 1970s, pushed by the extreme Right and the Left, official and unofficial violence escalated.

By 1977, General Carlos Humberto Romero was elected president in the most blatant fraud El Salvador had ever known. Police and ORDEN, a paramilitary group of informers and enforcers, forcibly removed or arrested opposition party poll watchers. Some ballot boxes were full before the voting even began. Orders went out over two-way radios to stuff more ballots wherever necessary. The day after the election, people began gathering in the Plaza Libertad, where the opposition candidates, Claramont and Morales, vowed to stay with them as long as the people wanted, to show the government they would not accept this fraud. At the end of the week, on February 28, military forces charged the crowd, firing machine guns that killed over a hundred innocent people. Morales fled into exile in Costa Rica.

General Romero presided while the Right attempted to fight terror with terror. The guerrillas kidnapped for ransom and revenge, the right-wing death squads looked only for revenge through the elimination of nonviolent leaders, priests and peasants. Christian Democrats were persecuted throughout the country, and many of my colleagues left the country.

While I was in exile, there were attempts to unite leading opposition figures abroad into a front such as the one formed among Nicaraguan politicians, educators and businessmen prior to the Sandinista revolution. Many democratic leaders were united with the Sandinista guerrillas to overthrow Somoza. But I always turned down such approaches from the Salvadoran guerrillas. I would see Shafik Handal, still the pacifist leader of the Communists, who stopped by to see me in Caracas whenever he traveled abroad, but he never spoke to me about the armed struggle.

The Communist Party was the last to form its own guerrilla group, which it finally did in 1979, calling it the Armed Forces of Liberation (FAL). At that point, the Communists believed that other Central American countries were bound to follow the Nicaraguan pattern of mass insurrection. Even before the Nicaraguan democrats became disillusioned with the Sandinistas, I was skeptical about their alliance with the Left. I suspected that the guerrillas were posing as democrats only to impose their own Marxist theories on the people after they had won.

It was not until after the Sandinista guerrillas marched victoriously into Managua in July 1979 that any U.S. government official tried to reach me to discuss the problems in El Salvador. Suddenly, thanks to the Sandinistas, Central America's tragedy caught the attention of the United States.

I was invited to the house of a friend in Caracas to meet with the U.S. Assistant Secretary of State for Inter-American Affairs, Viron Vaky. He wanted to know what could be done to save El Salvador. I told him the opposition parties were already working with the important sectors of Salvadoran society to present a democratic plan to General Romero.

We had already formed the working groups of the People's Forum from the parties, the private sector, the unions and the

The Duarte Family (circa 1934). The children are, from left, Rolando,
José Napoleón and Alejandro.

The Duarte and the Durán families. José Napoleón is second from the right, his future wife Inés is the second girl from the left.

The Boy Scout troop. José Napoleón is left center, the scoutmaster's arm on his shoulder. The scoutmaster then is today Cardinal Sebastian Baggio, Camerlengo of the Sacred Roman Curia and President of the Pontifical Commission for the State of the City of the Vatican.

The Liceo Salvadoreño graduating class of 1944. Duarte stands in the center row, sixth from the left.

The engagement photo of Inés Durán and José Napoleón Duarte.

Wedding portrait, August 14, 1949.

Dancing in Mexico on their honeymoon.

Duarte is sworn in as mayor of San Salvador, 1964.

A victory celebration for the mayor.

The mayor throws the switch that illuminates San Salvador's new system of street lights.

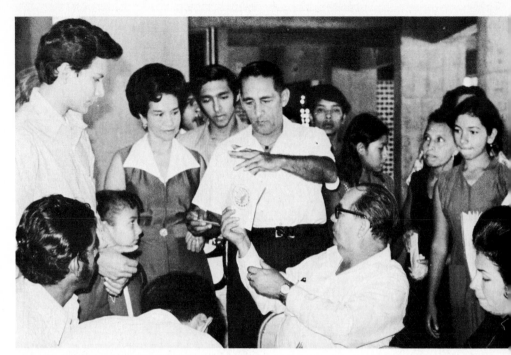

1972 Presidential candidate José Napoleón Duarte casts his own ballot, his wife at his side. Son José Napoleón, Jr., looks over between his parents. *La Prensa Gráfica.*

After being beaten, jailed and expelled to Guatemala, Duarte talks to reporters, the bruises from the beatings still evident. *La Prensa Gráfica.*

Church. Under Archbishop Oscar Romero, the Church criticized the government and defended the priests working with the poor. Archbishop Romero even refused to attend General Romero's inauguration in 1977. (The Romeros were not related.)

Vaky went to see General Romero, who agreed to talk with the opposition, then reneged. The changes outlined by the People's Forum called for an end to right-wing paramilitary groups, for guaranteed freedom to organize and to strike, for opportunities to provide peasants with their own land, and for a transitional government leading to democracy. General Romero was not listening, but the military officers, particularly the younger lieutenants, captains and majors, began to speak candidly among themselves about the future of their caste. The marches, strikes and terrorism had gone beyond control by repression. The officers were afraid the armed forces might not be able to put out the fires of revolution. To save the armed forces, they would have to break their alliance to the oligarchy and realign with political forces that could win popular support. Many officers vacillated over this political choice until the Nicaraguan revolution convinced them. After Salvadoran officers watched the Nicaraguan people celebrate in the streets the defeat and dismemberment of Somoza's National Guard, the conspiracy against Romero gained firm adherents—even among normally conservative officers.

One of the problems with analyzing the military is that officers do not fit neatly into political categories. They change. Because they lack an ideological foundation, the military decide questions on a case-by-case basis, often influenced by whoever spoke to them most recently. Coups d'état depend on the convergence of forces in a society more than on a few tireless instigators. Those military men working for a coup in 1979 seized the moment of confluence, but they were not strong enough to dominate without negotiating, even after they launched the revolt.

On October 15, 1979, my son Alejandro called me from San Salvador. "I'm seeing a number of strange things going on in the capital," he said. "There are lots of Air Force planes flying around. I think there's been a coup."

Shortly after, the American ambassador in Caracas called to say he was sending over an embassy official to speak to me. The State Department wanted to know what I could tell them about the coup in El Salvador. They seemed worried about their lack of information. They wanted to know if I was returning to San Salvador to join the new government. In all honesty, I told them I didn't even know who had led this coup.

The coup leaders themselves were not sure who would be in charge. They first agreed to organize a ruling junta formed of five members. One of the military officers on the ruling junta should be Colonel Adolfo Majano, who had been a favorite professor at the Military Academy. Majano had learned about the plot only a week beforehand. Colonel Jaime Abdul Gutierrez, the highest-ranking of the conspirators since August, took another position on the junta. The officers asked the People's Forum to name a candidate for the junta, and Guillermo Ungo, my former vice-presidential running mate who would later join the guerrillas, became the third junta member. The officers then asked the president of the Jesuit Central American University, Román Mayorga Quiroz, and Mario Andino, a Phelps Dodge factory manager active with the Chamber of Commerce, also to serve with them on the junta.

The armed-forces proclamation of October 15, giving the objectives of the coup, was a popular document. It was similar in many ways to the platform drawn up by the People's Forum. The military themselves denounced the violence of the ORDEN thugs, the corruption in the government and the abuse of human rights. They called for agrarian reform, respect for labor unions, and free elections "within a reasonable period." But when Fidel Chávez Mena called to advise me that the Christian Democrats were considering participation in the new government, my recommendation was to stay out.

"I don't think we should accept any role in the government," I told him. "Let the military govern alone. Let them set the date for elections quickly and we'll begin preparing our plan for a democracy. The coup hasn't weakened our call for democracy. It has strengthened it."

I was convinced that by participating in a government through a pact with the military, our party would be weak from the start. We would be granted power only at the convenience of the armed forces. Chávez Mena presented my view to the Christian Democratic political committee, but the committee went along with Rubén Zamora's position. He felt our participation was essential for the country. Zamora and the younger members of our party shared the conviction that elections were discredited by so many frauds and that reforms could be implemented if we used this opportunity to govern instead of worrying about setting up a democracy first.

The Zamora group did not want me to return to the country. They were afraid that my presence would sway many party members against their plans. But they still could not control the Christian Democrats' national directorate. The party leaders voted to have me return as soon as possible. On October 25, ten days after the coup, I came home.

Before the party's decision, I had gone to talk with Venezuelan President Luis Herrera Campins about the military-civilian government being formed in my country. Herrera looked at me quietly for a moment, then said, "I think your country needs you. I'll provide a plane and protection until you land in El Salvador."

Venezuelan security agents, journalists and a German television crew accompanied me on a small plane headed for San Salvador. We flew first to Panama to spend the night. At the airport, a man who identified himself as a representative of the Sandinista government in Nicaragua asked me where I was staying. He and three other men with him said they were sent to protect me. Their names have since become known for their commando-type missions abroad. The Venezuelan agents became so suspicious of these Nicaraguans that they insisted I go to another hotel. At the hotel where I had my reservations, the Venezuelan investigation uncovered a plot to kill me with a bomb in the elevator.

There was every indication that my assassination had been ordered by a group in the Sandinista security forces, probably in collaboration with the Salvadoran guerrillas. The Panamanian government was not involved. There was no need for me to contact Panama's leader, General Omar Torrijos, who happened to have been a student of mine when he studied at the Salvadoran Military Academy.

My next stop was Costa Rica, where President Rodrigo Carazo met me at the airport. Again, the same four Nicaraguans who had been in Panama were waiting for me in San José. The Venezuelan security men insisted I cut short my stay there and fly directly to San Salvador.

When our plane made its landing pass over San Salvador, I felt with sadness how different this homecoming could be from the joyous welcome that greeted me five years before. Down below, the streets looked deserted. Perhaps no one will turn out for my return, I thought.

My heart warmed when I saw several thousand people gathered at the airport. The crowd included my mother, other family members and Christian Democratic Party leaders. Rey Prendes, Morales, Mario Zamora, Antonio Guevara, Ovidio Hernández

and my son Alejandro formed the committee planning my welcome, with my son in charge of security. When Alejandro asked
the new government to help organize protection, he was told to
work with Colonel Eugenio Vides Casanova, chief of the National
Guard. Vides assigned Guardsmen to provide security at the airport, but the ten-day-old government was unwilling to police the
streets or try to maintain order if this meant confrontation with
the leftists. My party had learned from friends within the more
radical organizations that the guerrillas planned to kill me as soon
as I arrived.

The word among the Left was that I would never reach the
Plaza Libertad. The Left could see no use for me since I had
refused to work with them. But their efforts to eliminate me
showed that, unlike the military government in 1974, they believed I still had political support. They feared the man they said
was out of touch with reality in El Salvador. One attempt on my
life was meant to take place at the airport, but strict security there
meant they had to wait for opportunities along the route to the
plaza.

For the drive into the city, I mounted a box on the back of an
eight-ton truck, with twenty-five men forming a human wall
around me. As we drove down the highway lined by factories, the
workers again came out to cheer. The press estimated 100,000
people crowding along the streets and waiting in the plaza. But
leaning above the walls of one factory occupied by a guerrilla
group, men with machine guns kept us in their sights. When the
truck reached the Flower Clock intersection, thousands of waving
people slowed it down. A man leaped up on the side, a gun in his
hand. One of my bodyguards knocked the gun into the air, while
the other men pushed the man off the truck. He sank into the
crowd like a pebble in the sea.

As the truck reached a downtown corner between two tall

buildings, Alejandro could see a line of leftist demonstrators blocking our way. "Turn the truck now, into that side street," he told the driver, pounding on his arm. "Move it."

Our party supporters, marching in front of the truck, charged at the leftists. Rocks and bottles started flying, but the truck had already wedged itself into the narrow side street when gunshots rang out.

The street skirmish had been planned to slow the truck down so that snipers on the roof of one of the tall buildings would have a clear shot at me. They lost that chance when the truck wound around the back street to reach the Plaza Libertad from the opposite direction. I mounted the platform there before anyone knew I had arrived. The crowd was looking in the direction of the fighting between the leftists and the Christian Democrats.

I was taking a microphone to speak when a Molotov cocktail suddenly exploded at the foot of the platform, setting it on fire. The fire, the rocks and the gunshots forced me to abandon my speech.

Perhaps this was a fitting welcome to the country El Salvador had become by 1979. No one seemed to be in control, neither the junta, the security forces nor the leftists. The army officers were fighting among themselves, dissatisfied with the direction the government was going. They had staged the coup, but they did not control the government. Nor did the government control them. In October of 1979 there was a power vacuum, with everyone trying to grab power but no one in charge. The ministries were divided among the political groups. Fighting among themselves, they talked eloquently about ideals, but they were unable to administer the government.

In my opinion, the weakness of the government lay in its lack of political support, which was exactly where I could help. The day after my return, I asked to meet with members of the junta, but none of them would receive me. Even Ungo, my former running mate, refused. Only the undersecretary of the Economy Minister, a Christian Democrat, came to me when the new government had no money to pay for oil. They wanted me to use my influence in Venezuela to ask for credit. I made a trip back and arranged for petroleum and financial aid. Still, the junta found no reason to see me.

The ones who did want to talk with me were the oligarchs, the leaders of the Right. They were worried by the threat of agrarian reform. The fact that the coup proclamation included land reform among its objectives would not normally have bothered them; all military coups pledged social reforms, then did nothing. But the pressure of the Left, with its power within the government, did frighten the Right. They thought of converting me into a spearhead for the Right, to lead a popular movement against the Left. But after talking to me, they concluded I would not be manageable, nor was I conservative enough. These same men would later found the ARENA party, using Major Roberto d'Aubuisson as their voice.

The Right wanted to use me. The Left wanted to kill me. And the junta government didn't want anything to do with me. After my seven years in exile, only the people seemed to care.

5

The Worst of Times

THE October junta was probably doomed as a multiheaded monster from its birth. Not even the colonels on the junta, Jaime Gutierrez and Adolfo Majano, agreed on where the government was headed. The differences between these two military officers would eventually lead to a confrontation within the Army. Meanwhile, the tension between the officers and the civilians grew. Two of the civilian junta members, Ungo and Mayorga, identified with the Left and were frequently at odds with the businessman on the junta, Mario Andino.

Below the junta, the crevices widened even deeper among the ministers from opposing political philosophies, giving El Salvador a government of national disunity. The Labor Ministry was under a Communist, Gabriel Gallegos. It was taken over by the leftist mass organizations, as was the Education Ministry. The Defense Minister, Colonel José Guillermo García, continued the repressive policies of the deposed Romero government, letting the security forces use brute force and terror against leftist demonstrations. The junta ordered the disbanding of ORDEN, a paramilitary network of informers and vigilantes, but, under the protection of the armed forces, ORDEN continued to operate. The junta appointed a committee to investigate the fate of political prisoners who had disappeared, with obvious aims to destroy the army structure, and the armed forces refused to be held accountable.

By December, as the government tottered, the junta's own Minister of the Presidency, Rubén Zamora, was eager for its collapse. Zamora and his brother Mario were both leaders of the Christian Democratic Party, members of its key political committee. Mario, a true believer in Christian Democratic concepts, would pay for his commitment with his life. Rubén, a Marxist-minded political scientist, would later join the guerrillas. Back then, he believed that the disintegration of the junta government would enable him to dictate new terms to the military. Zamora thought that when the Army faced the alternative of either the complete collapse of the government or its own submission to the junta's control, the armed forces would accept any order, especially those aimed at stopping the abuses. If not, then the Army would be left without any political allies.

"We'll make the Army accept a second junta," Zamora told me. "But this time, we, the Christian Democrats, will lead the junta and we'll bring in other parties as we see fit."

"It won't work," I cautioned. "The other parties will not go along, and you are trying to get the Army to surrender. It's impossible." Even if the Army promised us complete control of the government, I knew they would still have the rifles in their hands. All that time, the majority of the high-ranking officers had antidemocratic ideas in their heads, and military men who give power away on a basis of convenience, not conviction, can take it back at their whim.

Zamora thought he could impose control on the Army without laying the groundwork, without weeding out the incorrigibles, and, most important, without leading the military to the reasoned conclusion that working within a democracy is the best way the Army can serve the people and defend the nation. Over the years, this would be my task, while Zamora's was to represent the FMLN guerrillas abroad.

I came to the conclusion that if I were forced to choose between converting the Marxist guerrillas to my democratic philosophy and trying to convince the officers, I stood a better chance with the armed forces. If I had understood the armed forces better years ago, my work would have been easier. My prejudice against the military was deeply rooted in the history of El Salvador, and I regret not having learned how to analyze the philosophy of the military much earlier. It is hard to categorize officers. They move along the spectrum of political thought, responding to a particular issue or to whom they spoke to last. But it is this flexibility that has led to the changes that are now evident in the Salvadoran armed forces.

Back in December 1979, I advised my party not to join the second junta government. Elections were the only basis for governing. By deriving power from elections, ones sanctioned by the armed forces, a civilian government would have more control than we could win through concessions from the Army. But everyone thought I was unrealistic. Why insist on elections when the country was verging on chaos? The Christian Democratic national committee backed Zamora's strategy of negotiating with the military.

The Left took strength from the chaos, from the bloodshed, the hundreds of victims each month. This made a mass insurrection more likely. The Left was counting on a broad-based uprising, not a guerrilla victory. At that time, the tiny guerrilla cells had no hope of defeating the Army. They were capable only of destabilizing the government.

Their plan was to lead a massive revolt by the population, the way the Sandinista guerrillas led the people against Somoza's dictatorship. First the Left needed to totally discredit the junta by turning everyone against it. The Left began by dismantling the government. The first group to resign was the Communists—the Labor Minister and the Education Minister, Salvador Samayoa, who announced that he was joining the guerrillas.

Next to resign was the Minister of Agriculture, Enrique Alvarez, protesting at the lack of support for agrarian reform. Alvarez, who was a friend of mine, had taken the first step toward land reform by freezing ownership of all landholdings over 100 hectares (247 acres). He went off to head the political alliance representing the Left, the Democratic Revolutionary Front, known as the FDR.

Although he was rich and I was not, I had known Alvarez all my life, because we formed the basketball team that became the national champion. But when I returned from exile I found a different Enrique Alvarez—resentful, reserved. We saw each other only once while he was a minister of the junta. Still, I considered him a friend, a noble man with a big heart. On November 27, 1980, less than a year after resigning from the government, he was kidnapped with five other leaders by a paramilitary hit squad that invaded an FDR meeting. Their bodies were found a few days later. His death hit me hard.

The third wave of resignations from the junta government, on January 3, 1980, included all the non-Communist Left and the Christian Democrats. But this group had a plan to come back as the next government. Their resignation letter read like a political platform.

Following Zamora's plan, the Christian Democratic Party laid down a set of conditions under which we would agree to participate in the government. There had to be a public commitment on the part of the armed forces to the changes we demanded and a timetable for their implementation. The junta had to be restructured. It had to exercise authority over the military forces. The agrarian reforms and economic changes promised by the October 15 declaration had to take place. In the Army's mind, the issue was whether our political plan would help them to defeat the leftist guerrillas or handicap the Army by our insistence on applying the law and respecting human rights.

In every discussion they asked, "Are you willing to fight the guerrillas?" It was a clash of two mentalities. They considered any controls on the abuses of authority as our way of avoiding confrontation with the guerrillas. We considered the controls essential because we had suffered the abuses ourselves—we were the ones being killed.

A decisive meeting took place January 5 in the Presidential Palace's Blue Room. On one side of the long table sat Colonels Gutierrez and Majano, Defense Minister Colonel García and his deputies: Colonel Francisco Castillo and the officer who would rather have eliminated Christian Democrats than negotiate with them—Colonel Nicolás Carranza. All the party leaders—including Zamora and me—faced them across the table.

The night before, I had made a televised speech explaining our position. The Christian Democrats offered the armed forces a political program, based on our ideology. We were not merely seeking a share of government power, we were offering the blueprint for a new form of government—democracy. The transitional form of government should not be based on a corporative model, one that allotted representation to sectors such as business or labor. For this reason, Mario Andino, the spokesman of the business sector, did not belong on the junta. But the Right was pushing the military to keep Andino on the junta.

The discussion of this issue between the colonels and the Christian Democrats became very tense. I finally asked to make a statement.

"We, as a party, have no interest in being a part of the junta government, because our only interest is leading the country toward a democracy," I began. "The points we have presented as a basis for participation are not points of honor with us personally. They are the points of honor that define democracy. Without these essential conditions, while we could resolve circumstantial differences, we would never reach a democracy."

There were other solutions the armed forces could choose, I explained. The armed forces could govern alone. They could find technocrats to administer the government. They could work out an alliance with the business or labor sector that would lead to a corporate state. But none of these alternatives would resolve the basic political conflict of how a society agrees to be governed. If the armed forces wanted a political foundation, then the basis of our endeavor had to be an agreement on a political concept, democracy. We were not proposing a coalition or a corporate state, so a person allied with the Right, as Andino was, had no reason to be part of the government we planned.

"The junta should be composed of two Christian Democrats, two representatives of the armed forces and one respected person whom we both agree on," I concluded.

When I finished this statement, no one said anything. In the midst of the silence, Mario Andino walked into the room, uninvited. He took a chair on the military side of the table and asked to speak.

"I heard Napoleón say last night that as long as I remain in the government, the Christian Democrats cannot participate," Andino said. "I do not wish to be an obstacle, therefore I resign from the junta. But I will warn you that this is a bad mistake. From now on, the business sector will consider the government their enemy and you will not be able to govern. This situation won't last very long. God help you."

He got up and walked out of the room.

After he left, there was no further discussion. We would meet the next day. This allowed the armed forces time to consider all that had been said. They decided to accept Andino's resignation.

On January 9, 1980, the armed forces published their promises to implement reforms, bring forth a democracy and respect human rights. The Christian Democrats' convention then chose Antonio Morales Erlich and Hector Dada Hirezi to join the new junta with Colonels Gutierrez and Majano. Neither I nor the party wished for me to be a member of the junta. My character and experience were suited for a democratic environment, not a military junta. If our pact with the armed forces meant anything, elections must come someday. I was being held in reserve for that time.

Selecting the fifth member of the junta was a problem. The Army kept proposing names from the Right which we rejected, and they turned down our nominees. The compromise, suggested by my wife, was Dr. Ramón Avalos, an apolitical doctor with a social conscience whom the military respected.

Next, I knew we had to build popular support for the new junta if it was to have strength against the Left and the Right. "If we're going to be part of this government," I argued within the party, "we should call a meeting of the people and tell them that we need their help." The rally we tried to organize failed. The Christian Democrats were too afraid of violent attacks from the Right and the Left.

Even our party veterans, including Rey Prendes, who was then mayor of San Salvador, and my son Alejandro, organized the plan timidly, adding so many precautions that no one knew what to do or where to go. Instead of twenty thousand people, five hundred turned up. That was how our junta period began—with the image of a government that no one seemed to want.

When the Left saw our failure, they seized the moment. Their mass organizations had grown over the past eight years while our grass roots withered. They had recruited many of those who had voted as Christian Democrats in the past—the unionized laborers, the teachers, the Church activists.

On January 11, all the leftist parties, the Communists and the mass organizations of the guerrilla groups, united under the name of Revolutionary Coordinator of the Masses, known as the CRM. They called a demonstration for January 22, the anniversary of the 1932 Communist revolt. Over 100,000 people went into the streets. Some security forces fired on the marchers from the National Palace. In protest, militants from one of the mass organizations, the LP-28, took over our party headquarters, holding about thirty hostages including the daughter of Morales Erlich, one of the junta. The LP-28 wanted to obtain the release of some of their militants taken by the police and to denounce the Christian Democrats for belonging to such a repressive junta.

These seizures of offices, embassies and businesses by leftist organizations happened frequently. The leftists wanted publicity. If the police reacted brutally to the seizures, then the Left knew they would win more sympathy. At this stage, the leftists needed international solidarity to prepare for the armed insurrection.

We asked the armed forces to let us handle the LP-28 seizure of our headquarters, but after they had agreed to this the military's actions belied their words. We could have ended the confrontation with the LP-28 peacefully. It was tiring, but we had almost convinced them to leave when the Treasury Police stormed the building on February 12, 1980. Colonel Francisco Morán had ignored our instructions and ordered his men to take the party headquarters by force. The LP-28 leaders were killed after they surrendered.

Less than a month after joining the junta, we threatened to walk out. We demanded that Morán be dismissed. To mollify us, his commanders promised he would be ousted, but they said a few days were necessary to ensure that it went smoothly. Of course he stayed on. This was the beginning of a sordid struggle between the Christian Democrats, allegedly governing, and officers such as García and Carranza, exercising their personal power within the armed forces.

The Right was already working to get rid of our junta government before we could enact any agrarian-reform laws. A coup was planned for February 23. Retired Major Roberto d'Aubuisson emerged at this time as the spokesman of the Right, launching television attacks against those he called Communist infiltrators in the government. The junta looked weak at this moment. Colonel Gutierrez had left the country for medical treatment, leaving Colonel Majano the sole military member on the junta.

The García-Carranza cabal began maneuvering to increase their power in the government. I was unaware of what was happening when a group of officers invited me to dinner. They asked many questions concerning the Christian Democrats' view of what the high command was doing. The day after that dinner, a countermove by Majano's backers in the capital's San Carlos barracks, with the support of seven other bases, threatened to overthrow the junta if García was not removed as defense minister. Gutierrez rushed back to El Salvador. To save the junta, he and Majano promised the officers they would resolve the problem of García. But he stayed on as defense minister.

Meanwhile, the United States was putting its full weight against any coup. U.S. military aid had been cut off under General Romero's regime. Now, to support the slim chance of a democratic regime, the United States was offering $50 million in aid, including $4.8 million destined for nonlethal military supplies—trucks, radio equipment, tear gas. In Washington and El Salvador, publicly and privately, President Carter's diplomats sent out the word to the military: no coups.

The extreme Right's death squads continued killing Christian Democrats, carrying out d'Aubuisson's strategy to force the party out of the government. On the night of February 22, a small group of Christian Democrats got together for a party at the home of Mario Zamora, who held the post of attorney general for the poor. Morales Erlich stayed until midnight, and the bodyguards assigned to him later recalled a car circling the block several times. Minutes after Morales left, hooded men broke into the Zamora home. They forced everyone to lie face down on the floor, then took Mario into the bathroom and shot him.

Mario's murder shocked us deeply. His loss made the Christian Democrats wonder how long we could continue to try to govern if our best men were being systematically assassinated. Some of us thought the Right had killed Zamora because he was one of our most articulate leaders. They intended to destroy our party along with the government. D'Aubuisson had picked out Zamora to denounce by name only days before the assassination, accusing him of links with the guerrillas. D'Aubuisson's pointed finger would prove deadly time and again.

But some within our party wondered if the Left could have killed Zamora: by making us blame the Right and the Army, they might cause us to resign from the government and join the rebellion.

Whoever killed him, the objective was the same—to force us

out of the government. We were determined not to let them succeed. But Hector Dada could no longer take the pressure, and he resigned from the junta. Dada was influenced by Rubén Zamora, who, after his brother's murder, decided to go into exile and work with the guerrilla front. Dada was a theorist who could never stand reality. He was always saying, "This is intolerable, I won't take it"—first as a legislator, later as the first junta's foreign minister, then as a junta member. After he went to Mexico to join the guerrillas, he threw up his hands and left them too. He is an idealist and could not bear the harsh choices of El Salvador.

Dada provoked a crisis among the Christian Democrats by resigning just before the agrarian-reform decree. He chose to quit March 6, two days before it was enacted. I think it was because he did not want to sign the decree. Dada knew that if the reforms were successful his rationale for going off to join those who advocated a violent revolution would be undercut; and if the reforms failed, he did not want to be associated with them.

The decree, enforced by the military seizure of many plantations under a state of siege, affected 25 percent of El Salvador's arable land. These were the landholdings of just 244 owners who each held more than 1,250 acres. At the same time, the banks were nationalized. This was a necessary attempt to keep Salvadoran agriculture from being decapitalized by the bank-owning oligarchs based in Miami. That same week, the Christian Democratic Party, after working hard to begin these reforms, had to decide whether to name another junta member and stay in the government. Dada had asked for a party convention to receive his resignation. On March 9 the delegates convened. The majority wanted me to serve on the junta. They no longer believed I could wait to be a candidate in elections. The party needed the strongest individual we could get on the junta.

Rey Prendes warned the convention that staying in the junta

was a no-win situation for the party. I remember him saying, "If we stay in this government and we win [by creating a democracy], we'll lose. And if we stay in this government and fail, we lose." In Rey Prendes' analysis, even by achieving our primary objective the party was going to be sullied by the compromises it would have to make to create a democracy out of a military junta. But the alternative of leaving the government also meant that the Christian Democrats would lose—to either a leftist insurrection or a rightist dictatorship. The party would suffer either way, but with the agrarian reforms enacted, and a chance to create the conditions for democracy, could we turn our back on the junta?

My personal desire was to stay out of the junta. Until this moment, all the difficulties with the armed forces, all the killings, were not mine to resolve. By becoming a junta member, I would have to accept that the violence would be my responsibility.

I wanted my legacy to be democracy, not deaths. Was the junta the only way to take El Salvador toward a democracy? The Right and the Left both assumed the junta could not survive. Those in my party, like Zamora, who expected the Left to win wanted to play a role in the revolution in order to ride into power with the guerrillas. The only force holding back the leftist revolution was the Army.

But this Army was different from the old military that the Right thought they controlled. Twice in the last six months, this Army had taken as its own objectives the program of the Christian Democrats—at least some elements in the armed forces who were more concerned about appalling misery and injustice in El Salvador than I would ever have believed. In fact, I did not fully understand the armed forces. We had been enemies for so long. It was hard for me to estimate how many officers were really committed to establishing a real democracy in El Salvador.

The chances of using my position on the junta to influence the

Army seemed very slight. But what was the alternative? I probably knew the guerrillas' thinking better than I did the Army's. I had known some of their leaders, such as Shafik Handal, for years. The Communists may have split over tactics, but their ideological commitment is coherent and unvarying. It was not the one I wanted to see imposed on my country.

The night before the party convention I was driving home with my son Alejandro, full of doubts about becoming a member of the junta.

"What do you think I should do?" I asked Alejandro, who never tells me what he thinks I should do unless I ask.

"Let me put it this way," Alejandro replied. "If you ask me as a politician do I think democracy has any future in this country, do I think it can be saved, then the answer is this: There's an exact moment in history when the right man is needed for a crisis. Unless this man can keep the country from giving up, from going to the extremes, then neither the Christian Democrats nor the country will be saved. There isn't anyone but you with the stamina and conviction to take on this responsibility."

As a father, I felt the burden my son's estimation placed on me. I knew I had to try. My decision to join the junta was the only positive response I could make to the threatening disaster in El Salvador. To refuse the position would have been to abandon my life's work for my country.

The party directorate voted 136 to 5 to send me into the junta government. The five who were opposed resigned eventually. Those who quit claimed that the party split over my participation in the junta. But the lopsided vote speaks for itself. Rubén Zamora had lost his influence over the party delegates, the same ones who had followed his lead in electing Dada to the junta.

Within two weeks, my faith in our ability to save El Salvador was put to a severe test. Our beloved Archbishop Oscar Romero was assassinated. The Archbishop preached his last homily at San Salvador's Metropolitan Cathedral March 23, calling on soldiers to disobey their superiors if ordered to kill. He said, "No soldier is obliged to obey an order against the law of God." The next day, as the Archbishop said Mass in a hospital chapel, an assassin killed him with a single shot to his heart.

Minutes later, a secretary ran desperately into the room on the second floor of the Presidential Palace where the junta was meeting.

"They've just killed Monsignor Romero!" she cried.

I felt as if the world were ending. "It's all over," I said aloud, walking out of the room onto the balcony. Three Cabinet officials followed me, in shock, asking what should they do.

"Stay here in the palace, we have to be ready for the worst," I answered, thinking that mass rioting, even a revolt, would erupt.

But the police reported that no one was in the streets. San Salvador appeared totally deserted, the houses blackened out, no lights. The silence was suffocating. I listened, hoping to hear something, any normal sound. All night I waited in the palace, receiving the police reports.

I knew we had to bring the killers of Monsignor Romero to justice if the country was ever to emerge from its moral decline. But that investigation still goes on today. The police photographer reached the chapel shortly after the murder, taking a sequence of photos which we have. This was practically the only attempt made then at gathering evidence. Finding witnesses has been almost impossible. There were about fifty people in the chapel, all of whom said they saw nothing. Not one word of useful testimony could be obtained. The Church would not allow even the nuns who were with Archbishop Romero at the time to be questioned. No autopsy was permitted by the Church, so the fatal bullet could not be obtained for analysis. Only recently have we made some progress in the investigation. The Church reluctantly agreed to help collect testimony.

Who killed Archbishop Romero? We went through the same reasoning we did after Zamora's death. D'Aubuisson had denounced Romero. Days later he was dead. The Right hated Monsignor Romero because he had supported the economic reforms. As the rich abandoned San Salvador for their Miami homes, they were willing to pay huge sums for vengeance. They wanted to kill everyone on the junta, but we had armed bodyguards, while Romero would not take the precautions we all urged on him. On the other hand, if the Left wanted a create a martyr to spark a rebellion, the way Pedro Joaquín Chamorro's assassination had touched off the Nicaraguan revolution, then there was no one better loved than Archbishop Romero. The Right would be blamed, and the national outrage would unite people behind the Left.

The last time I had seen the Archbishop was with Colonel Majano, who asked us both to meet with him one night just after I joined the junta. Majano apparently thought that if he could establish his rapport with Romero, I would be convinced to side with Majano in his struggle for personal power. What I remember most clearly about that meeting is that the Archbishop had no concern about his own safety. I asked him to be careful. "The country needs you, we can't do without you," was one of the last things I said to him.

The next day Gutierrez stormed into my office furious because he had learned about my meeting with the Archbishop and Majano. It seems that Gutierrez had proposed a meeting between the junta and the Archbishop to try to work on whatever problems the Church wanted to raise. But Majano had preempted him. The two colonels always worked against each other.

As the plans for Romero's funeral proceeded, I was able—for the first time—to influence the armed forces into thinking politically. I met several times with the commanders prior to the March 30 funeral. The Church was preparing for cardinals, bishops and priests from all over Latin America to take part in the huge procession from Sagrado Corazón Basilica to the Cathedral. The armed forces worried because they had heard that large numbers of armed guerrillas, who would march in the procession, planned to steal the coffin. After being warned, the Church decided that during the ceremony the coffin would be placed behind iron grates just inside the Cathedral doors. The Church knew that guerrilla delegations were coming to the funeral and had asked them to enter the Cathedral last.

The armed-forces commanders wanted to stop the guerrillas from taking over the funeral, but I advised them to leave the funeral alone.

"But we can't let guerrillas infiltrate San Salvador," one officer said. "We have to cordon off the city for two days beforehand and search everyone entering or leaving the metropolitan area."

"No. Please listen to me," I said to him. "I'm going to suggest a different political strategy. If I were a guerrilla, I'd see this funeral as our best opportunity to capture the world's sympathy by creating a disturbance, to cause bloodshed and then blame it on the armed forces. I'd wait until the plaza was totally full, then provoke a soldier or a policeman into firing shots and starting a panic. It will be on television for all the world to see—hundreds of pathetic mourners, women and children, falling in the street under fire. Who do you think will be blamed?"

There was silence.

"My counterstrategy is this: there must not be one single soldier or policeman in the streets of San Salvador during the funeral."

"You're proposing that we just let the guerrillas take over the city?" one of the officers said, sneering.

"Yes, let them," I said. "We will take pictures and film everything. We'll have copies of the photographs, the videotapes, the film of the news reporters from all over the world, to prove that nothing happened. Or if something happens, we can show that the guerrillas were the only ones provoking trouble. But the troops must be confined to the barracks, because if anyone disobeys this order, our strategy will fail."

"We can't leave the National Palace without any guards," someone protested.

"All right, then keep six men inside the palace. But they have to stay where I say, under the stairs, and I want to have radio contact with their commanding officer the whole time. No soldiers at any window, no one on any roof," I warned.

The officers stared at me skeptically. But then Colonel Vides Casanova, head of the National Guard, spoke up. "That sounds to me like an intelligent strategy," he said. "I propose we approve it."

Vides Casanova's influence was disproportionate to his rank. He was like a barometer of the armed forces. When he moved in one direction, others followed. The high command agreed to the plan, giving strict orders to all officers in the city that not one of their men was to be on the streets.

The junta members were advised not to attend Archbishop Romero's funeral, because no security forces could go along to protect us from the guerrillas. We were waiting at the Presidential Palace when Majano returned from the funeral, where he had gone briefly, disguised in civilian clothes. I wanted to go, too, but my security officer stubbornly refused to let me go alone. There was nothing to do but wait until the ceremony ended.

Later, on films we bought from the media, I was able to see what had happened. The guerrillas came into the plaza masked but flaunting their banners, carrying their weapons in bags that did not fully hide them. They planted noise bombs in the four corners of the plaza. At one moment, they all exploded. The crowd felt they were under attack from all sides. There was no place to flee to except into the Cathedral, which was closed by the iron grate. Before the Church could unlock the iron door, the crowd surged forward, crushing and killing those closest to the gate. At least thirty people died in the stampede.

The journalists' cameras searched for the source of the panic. They could not find any soldiers. In the film, voices yell, "There they are, up in that window," but the camera lens focuses on the empty windows, panning the area to reveal no one. Only the guerrillas are seen firing guns, casually, without even seeming to take aim.

Soon after the funeral, I called a press conference to denounce the violence of the Left and deny reports that guards fired from the National Palace. These accusations were made by leftist journalists, such as the reporter from Mexico's *UnomásUno*, a newspaper openly sympathetic to the guerrillas. No one else, and all the films and pictures proved it, saw any security forces firing.

The new U.S. ambassador, Robert White, who had arrived in San Salvador only two weeks earlier, backed me up. He told the press that the Left, not the government, was to blame for the bloodshed. "As far as we know, the security forces followed their orders meticulously. There is no evidence at all that the security forces took any part in this," White said.

More important than the foreign observers, there were 100,000 Salvadoran witnesses in that plaza. These people did not see any soldiers, but they saw the guerrillas shooting. From this moment on, there was doubt when the Left claimed they tried only to help and defend the people. Their appeal to the masses began to diminish. This day was pivotal for me, because the armed forces realized that I could take effective decisions, that I would assume responsibility for defending the armed forces, and that there were methods of countering the Left other than repression.

There were other occasions when I showed the armed forces

how a political strategy could be more effective than brute force. During the summer of 1980, the Left tried to build up momentum for their final offensive through strikes—first single unions, then general strikes, increasing from one- to two- and three-day shutdowns of the nation. I wanted to show the guerrillas several things: that the willingness to negotiate does not mean weakness, that I would not allow illegal activities, and that I was going to fight them politically.

In June, the teachers' union struck for the release of Salvador Samayoa, the first junta's education minister, who had quit to join the guerrillas. He had been captured by the armed forces, and I asked them to let him go into exile. Although he declared himself a guerrilla, we had no evidence he had taken part in any violent action. We had to differentiate, I explained, between those who took up arms and those who simply declared their opposition. Besides making this point, we also ended the strike by taking away its cause when he was freed.

The same month, while I was in Europe, the Left staged a two-day general strike, and the uncontrolled response of the security forces was to wage war on the National University, storming it and killing dozens of people. I knew this only made matters worse.

In August, when the Left called a three-day general strike, I asked the military commanders to allow me to handle this one. Many workers stayed home out of fear rather than support for the strike, and they needed a reason to risk going to work when the guerrillas were burning buses or trucks that ignored the strike. They had burned nine hundred buses! On television and radio, I appealed to the people to go to work for the sake of the country. Employers were asked to allow workers to spend the night in the factories or accept those who arrived two or three hours late due to transportation difficulties. I went into the streets myself and encouraged people who were trying to get to work. The strike was a failure. Only 10 to 20 percent of the work force stayed out, and most businesses remained open.

A week later, the Left chose another weapon. They decided to paralyze the country through a strategic union they thoroughly controlled, the electric-power workers. The union, known as STECEL, was well organized and so brazen that union leaders used the electric company's own radio network to plan the strike. We listened to their plans to shut down the country's energy supply by simultaneously seizing all the hydroelectric dams, the generating plants and the distribution centers. They openly talked about the bombs they would plant in the generators and the switching system so that we would not dare storm the power plants. The armed-forces commanders came to me with this information and their own plan to take over the power grid before the union did.

"You can occupy the electric facilities, but that won't give you any political advantage," I told the officers. "This is a political battle. If you're going to apply the method I've advocated, here is what must be done." First, we had to try to negotiate. We should listen to the workers' grievances and offer some concessions. We wanted to show that the government was reasonable and that the Left's labor demands were only an excuse to stage the strike and prepare for the final offensive.

Of course the union rejected everything. Once the strike started, we had to let people know who was to blame for their being without lights and water. The union could not close down the system entirely, because of the danger of too much pressure building up at the dams. There had to be some discharge of electricity, so they rotated the cuts, always leaving some section of the country with electrical power. To reach the people, I would find one radio station that temporarily had power or had a generator of its own. I asked the people for their confidence and pledged to do my best to end the hardship imposed by this small group of workers. Slowly, the Salvadoran people became angry with STECEL.

On the second day of the strike, I called in the military commanders and asked them to prepare a plan to take all thirty power stations and grids without any loss of life, without any casualties.

"You're asking us to do the impossible," one officer said.

"That's right, because we're going to have to do the impossible to save this country," I answered. The following day I approved the plan to storm the dams and the power plants, but with a warning that the Army must follow it to the letter. All the attacks were carried out at the same minute without giving the union leaders time to warn one another or set off their bombs. No one was killed. The Army captured all the leaders, including the union's secretary general, who held the rank of commander in the FPL guerrilla group. They were charged with sedition under the law. This successful commando operation, at a time when the Army had no American aid or training, became a source of pride for the armed forces. I had taken the first steps toward teaching the armed forces a more successful way to fight subversion than brutal repression.

The Right, however, still thought that with enough repression the guerrillas could be wiped out, strikes abolished and the old system restored. D'Aubuisson established a sophisticated organization, divided between a political front, for propaganda and fund-raising, and a paramilitary arm, known as the death squads. The idea was that to defeat Communism you must match all the Communist tactics. In front there would be legitimate political fronts, but behind them the cadres prepared to use violence. The clandestine cells the Right planned would kill, kidnap and terrorize just as did the leftist guerrillas. The rightist terror would be freed from any restraint a government might place on its security forces, but the death squads could count on sympathetic members of the security forces to protect and facilitate their actions. There were exchanges of information, recruitment, training and financing that linked the overt and covert rightist organizations. The Salvadoran Right did not originate this anti-Communist strategy. They copied it from their Guatemalan counterparts, who put down all opposition, from guerrillas, unions, intellectuals and political reformers, by systematic terror. Before d'Aubuisson surfaced in El Salvador organizing his political front and pointing out targets for the death squads, he spent some time in Guatemala, consulting Mario Sandoval Alarcón. Sandoval heads the National Liberation Movement, a party that, despite its leftist-sounding name, represents the Far Right. Guatemala, where they went about trying to exterminate guerrilla suspects, without U.S. military aid, without any concern for human rights, was the model the Right admired.

To take power away from the junta, the Right had two plans. They intended to destabilize our government through selective assassinations and to organize a coup within the armed forces. Both the Left and the Right utilized the split within the armed forces, but the Right could maneuver its men better during crises from inside.

There were at least three groups within the armed forces. One was led by Colonel Majano and included many younger officers who favored the reforms. Opposing them were the officers manipulated by d'Aubuisson, who counted on Carranza inside the high command. The Defense Minister, Colonel García, did not actually support d'Aubuisson, but he was indulgent. He preferred to do nothing and increase his own power at the expense of the two opposing factions. In the middle was the third group, the "institutional" majority, led by Vides Casanova. Their loyalty was to the Army itself, and they judged a political position on the basis of how it would affect their institution. The 1979 coup, for example, split the Army away from the oligarchy in order to save the Salvadoran soldiers from the fate of Somoza's National Guard. The primary concern was always how an action would affect the Army.

The events following the night of May 7 illustrate this point. On that date, our Soldiers' Day, a conclave of d'Aubuisson's allies assembled at a country home near Santa Tecla to plot a coup against our junta. Majano, who learned about this gathering, ordered an officer he trusted in the First Brigade to take a company of soldiers, surround the estate and arrest everyone inside. The army troops disarmed the guards outside, stormed into the house and found over a dozen military officers, plus a few civilians, with some highly compromising documents. With these documents in his possession, Majano thought he could confront the Right and dominate the armed forces.

All along, Majano had been ambitious but indecisive. He came late to junta meetings, spent the whole time writing in a notebook, then would leave just before a vote was taken. He avoided decisions. The only decisive action he ever took was to raid the Santa Tecla meeting, and the outcome was the exact opposite of what he hoped. Majano wanted to be president himself and was using his contacts with the intellectual Left to give himself a public image as the military moderate.

Astutely, Majano made U.S. Ambassador White his ally. In fact, White fought to the very end to keep Majano on the junta even after he had no military support left. Majano saw me as his rival for popular support. He would get angry when I asked for studies to be conducted of areas he considered his domain, particularly agrarian reform. With his collaborators, Majano was running a government within the government.

On the night he raided d'Aubuisson's hideout, Majano advised

Morales Erlich that he had some disturbing facts to reveal. A late-night session of the junta was convened at the palace. From the few pages of documents that Majano permitted me to see, it was clear that they included assassination plans: kinds of weapons to be used, codes, who would be paid for what. Only the name of the victim was not specified—it could have been Mario Zamora or Archbishop Romero or someone else. There was also evidence of their coup plot, even the list of future Cabinet members. The problem was that Majano's method of obtaining this evidence had gone against the military grain.

Colonel Gutierrez was appalled. He felt Majano's raid might actually precipitate a coup rather than stop one. Majano's troops had come close to provoking a shootout between army officers, and those inside the Santa Tecla estate included representatives of almost every military unit in the country. The armed forces decided to conduct an internal investigation, which eventually let everyone arrested go free. Majano and the high command argued over lines of authority and discipline. The Right turned the issue into one touching the soul of the armed forces: Majano had broken the chain of command; he had given commands to lower-ranking officers without informing their superiors.

Those arrested denied any complicity, and there was no proof that the documents implicated any of them individually. The most dangerous one was d'Aubuisson, but the charges could not be brought against him alone. And he had been arrested with a group large enough so that every officer had a classmate friend among them. When Majano tried to condemn all the Santa Tecla plotters, army officers from the rank of captain up said, "No."

The high command would not ignore the large number of junior officers who had friends among those arrested. Internal investigation in the Army always takes into account the consensus of the officers. The consensus in this case turned against

Majano. On May 12, the armed-forces officer corps voted to make Gutierrez their spokesman on the junta. From then on, Majano lost his power bit by bit. Colonel García quietly took every advantage of the split in the junta, making his own decisions. But the real leader emerging was Colonel Vides Casanova, who mediated the internal disputes. He would be called in by one side, then the other.

The tension peaked every month when the Defense Ministry prepared the orders assigning officers to different posts. In September, García gave the order transferring several key officers of Majano's group from troop commands to diplomatic posts abroad. Majano marched across from the Presidential Palace to the El Zapote barracks next door and organized a mutiny, ordering his supporters not to obey any commands from García. Gutierrez and García got ready to strike back. At this point, the civilian junta members went from barracks to barracks, telling the officers that something had to be done.

"Gentlemen, this can't go on," I said. "The country has enough problems without a battle within the military forces. You have to decide who is the commander, and we think it should be the junta. The majority of the five should determine what should be done."

The officers took a vote and approved my thesis that the commander was the junta. They also decided that Colonel Gutierrez would be commander in chief of the armed forces. A compromise was worked out on the transfers. Gutierrez and Majano continued on their separate ways. Majano irritated many of the officers who had supported him, because he forced these confrontations, then caved in. Those who backed Majano recognized that his own behavior was isolating him. As Majano lost support in the armed forces, he spent more time cultivating his contacts with the Left, becoming more secretive.

At this point, similar successive assassination attempts were made on Majano, Gutierrez and me.

The junta made the bad mistake of having a regular routine. The cars and armed escort sent to pick us up for our meetings always came at the same time and never varied our route. The captain in charge of the transport came to my house to call for me one November day, and Inés offered him a cup of coffee. I marched into the room saying, "Let's go." But as the captain put down the cup, Inés chided me, "Won't you even let him finish his coffee?"

I apologized, asking the captain to sit down. The poor captain stayed only a moment to gulp down his coffee. As we left the house, a bomb exploded three blocks away from our house. It was the very place my car would have been passing if Inés had not slowed us down. That cup of coffee saved my life. People who had been waiting at a bus stop along the street were blown to pieces. How could the criminals who wanted to kill me care so little about people who just happened to be on the street?

Another bomb exploded in a street just as Majano's car passed, but somehow Majano escaped unharmed. When I went into Majano's office, he acted offended, ready to accuse even the junta members of being behind the attack. But the killers' aim was obviously to eliminate the junta government.

Majano was finally forced out. What eroded the last of his support was the intrigue surrounding the killing of Captain Amilcar Molina Panameño. Molina Panameño had studied at a seminary before turning to a military career. He had contacts with radicalized sectors of the Church, which may have led to ties with the Left. He was among the early plotters of the October 15 coup to end the military alignment with the oligarchy. In 1980 his duties concerned police intelligence.

Who killed him remains unknown, but the night he was found

dead—he'd been shot to death in his home—Majano called a lieutenant at El Zapote barracks with a strange order. The lieutenant was told to go to Molina Panameño's house, search for a briefcase and bring it to Majano. The officer found the briefcase, but after looking at what was inside he turned it over instead to his own commander. The commander advised Gutierrez and García, because the briefcase contained leftist guerrilla documents. Gutierrez told me there were plans for kidnappings, false passports, photographs of guerrillas. Why was Captain Molina Panameño concealing these documents and how did Majano know about the briefcase?

The lieutenant was shipped out of the country with a scholarship. Shortly afterward, Majano used a personal trip to the United States to disappear abroad. He turned up in Panama, under the protection of General Torrijos, who provided a plane and guards to bring him back to San Salvador after receiving a promise that Majano would not be arrested.

The crisis led to a new agreement between the Christian Democrats and the armed forces. It came during the first week of December 1980, a month after Ronald Reagan defeated Jimmy Carter, a month before the guerrillas' "final" offensive. Four American religious women were murdered during that week, leading to a suspension of American aid and the dispatch of a high-level U.S. diplomatic mission to San Salvador. All these facts are related. Both the Salvadoran and American governments were caught in a transition process and trying to deal with each other at the same time.

The deaths of the four American women disturbed me more than anything else during my years on the junta, and I will discuss the investigation separately. The effect of U.S. politics on El Salvador also requires more explanation later.

On December 7, after two days of debate, the armed forces'

general assembly voted three hundred to four to oust Majano from the junta. Once he had been removed, Majano went underground. He had rejected the Army's offer of a diplomatic post in Spain, choosing to live clandestinely and publish bitter accusations against the armed forces. A few months later, Guatemalan authorities arrested a man with an irregular passport, who turned out to be Majano in disguise. Guatemala turned him over to the Salvadoran security forces, who eventually released him to go into exile.

With Majano gone, the junta government had to be reconstructed. The armed forces wanted me to become the figurehead president. I argued that if I was going to be given the title of president, I should have some executive powers. I proposed that legislative powers should reside in the junta, while I would serve as the chief executive. Not only the officers but the Christian Democrats objected to this, saying it would downgrade the junta and give us less power. I did not see how we could have any less power, because the junta was already debilitated. Unable to convince my colleagues or the army officers, I went along with the party, although I was not pleased with the situation.

Vides Casanova then surprised me. "We [the armed forces] have a debt to pay to you," he told me at the time. "The debt is left from the time we denied you the presidency in 1972. We'll have to pay it someday, but now isn't the time. Accept the presidency of the junta with all its limitations because we have to move forward. Someday the armed forces will realize that they can trust you." He sounded prophetic. "Someday you'll need the support of the armed forces. And you'll have it."

Accepting that the armed forces would not give me the authority I needed to be an effective president, I still insisted on some conditions. The first was the removal of Carranza, d'Aubuisson's ally, as undersecretary of defense. Carranza was sitting in front of me when I made this demand. He was sent to head the telephone company. But on my other demands I received promises that were not totally fulfilled. Ten other officers were supposed to be sent abroad. The infamous Colonel Morán of the Treasury Police was supposed to be transferred by the next month. But as long as García was defense minister, I could never dislodge Morán. I wanted influence over who would be in the Cabinet, and I never got it. Another demand was for García to hold a meeting where he would order all officers to respect human rights and to end the internal support of the death squads. At this time, the extremist right organization was at its largest size, and thousands of people were being dragged into the night, tortured and killed. The FDR leaders had been seized from a meeting and slaughtered. The four American religious women had been murdered.

Why didn't I quit? Why did I stay in a government that allowed such things to happen? These questions went through my mind many times. I would say to myself, There's nothing more I can do. But I knew that if I gave up and resigned because of some atrocity the Right or the Left had committed, they would have won. There was no doubt in my mind, and we had all the supporting evidence, that the Left was mounting their final offensive. The Right was getting ready to take over the government, convinced they could count on Reagan's support for a coup. If I left, who would present an alternative between these two? My belief in the third way, the democratic way, had to be kept alive. Resignation would be an admission that I had failed in my lifelong struggle. I asked myself, Is it worth the suffering? Do I have the slightest chance of success?

I found the answer in the Salvadoran people. When I talked to people in the streets, not the ones involved in politics, my belief would be renewed. The people were caught in the middle between the Right, with its military allies and backers in the United States, and the Left, with its armed organizations and international solidarity movements. But the ones who were being hurt, the Salvadoran people, deserved a democratic revolution.

There have been democratic revolutions—José Figueres led one in Costa Rica that continues to this day. Figueres never lost sight of his objective. When he won the war, he dismantled his own army to prevent any threat to democracy. Costa Ricans have enjoyed almost four peaceful decades of democracy. If I were going to join an insurrection, I would want to fight for my own ideals of democracy, not for someone else's philosophy of terrorism and a return to totalitarianism.

Emotionally, it would have been easy to resign—to go abroad to live in comfort, speaking at forums around the world as Ungo does for the FDR-FMLN. But by taking that course, I would only help bring another form of totalitarianism to El Salvador.

Before Somoza fell in Nicaragua, I had talked to Sergio Ramírez in Costa Rica. I warned him against working with the Sandinista guerrillas. Ramírez, an intellectual and a writer, was not thought to be a Communist then. "You are being used by the Communists," I told him. He had no qualms about it and is now vice-president of Nicaragua. But I could not lend myself to Marxist guerrillas, broaden their base of support, then stand by and watch them impose their own police state on my country.

Even so, I fought with my conscience about being in the junta government. Many times I came close to resigning. I sought counsel from Archbishop Arturo Rivera Damas. We talked about the violence, and I asked if, to live in good Christian conscience, I should resign the junta presidency. He told me that my duty as a Christian was not to resign, but to work to end the violence and to bring peace to the nation. He asked me to make a personal effort for justice. In thinking through my decision, I agreed. I came back to my belief that man can change history.

I do not believe in historical determinism. Men make history, and men can change history. My Christianity teaches me that all men have free will. They can use it positively or negatively to create their societies. Leaders emerge when they manage to express the collective will of their societies. That is when a single leader makes a difference.

But a leader cannot change the history of a country according to his beliefs by giving up. I knew I must stay to continue my fight. The killing in El Salvador was going on and on. I could not stop it as yet, but I had to work toward that day, one step at a time. The next step was for me to be named president of El Salvador, even without the conditions I wanted. I was sworn in three days before Christmas 1980.

6

The Women
of God

THREE weeks before, on December 2, 1980, El Salvador's Comalapa International Airport became chaotic late that afternoon as the flights from the United States arrived. TACA airlines also had a planeful coming from the Nicaraguan capital. There was a strange assortment of people among those arriving and those waiting for them. A Christian Democratic politician wished a family member bon voyage. The U.S. Embassy chauffeur waited, some nuns and priests chatted, and a National Guardsman eyed everyone nervously, looking for "subversives."

Some of the arriving passengers came grimly to attend the funeral of five leaders of the Revolutionary Democratic Front, kidnapped and killed three days earlier by armed men everyone believed were members of some security force. The nights were filled with terror. The streets of San Salvador would be deserted after sundown, because ordinary people were afraid—of the terrorist bombs, of the security forces abusing their power and of criminals who took advantage of the collapse of our social order. No one wanted to drive the highways at night. The new Comalapa Airport lay twenty-five miles down from the hills surrounding San Salvador, but most flights came in early enough for passengers to hustle through before dark.

Two Maryknoll nuns, returning from their annual assembly in Managua, came in at 4 P.M. on the TACA flight. But because the plane was full, two other nuns had had to wait for the next flight on the Panamanian airline COPA. A twenty-seven-year-old lay missionary named Jean Donovan and an Ursuline nun, Dorothy Kazel, both of whom worked at a nearby orphanage run by the Cleveland archdiocese, had to make a second trip to the airport at 6 P.M. to pick up Sister Maura Clarke and Sister Ita Ford.

Corporal Pérez thought these foreign women who kept coming and going, carrying large purses which could conceal weapons, must be reported. He called his sergeant, Colindres Alemán, who was in charge of the National Guard's airport patrol.

On December 3, the junta meeting had dragged on all day. I came home exhausted after long hours with the budget committee and the armed-forces high command. The internal crisis in the armed forces reached the point where Colonel Majano was removed from the junta. We had to forge a stronger government in order to forestall a rightist coup and the leftist insurrection we knew was coming. In front of my house, a market woman and a worker, who could not get in to see me at the Presidential Palace, were camped on my doorstep. I made time for them before dinner. While I was eating, my daughter Inés Guadalupe answered the phone and told me the Archbishop of Cleveland was calling. Archbishop Hickey wanted me to help him find four American religious women who had disappeared the day before after leaving the airport. I promised to do everything I could.

My first call was to Monsignor Rivera Damas, acting archbishop of San Salvador. He told me Father Paul Schindler, the American priest from La Libertad, where the women had intended to spend the night, could find no trace of them. I called Colonel Gutierrez and the Defense Minister to begin a search for the women through all the different branches of the security forces. I phoned my brother Alejandro, himself a former priest, to see what else he could learn from Father Schindler. I left messages for the chiefs of the National Police and the National Guard telling them to call me. When I reached Vides Casanova, who had already heard from Colonel García, he said he would relay any information he received from Guard posts in the airport zone.

Staring at my silent telephone, waiting for some word, I went over all the possibilities. Could Sister Dorothy and Jean Donovan have decided to drive Sisters Maura and Ita all the way home to Chalatenango province, where they worked with refugees? Could there have been an auto accident? Could the guerrillas have captured them? What if they had been arrested for some reason? God, help me find them, I kept repeating to myself.

A headache was hammering inside my head, but finally the phone rang. Colonel López Nuila called to say that nothing had been reported by the highway police whom he had alerted. Then Vides Casanova informed me the Guard knew nothing. Gutierrez called to talk for some time about the implications of these disappearances—how the Left could use it against us, and the Right would revel in the weakness of our government. After letting Archbishops Hickey and Rivera Damas know that I had alerted everyone, I tried to sleep, staring at the ceiling, feeling completely powerless. I kept praying.

At dawn I went to my office and made more phone calls, trying to reach Father Schindler. My brother Alejandro told me the American father was completely trustworthy. Alejandro had learned from him that some Canadian priests had seen Jean Donovan and Dorothy Kazel at the airport. The Canadians had driven on to San Salvador, but had been stopped at a roadblock. Alejandro called again to tell me the white Toyota van the women had been driving had been found on a road near the airport, totally burned out. There was no sign of the women.

Gutierrez phoned García in my presence to confirm that the wreck of the Toyota van had been found. We had just called the junta together to discuss the situation when our press secretary took a call from a journalist. He asked for an official statement on the discovery of the women's bodies. We called García back, asking if he knew that bodies had been found. We instructed him to get police investigators to the scene immediately, then to convene a meeting of the high command.

The government was the last to know what had happened to the nuns. The priest in the village of Santiago Nonualco, fifteen miles northeast of the airport, learned from some peasants that they had been ordered by the local Guard and Civil Defense patrol to bury the bodies of four foreign-looking women. The priest informed his superiors, and the archdiocese called the U.S. Embassy. Ambassador White happened to be at the airport, ensuring that the Canadian priests left safely for home, when he was alerted by his car radio. He drove directly to the village, finding Father Schindler already there, along with members of the press. White ordered the graves to be dug up, uncovering the partially clothed bodies of the four women. They had been shot repeatedly.

From that day, I knew that the dreadful death of those women must not be in vain. This crime, of all crimes against the innocent, against God's people, could not go unpunished. Nine months had gone by since Archbishop Romero's murder, and where was justice? I had to try again to make the dormant and decaying legal system work, but this time I knew we could not carry out the investigation alone. I knew where to turn for help. The victims were American. The expertise and diligence we needed could come in part from the United States, with its scientific criminal-investigation techniques. What I did not consider at the time was how the best evidence could be irrelevant in our antiquated legal system. My mind was on the criminal investigation, not the judicial problems. I told the junta we needed investigators who were technically competent and determined to probe deeply. No one with these qualifications would be found in El Salvador. The junta agreed that we must seek help from INTERPOL or the FBI.

Besides gathering evidence and testimony, our investigation had to ensure that there were no legal errors that could be used to unravel the case once the courts had it. Our justice would not only have to meet our standards, but those in other nations that felt outrage at these depraved murderers. We decided to form a high-level investigating commission, asking the armed forces to designate three respected officers to serve with three lawyers from the Attorney General's office, along with our Minister of the Presidency, Pablo Mauricio Alvergue.

On December 5, the United States suspended military aid to El Salvador in response to the killing of the nuns. President Carter sent a bipartisan commission to recommend what should be done. William Bowdler, Carter's assistant secretary of state for inter-American affairs, and William D. Rogers, who had held the same position in a Republican administration, spent December 6–9 in San Salvador. They presented their report December 12.

The Bowdler-Rogers report was fair. It presented all the points to be investigated, including the complicity in the murders by members of the security forces. The most incriminating fact was that members of the security forces had ordered the secret burial of women they obviously knew were foreigners. Then, despite the government-announced search for the women, the Guardsmen and the justice of the peace in Santiago Nonualco had kept the burial secret. The justice of the peace excused himself by saying two or three unidentified bodies were buried each week, but even the peasants who dug the grave recognized that these victims were different.

An indication of possible premeditation in the murders was the threat made against the Maryknoll nuns working in Chalatenango just a few weeks before their death. A note pinned to the door of the parish house said: "Those living here are Communists and anyone who enters here will die." But threats against the clergy had become so common no one paid much attention to this note.

Without openly expressing suspicion about the possible killers, the report mentioned that both the Canadian priests and a U.S. Embassy chauffeur had seen a security-force patrol stopping cars at random outside the airport.

Our investigating commission found Bowdler and Rogers ready to help provide the technical expertise we needed to get fingerprints and ballistics evidence. We also asked them to aid in getting autopsies on the bodies that were sent home for burial, and testimony from the Canadian priests who were the last ones to see Jean Donovan and Dorothy Kazel. The embassy chauffeur at the airport was never identified, nor was his mission ever explained, and he was kept out of the investigation. The FBI sent a team of four experts, who worked on the van and at the gravesite collecting evidence. In early January, the FBI representative asked to present their findings to me. He suggested that autopsies should be done on the two nuns buried in Chalatenango, that more digging be carried out at the gravesite for bullets, and that additional people living in the area of the crime should be questioned.

Once the FBI team had taken fingerprints off the van and the bullets that I had found at the scene, they recommended that we fingerprint and use a lie detector to question the Guardsmen who buried the women and who manned the roadblock near the airport. The FBI also found traces of red paint on the Toyota van's bumper, which could have come from a red pickup truck seen speeding away from the area where the van was burning. We had to search for a red pickup that belonged to the security forces.

The FBI assumed we knew who had set up the roadblock near the airport. But none of the official reports to the investigating commission from the security forces nor the testimony of witnesses had established who was stopping cars near the airport December 2. In El Salvador, we have the Army, the National Guard, the National Police, the Treasury Police and the Customs agents—all operating independently. The first inquiry by the government, on December 8, had been an order from the Defense Minister to all security forces to provide a list of their personnel assigned to the area around the airport.

What I did not know at the time was that the list given to me did not include the names of the National Guardsmen assigned to the airport itself. Military men never volunteer information, they answer strictly the question asked. We asked for the area around the airport, therefore they excluded the airport post itself.

I was discouraged. The information gathered to date showed the total inefficiency of our system of justice, the lack of cooperation from citizens and authorities, all of whom turned a blind eye to the crimes happening around them. Just listening to our investigating commission, I could sense that they felt weak. They were carrying out their mission with caution because they were not sure what results the high command really wanted. I knew they suspected that the security forces were involved, just as I did. But they blamed the Church and the U.S. Embassy for not cooperating with them as an excuse for their failure to get more information.

Who could blame their timidity? We had a system which served to cover up the truth for decades. It was supposed to protect the prestige of the armed forces and it destroyed those who challenged its authority. The cover-up was an automatic reflex in El Salvador—just as the conviction that security forces should be blamed was the automatic response of the Church and the U.S. Embassy.

In my opinion Ambassador White acted as a proconsul, assuming that no local system of justice existed. Thus he could order the excavation of the bodies without waiting for any legal or police authority. In the case of the Canadians, he helped to protect witnesses who wanted to leave the country before they could be questioned. He kept the embassy's driver from being involved in the inquiry. He learned of information about a radio communication that suggested someone in the security forces was looking for the nuns at the airport, but never revealed it to me. Months later White told reporters about this strange message, but only after he had left the diplomatic service to become a leading critic of Reagan's policies in Central America.

White's authority had been undercut by Reagan's transition team after the U.S. election, and he was one of the first ambassadors to be relieved by the new administration. White's replacement, Chargé d'Affaires Frederic Chapin, arrived in February 1981. The military officers who had considered White their antagonist, referring to him as the "Communist White," looked carefully at Chapin for signs of a change in U.S. policy. But Chapin's firm stand against the violent abuses by the security forces irritated more than one high-ranking officer. Chapin once met with the junta to present a stern warning about the unrestrained rightist crimes, using as his example the killing of Christian Democratic mayors. The tension in the room could have triggered an explosion. The officers concluded that it was the Christian Democrats who were manipulating U.S. influence against the Army. They thought Chapin's attitude confirmed their suspicions that Ambassador White had been used by Majano and me to sow dissension among the armed forces. The junta nearly fell after Chapin's speech. It took us three days to convince the military officers that they had exaggerated our influence over the United States and its ambassadors.

Chapin did work closely with me. Solving the case of the nuns' murder was more than just part of his job to him. He invited me to the ambassador's residence for dinner one night soon after he moved in. We talked about the political and economic situation in general, then the conversation turned to the violence and finally to the murder of the nuns. With tears in his eyes, Chapin spoke of a tragedy in his own family, relating it to the death of the nuns. Suddenly he took a piece of paper from his pocket and handed it to me. Typed in English on a blank sheet was this message: "One might look at the National Guard post at San Juan Talpa. Reportedly, the National Guardsmen stationed at San Juan Talpa on the night of December 2 formed a roadblock some ten kilometers from the National Airport."

Chapin offered no explanation, no more information. This was the break I was waiting for. Immediately, I asked the investigating commission to fingerprint all security personnel in San Juan Talpa, make ballistics tests of their guns to see if any matched the bullets I had found. Then I asked my brother Alejandro to talk to Father Schindler, to see if he had any other clues related to the San Juan Talpa tip. It turned out that Schindler, after identifying the burned-out Toyota, had gone not to San Juan Talpa but to San Luis Talpa, a village only four miles from the airport, to talk to the police. When the priest asked about the missing nuns, the commander was evasive and insolent, saying, "No one has seen any nuns around here." Schindler later commented on this incident to the embassy.

Our investigation revealed that the National Guard did not

have any post in San Juan Talpa or San Luis Talpa. It was the Treasury Police whom Father Schindler had run up against in San Luis Talpa, and they had not conducted any roadblock operations on December 2. No red pickup was found there, and none of the fingerprints or guns matched our evidence. Frustration possessed me; the case was bogged down again. We still did not have suspects.

When I forced myself to call in Ambassador Chapin to tell him we had run into a dead end, he surprised me. He handed me another piece of paper. This time, written by hand, there were the names of nine National Guardsmen assigned to duties at the airport post December 2. There was an x at the name Luis Antonio Colindres Alemán—he was the sergeant. The word "driver" was written beside the name Francisco Contreras. There was a question mark at one name, noted as "(Andrés) ? Palacios."

None of these names had appeared on the list provided to me by the security forces, but I had since learned that there was a Guard post at the airport itself. These were the men assigned there. During a junta meeting at the end of February, Gutierrez reported that the fingerprints and guns of the Guardsmen at the airport had been sent to the FBI for comparison. I asked Colonel Vides Casanova to brief me on how the Guard's own internal investigation was going.

Vides Casanova reported back that most of the voluminous testimony collected offered no new information about the crime. I asked to see the report. He said only the high command could release the report and needed a written order, because it was classified secret. I understood his position and made a formal request. When I received the report a week later, there was little to learn from it. The Guard's investigation was strictly routine. The contradictions and incongruent details of the testimony were not followed up.

Major Lisandro Zepeda, the investigating officer, did make one uncharacteristic observation. "There is a possibility the murderers had advance knowledge of the airport arrival of the four American religious women and carried out a premeditated plan to kill them," he noted. If Zepeda had thought that any military officer had given orders to seize the women, then I doubt he would have brought up the possibility of premeditated murder. He could have left that sentence out, sticking to the factual testimony. Its inclusion showed he felt no constraint or concern about avoiding the issue.

When I asked Vides Casanova about the suspects named by the embassy, he said three of the nine had proven alibis. "There are valid reasons for suspecting that the other six are responsible for killing the nuns," he said, "but they deny everything. You know Guardsmen are trained in legal investigative techniques, and these men have stuck to their story under cross-examination. They know there isn't enough evidence to charge them. If we bring them before a judge, they'll be out free in seventy-two hours. We have to find more evidence, but the truth will come out.

"Nonetheless, if we try to invent proof or obtain confessions by force, there will be trouble," the colonel added, knowing full well that El Salvador had a bad record on the torture of prisoners. He indicated that such treatment not only went against our principles, but would not be tolerated by the armed forces against their own. "There would be dangerous consequences," he warned. "The only thing to do is to try to get more proof and arrest them in the meantime so they can't leave the country."

Vides Casanova recommended they be held under military arrest, otherwise any smart civilian lawyer could get them out. Colonel Gutierrez later informed me that the six Guardsmen were arrested on April 29.

Even when the FBI reported that some of their fingerprints matched those taken from the nuns' van, and the bullets proved to have come from their guns, the Guardsmen continued to deny their guilt. Sergeant Colindres Alemán, who commanded the group, stubbornly insisted the FBI was wrong, those could not be his fingerprints on the van. Scientific crime detection had never existed in El Salvador. In our courts, the fingerprints and the ballistics evidence would not be enough to convict the Guardsmen. They knew it and we knew it.

The conclusion of the National Guard's internal investigation was that "the responsibility in an extremely delicate case like this one is hard to determine," and "there are no concrete charges that can be made against our personnel. It is all supposition."

I felt very discouraged. How could we find any more solid evidence? What we needed were witnesses to prove these men abducted the nuns, and if there were any they would be too afraid to come forward. Somehow we had to expose the lies in the men's denials. Once again we turned toward technology: the lie detector. We asked the United States for the equipment and for help in the cross-examination. Our interrogators obviously had not asked the right questions.

U.S. congressional restraints on providing any advisers to police forces complicated the situation. But I knew we had to find a way. Every single congressional delegation, coming through almost weekly, asked about our investigation of the nuns' deaths. The new U.S. ambassador, Deane Hinton, who arrived in June 1981, was as dedicated as Chapin to seeing that the killers were brought to justice. To his credit, he too would also alienate the Right. When I headed for the United States in September, the lie detectors were on my agenda. My mission was not to seek more military or economic aid, but to ensure that Americans understood the problems we were facing in our fight for democracy.

The question of how we were going to bring the murderers of the nuns to justice was bound to be asked everywhere I went in the United States.

In one session with U.S. legislators, Representative Mary Rose Oakar probed hard on the legal mechanics of bringing the suspects to trial. I denied the rumor that the six Guardsmen had been released. But I did admit that under Salvadoran law we lacked the conclusive evidence, even with the fingerprints, to convince a judge to indict them.

Americans find it hard to believe that our legal system is so different from theirs, or that I had so little influence with the courts. In the case of the two American advisers murdered with our agrarian-reform director, we had confessions from the killers, who had acted under orders from Lieutenant Rodolfo Isidro López Sibrián. The prosecutors, goaded by U.S. assurances that they had enough evidence, presented it to a judge, who allowed López Sibrián to go free. In El Salvador, confessed killers cannot be witnesses against a co-defendant. To make matters worse, López Sibrián had been allowed to dye his hair and grow a mustache before appearing in a lineup. This was the kind of justice system I was trying to make effective!

To try to use this system, I suggested that the families of murdered Americans hire their own private prosecuting attorneys. This device has allowed Salvadorans to bring better-qualified lawyers, who will not work for public-sector wages, into the prosecution. Unfortunately, my suggestion was seen by Americans as an attempt to evade government responsibility for bringing the cases to justice.

At the end of the discussion, Congresswoman Oakar came and looked me in the eye. "Would you be willing to meet with the families of the murdered women?" she asked. I felt this was the least I could do. To schedule it, I offered to return to Washington after my other U.S. stops. My advisers thought I had been trapped. "These people are bitter. They're going to take out their anger on you. It will be bad for our country," said my advisers. But they could not change my mind. The arrangements were made for a meeting October 1 at the residence of Archbishop Hickey, now in charge of Washington's Catholic archdiocese.

Ambassador Hinton and El Salvador's ambassador to Washington, Ernesto Rivas Gallont, accompanied me, along with Dina Callejas, the undersecretary for justice. We found the parents of Jean Donovan; parents, brothers and sisters of Ita Ford, Dorothy Kazel and Maura Clarke; representatives from the Maryknoll and Ursuline orders; Representative Oakar; and Archbishop Hickey.

When I entered the room I felt a chill that almost made my teeth chatter. My heart beat faster as I looked at those faces around me, with their penetrating stares and expressive silences. The Archbishop asked us to pray, which helped me a little. I heard the words of the Lord's Prayer, "Thy will be done," as never before. I asked God to help me assure these families that justice would be done.

Monsignor Hickey spoke of the pain, the doubts and anguish of the families of the four women who worked for God in the midst of violence. He reminded us that everyone in the room came as a Catholic believer in Christ. No one with me had a tape recorder or took notes, out of respect for the families, although Representative Oakar's secretary and a nun took notes as we talked. Most of my memories of that meeting, however, are vivid.

William Ford, a lawyer, was clearly the spokesman for the families. He asked incisive questions about the investigative process, about the commitment of the U.S. government and whether too much would be swept under the rug. I asked Mrs. Callejas, our legal expert, to answer some questions because I am not a lawyer and did not want to mislead anyone. Mr. Ford asked whether I had known before coming to the United States how deeply the American people felt about these murders. In my answer, by trying to explain my purpose on this trip as speaking directly with the American people, I somehow gave the impression that the State Department was not conveying U.S. concern about solving this case. This was a misinterpretation.

Someone asked whether there was any basis for Secretary of State Alexander Haig's remark that the women might have run a roadblock or U.N. Ambassador Jeane Kirkpatrick's description of the nuns as political activists. I did not know the context of these remarks, but I carefully replied that General Haig and Mrs. Kirkpatrick must have made these statements based on information I did not have.

Ford said no one believed that six Guardsmen, on their own initiative, would have killed the four women. The families were convinced the crime had broader implications, involving other officers. It was hard for them to accept that, in the climate of violence I described, where most abuses are ignored, any local constable is capable of acting on impulse. There is a mentality created by years of repressive violence, by the fear of revolutionary violence and by the corruption of a legal system that permits atrocities to take place without any control.

Ambassador Hinton tried to add to my description of the tolerated violence. Ford interrupted, saying he was offended that his own ambassador would make excuses for the crimes of the Salvadoran military hierarchy. Hinton snapped back that he resented the distortion of his words and the false insinuations by Ford. After this heated exchange, the two calmed down. But they achieved only polite tolerance, not any mutual understanding.

The discussion centered on whether or not the Guardsmen were following orders when they seized the women. Ford asked about a radio message reportedly overheard at the airport. Ford said that former Ambassador White had publicly stated that an important Christian Democrat informed him of a radio transmission on the day of the murder. White had said a military source, disgusted at the security forces' unrestrained violence, informed our government of a military message that day which contained the phrase "She didn't arrive on this flight, we'll have to wait for the next one."

Why hadn't White brought this information to me earlier? This was the first I heard of the radioed message. What surprised me most was that it was supposed to have come from a Christian Democratic source. I asked Hinton if he could check the embassy files and find out who White's source was.

The families asked if I was willing to pursue this case no matter who was implicated, even if my own life was in danger.

"My life has been in danger for twenty years because of my principles," I reminded them. I told them my life and honor were dedicated to bringing justice to my country. Particularly in the case of their sisters and daughters, I would do whatever was necessary to convict those responsible. Then one of the women present wondered aloud, "What could these devout women have done that would make military men want to kill them in cold blood?"

"Nothing. They did nothing more than serve the poor, than help those in misery," I answered. "That's why they were killed. They were victims of this insane violence whipped up against anyone who tries to help those suffering from an unjust system. For me, these women were martyrs, perhaps saints."

After two and a half hours, when the meeting had ended, Archbishop Hickey invited me to his own chapel. To my surprise, the tiny chapel reflected El Salvador. It was adorned with colorful crosses and primitive scenes painted by the artisans of La Palma, along with photos of Archbishop Romero and the murdered women. I knelt and prayed there in Washington surrounded by reminders of the best and the worst of my country.

Back in San Salvador, Ambassador Hinton informed me that White's source about the radioed message was the Minister of the Presidency, Pablo Mauricio Alvergue. I immediately called him to my office and asked what he knew about the radio message. Alvergue said that, as a member of the investigating commission, he had used the Christian Democratic network to see if anyone had been around the airport on December 2. A friend told him that David Torres, a party member from La Unión, had spoken of seeing the two American women leave in the white van. Torres also remembered a man watching them, who spoke into a telephone or a two-way radio. The phrase Torres overheard was vague: "There they go" or "There go the nuns" or "The women are leaving the airport now."

Alvergue had talked to Torres himself, but Torres refused to give any testimony and his memories were confusing. Alvergue later mentioned the conversation to the U.S. Embassy's political officer, who obviously reported to Ambassador White. By the time White told the press, his recollection was that the source had been a disgruntled military officer, and the quote was "She didn't arrive on this flight," implying prior knowledge. No one in the embassy had mentioned this despite our continuous consultations on the case.

By the time I got to Torres myself, he was little help. He did not want to testify at all. He wished that his friend had never told Alvergue about his airport observations. He was not certain what he had seen or heard. Torres had gone to the airport between 2 and 4 P.M. to meet relatives arriving from the United States. He remembered seeing two American women drive off in a white van. He also remembered seeing National Guardsmen in uniform at the airport, and that men in civilian clothes were using a two-way radio. He could not remember the exact phrase he overheard or whether the man spoke into the radio or the telephone. After the communication, the man left the airport and followed the white van in another vehicle, according to Torres, who did not encounter any roadblock or checkpoint when he left the airport.

From what Torres had told Alvergue in December, while it was still fresh in his mind, Alvergue was sure the phrase had never been "She didn't arrive on this flight, we'll have to wait for the next." Now, using the lie detectors furnished by the United States, we questioned all the Guardsmen assigned to the airport. Corporal Margarito Pérez admitted phoning Sergeant Colindres to tell him about the two "suspicious" women he had observed. It was the first trip Jean Donovan and Dorothy Kazel made to the airport. This was the time when Torres was at the airport. But Pérez could not have followed the white van, because he had to stay at his post. Nothing would happen until hours later when the two nuns arrived on the COPA flight and their two friends came back to get them.

The question remains: Who would have spoken on a two-way radio? The National Guardsmen do not have two-way radios, which are reserved for high-ranking military officers. Certain agencies, such as the state telephone or power companies, and some private organizations have radio systems. The U.S. Embassy uses them, and the Bowdler-Rogers report mentioned the presence of an embassy chauffeur at the airport. It seems likely that Torres saw the embassy man talking and also heard Pérez. Torres' testimony fit with the pieces of the puzzle, but it did not provide any evidence of links to higher military involvement.

The fact that Colonel Vides' cousin, Edgardo Casanova, was the army officer in charge of the region has been brought out as a reason why Vides would not want a thorough investigation. The hypothesis that Edgardo Casanova gave an order to the Guardsmen regarding the nuns makes it unlikely that a cover-up would have worked. How would he have communicated with Sergeant Colindres? Using the chain of command, he would have called the Army Chiefs of Staff and asked them to relay a message to the National Guard, which would have contacted the airport post by telephone. Normally, Casanova would have given orders to soldiers under his command, not Guardsmen. Even if he bypassed the command chain, the Guardsmen would have been caught lying when they were asked whether they had acted under orders.

The lie-detector tests revealed many times that the suspects were lying when they denied their involvement. But they passed the polygraph test each time they stated there were no orders from their superiors regarding the nuns. Even with the lie-detector results, I still feared the courts would not convict the men. All we could prove was that they were lying. Where was the truth? God only knows, I thought. What more could we do to get evidence, to ensure that the courts would not be intimidated?

That night, as usual, my wife read the Bible before she went to sleep. Later, I picked it up, turning to where she had left her marker, John 16:

> . . . It is expedient for you that I go away; for if I go
> not away, the Comforter will not come unto you . . .
> And when he is come, he will reprove the world of sin,
> and of righteousness, and of judgement . . .

How would I answer the Comforter when He asked me about the nuns, about judgment? Wondering if it would be enough to tell Him of all the efforts I had made, my eyes followed down the page.

> . . . When he, the Spirit of truth, is come, he will
> guide you into all truth . . .

. . . Verily, verily, I say unto you, Whatsoever ye shall ask the Father in my name, he will give it you.

Hitherto have ye asked nothing in my name: ask, and ye shall receive, that your joy may be full.

Truly, I had never asked God's help in this investigation. I felt badly as I realized how little faith I had shown. It was sad to remember how I had prayed in Archbishop Hickey's house, only asking God to reassure the families that *we* would bring justice. Without any humility I had gone before God, who knew the weakness of man's justice in societies as corrupt and immoral as ours. Our effort to reach justice was valid, but I realized that only with God's help could justice be done. Now as I prayed, I felt that God heard me. God understood this world of lies, deceit, ignominy and oppression. God would show me the way.

A few days later, in early December, the lawyer of the investigating commission came to see me. He looked immensely pleased.

"Good news," he said. "We've found the driver of the pickup truck." This was the man who went to get the Guardsmen after their jeep broke down. He drove the pickup seen racing away from the burning van, although it turned out to have been blue, not red.

"Wait, that's not all," the lawyer said as I began interrupting with comments. "One of the Guardsmen we arrested eight months ago is the wrong man. He's innocent, but all this time he's been in jail he's heard the others admitting the crime. He'll serve as a witness. Not only that, but the guilty man, who's been free all this time, was converted by his wife to some Christian sect. He wants to testify to what he did, to free himself from his sins."

Three witnesses! Sitting in stunned silence, I just stared at the lawyer, recalling Moses' words: "One witness shall not rise up against a man for any iniquity, or for any sin . . . at the mouth of two witnesses, or at the mouth of three witnesses, shall the matter be established."

Adrián Ramírez Palacios did not choose to be an instrument of the Lord. He was innocent, but he spent 252 days in prison because his name seemed closest to the one on the embassy's slip of paper that said "(Andrés) ? Palacios," and because he had been assigned to the airport post. His denial of participation in the murders sounded like all the rest. Carlos Joaquín Contreras Palacios escaped lightly after he was questioned by the Guard, but then he found that Christ was questioning him. After Contreras Palacios was finally arrested and submitted to full questioning with the lie-detector equipment, several of those present commented to me that he was totally calm, looking far away. They said he seemed submissive. They had the impression he was not talking to them, but to God.

From the testimony of the three witnesses, we had enough evidence to build a case in our courts. It was January 1982. Ambassador Hinton wanted us to get the indictment process started quickly, before the Reagan Administration had to submit its January report required by Congress to certify El Salvador's progress in human rights. The conditions attached to U.S. aid to El Salvador were linked directly to justice in the cases of murdered American citizens. I explained that we had to wait until every last detail of our case had been prepared. I would not risk making a mistake now that we had a good chance of conviction. We still had to find a judge who would be courageous and fair enough to hear the case solely on its legal merits. Ambassador Hinton understood. The skeptical U.S. Congress was told there would be further developments within a few days.

The next step was working through the Supreme Court and the

Attorney General's office to find a judge. When someone recommended Judge Bernardo Rauda in Sensuntepeque, I called up my friends in that city. They told me he was a good man. We asked Rauda if he would take the case. His answer was succinct, categoric: "I'm a man of destiny."

For two years there were appeals and maneuvers by the defense. The legal technicalities dragged the case out. We also had to guarantee protection for the judge and the jury. All the obstacles that had to be overcome illustrated how our justice system was the result of a corrupt society, a social breakdown, a loss of human values. All Salvadorans have seen with their own eyes how judges and officials were appointed through political and personal favoritism. We all kept quiet when we knew about crimes or corruption. We accepted as routine a system oiled by money and ignored by those who considered themselves above the law.

I knew that one of the essential elements of a democratic revolution must be a fair legal system.

On May 24, 1984, after an all-night session, the jury convicted five Guardsmen of murdering the four American women. They were sentenced to the maximum penalty of thirty years in prison. It was the first time such a case had been brought and fairly adjudicated by the Salvadoran courts.

It will not be the last, God help us.

7

1981

WHEN Ronald Reagan was elected president, we did not
know what to expect. The Right celebrated his election
victory, firing guns into the air. They were sure that Reagan
would sympathize with their preference for a strong, au-
thoritarian government. The oligarchy did not believe that a good
conservative such as Reagan would prop up "leftist" Christian
Democrats in a government. Under President Carter, the United
States championed agrarian reform and human rights, opposing
the military officers who wanted to do away with the junta. The
Right believed that Reagan would accept the need for a new military government, and they began lobbying in Washington to
explain their point of view. The businessmen's delegation made
the rounds of Reagan's transition team in November.

To counteract the rightist influence, I decided to go to Washington myself. I had no contacts with the Republicans and won-

dered who would see me. By this time, the junta had captured documents showing that the guerrillas planned a major offensive before Reagan took office. I hoped someone in Washington during this awkward interregnum would realize that we needed military help quickly. A strengthened junta would be more effective in preventing a Marxist revolution than any new government the rightists would install.

There did not seem to be much point in trying to get to see President Carter, who was still absorbed in the Iran hostage crisis. But on my plane flight from Miami to Washington, I ran into Robert Pastor, the Latin America specialist on Carter's National Security Council. He listened to my concerns and promised to get me in to see Carter.

The first time I entered the White House was through the back door. For the quick interview with Carter, Pastor met me in the Old Executive Office Building. Fidel Chávez Mena, our foreign minister, came with me because he happened to be in Washington for the Organization of American States assembly. Pastor led us down through an underground passageway that connects to the White House. We were late, running all the way to make our Oval Office appointment on time. President Carter was standing in front of his desk. He was supposed to leave in his helicopter in ten minutes. Without any formalities, I summed up the situation in El Salvador, asking if he could speed up the delivery of four helicopters.

"You're leaving the government," I said, "but the Communists could attack and take over before your presidency ends, unless you help us defend ourselves."

He quickly consulted Pastor about the status of aid and agreed to see what he could do. But a week later the four American women were killed. All U.S. aid was suspended. No military supplies would be authorized by Carter until after the guerrilla offensive took place.

To forestall any offensive from the right flank and see what the attitude of the incoming Republican Administration would be, I sought out Reagan's foreign-policy advisers: Richard Allen, Jeane Kirkpatrick and Constantine Menges. Their attitudes ranged from skeptical to rude as they interrogated me. They seemed to have been coached by the Salvadoran Right to think that we Christian Democrats had no respect for private enterprise. I explained that we did believe in a healthy private sector and would treat business fairly, but that at the same time our government must ensure that Salvadoran society as a whole benefited and shared in the economy. They questioned me about agrarian reform, as if only a Communist would ever advocate such a plan. Allen, in particular, kept insisting on questions about whether I admired Fidel Castro.

Of all of them, Kirkpatrick, though doubtful at the beginning of our interview, showed more understanding and a willingness to listen. It may have been her influence that convinced Reagan to express support for our junta government, even before his inauguration. The coup from the Right did not materialize in December when I became president of the junta. But on January 10, ten days before Reagan took office, the guerrillas' final offensive exploded around us.

"I think Mr. Reagan will find an irreversible situation in El Salvador by the time he reaches the presidency," Fermán Cienfuegos, commander of one of the FMLN guerrilla groups, bragged to the press.

We did not know the exact date the guerrillas would strike, but the Army had captured two sets of guerrilla documents with plans for the coming offensive. One cache was discovered by luck. Some neighbors reported suspicious activities in a house on their street, but police raided the wrong address, only to find a real guerrilla safe house full of documents.

Back in 1980, the FMLN's command center was actually in San Salvador, although the guerrilla leaders frequently met abroad. Fidel Castro served as mentor, arbiter and backer. The guerrillas' alliance was a fractious one. Castro forced them to unite and to accept the late-joining Communist Party leaders in top positions. They had sent Shafik Handal traveling around the world to collect arms, receiving two hundred tons. With this supply of arms secured, Castro pushed the guerrillas toward the final offensive.

But there were disagreements over the plans. One group was working on the possibility of a leftist coup, using contacts with some of the younger officers who had links with Majano. Other guerrilla theorists insisted they could succeed only through a prolonged people's war, where the combatants are ideologically sound. Still another sector believed El Salvador was ripe for a mass insurrection, using every sector opposed to the government and assuming the Marxists would eventually control the new government.

I learned from captured guerrilla records years later that Cayetano Carpio of the FPL thought I was an obstacle to the revolution and had to be killed. Shafik Handal argued against killing me because he said I could be useful in helping unite the non-Communist opposition. Handal wanted to bring me over to their side to give the insurrection a broad-based front. But this was all before I entered the government.

From the information the Army found, we knew that the guerrillas finally patched together elements from their different plans into one "final offensive." They called for a general strike simultaneously with guerrilla assaults on towns throughout the country—as well as a move by "fifth column" leftist officers within the armed forces. These officers were meant to surrender their army garrisons during the offensive.

Nothing worried the Army more than the suspicion that some of their own might cooperate with the guerrillas. Fear of this led not only to Majano's downfall, but to sudden changes each month in the officers' assignments. Within the armed forces there was paranoia about officers labeled as "leftists," although the Army's definition ranged from anyone with a social conscience all the way to guerrilla supporters. On the other side, the hard-line rightists in the Army—d'Aubuisson's allies—did not worry their fellow officers. "They may commit crimes, but the victims are usually Communists," the officers would say.

On January 10, Captain Francisco Mena Sandoval, who was one of the original plotters behind the 1979 coup, took charge of the Santa Ana barracks. His colonel had gone home, and the battalion's commander was in San Salvador attending a military graduation ceremony. The guerrillas timed their offensive perfectly. Because of this ceremony, about a hundred officers were away from their posts. When a group of strange men came to the Santa Ana barracks asking for Mena Sandoval, the captain ordered the guard to admit them. They turned out to be guerrillas. Accompanied by the guerrillas, Mena Sandoval went into the room where the next officer in the chain of command was lying down and personally shot him. When another officer realized what was happening, Mena Sandoval killed him too.

During the ensuing gun battle inside the barracks, the armory caught fire. Soldiers panicked, running out into the surrounding streets. It was dark, flames lighting the sky. Word had reached Santa Ana's commanding officer, who rushed back to the city, bringing reinforcements. As he reached the barracks, the major encountered Mena Sandoval, who pretended to be on his way to occupy another part of the city where there was fighting. Mena Sandoval marched out of the barracks at the head of a company of soldiers defecting with him to the guerrilla ranks.

The guerrillas had seized other parts of the city, but the Army rallied forces from the surrounding area and retook the city. The Army then chased the guerrillas into the mountains, surrounding a group of three hundred in a valley and killing them all. Among the dead were engineers, doctors, nurses—all the university-educated elite who had brought the revolution to Santa Ana.

It is a miracle the guerrillas did not defeat the Army. The armed forces were at their weakest during the time of the final offensive. The guerrillas had the right timing and ingenious tactics. In towns such as San Francisco Gotera or Zacatecoluca, they took the church or the hospital, with all the patients still inside. Thus they could hold the highest buildings and the ones whose very nature offered a form of protection. They occupied houses around the barracks, breaking holes in adjoining walls so they could move from one to another without being seen, holding the residents hostage. There were very few soldiers in the barracks, because the new recruits had just started coming in and the released conscripts already had left.

The Chalatenango barracks was defended by a military band, with the musicians telling the green recruits how to shoot. Even so, the guerrillas could not overcome the Army's resistance in either town. One would have thought the Army, internally divided and infiltrated, would have panicked. We had received none of the U.S. military aid I requested, while the guerrillas were well armed with weapons which the Sandinista rebels no longer needed and passed on.

Why did the offensive fail? Perhaps the guerrillas suffered from inexperience. I think they made a major mistake in attacking so many places simultaneously. They mobilized about fifteen thousand people, but only three thousand of them were trained fighters. The rest were militia, and some were the elite who were not really prepared, such as the university students killed near Santa Ana. The Army was on the defensive, and when the numbers are even, the defenders have the advantage. But the most important factor in the failure of the offensive was that the people did not respond to the guerrillas. When they entered the villages, guerrillas were not received as an army of liberation, but as an army of occupation. The towns they attacked were areas where the Christian Democratic vote is strong and the leftists had not converted them.

One main reason why the people did not rally to the guerrillas' call for insurrection was our agrarian-reform program. After the seizure of the large estates was decreed in March 1980, the program was administered by the Salvadoran Institute for Agrarian Transformation (ISTA), headed by Rodolfo Viera. There had been an agreement between the Christian Democrats and the peasants' union (known as the UCS) that Viera would run the agrarian-reform program. These peasant leaders had come to us saying, "We represent two hundred fifty thousand farmworkers and they are ready to join the guerrillas unless you take action on agrarian reform and allow us a role in the management."

My answer was that we wanted agrarian reform as much as they did, but we would not accept blackmail. They had to work on the program with the party. We named a commission to draw up the agrarian-reform decree. To organize for its enactment, we sequestered our technical team in a hotel for eight days of intensive preparation on how to manage the reform process. Meanwhile, the military forces planned the occupation of the estates.

We made many errors in launching this agrarian-reform process. Some of the estates taken turned out to be smaller than our records showed, under the five-hundred-hectare limit set by the law. The agrarian-reform team seized sugar mills and agro-industries that did not come under the decree because, though located on the estates, they were owned by separate corporations. We had to pass three or four other laws to straighten this out. Of course, the former owners tied us up with lawsuits, jumping on the mistakes made.

Our greatest error may have been to seize the estates just at the end of the harvest. This meant we took on all the seasonal workers, who previously came to the estates only for harvests. Now they had to be salaried and aided well as the year-round workers on each farm, but there was no productive work for them to do. It was time to plant the next crop, but the landowners kept the proceeds from their harvest and left the estates owing debts to the banks. Thus it was impossible for new credit to be extended. On top of this, the farmworkers showed little enthusiasm because they did not believe we would be able to turn the land over to them. The Right swore that the reforms would be reversed within the year.

The U.S. Embassy had its own priorities in land reform, and these were imposed on top of ours. The Christian Democratic theory held that cooperatives should replace the large plantations. To subdivide these estates into minuscule plots would cause more economic stagnation for El Salvador. By creating cooperatives, the government would be better able to provide technical and financial assistance, and to maintain economies of scale within the farms. But our cooperativist theory clashed with the proposal favored by the U.S. Embassy. The embassy had brought in Roy Prosterman, the author of the land-to-the-tiller program in Vietnam. His plan would give sharecroppers and tenant farmers rights to the land they worked, up to seventeen acres in size though most plots were much smaller. The embassy introduced Prosterman to Colonel Gutierrez, whom he sold on the land-to-the-tiller program as the antidote to Communism that produced the economic miracles in Korea and Taiwan, even if it did not quite turn the tide in Vietnam.

Gutierrez championed this program against Majano's program with ISTA and the cooperativist movement. The Christian Democrats opposed land-to-the-tiller until Morales made a convincing argument. He said that, given the political crisis in the country, smallholdings might be an economic evil, but they would prove a social benefit because they would ensure the peasant's subsistence, despite their adverse effect on the national product. Economic survival by subsistence would buy time to transform our economic system out of its export-crop dependency.

I agreed with Morales on the need for the land-to-the-tiller program, but I did not see how we could afford it. The cash costs and the political costs were going to be high. In our junta discussion with Prosterman and Ambassador White, I opposed the mechanics of the plan. The large landowners were already out to get us, I argued. Enacting this plan would affect thousands of small property owners, spreading the conflict to every village, undercutting our support. Compensation would cost over $100 million, and the government was broke. The only way the plan could work was if we had the money to pay the landowners immediately, containing the backlash and enabling them to invest their money in other small businesses.

At this point, Prosterman intervened. He assured us that he could guarantee U.S. funding for the plan. His friends in Congress, he said, would provide the $100 million three days after we initiated the program. The junta voted four to one in favor of the land-to-the-tiller plan—mine was the sole dissenting vote. The decree was made April 28, 1980, seven weeks after the first agrarian-reform act. The U.S. funds never came, because Prosterman apparently had not reckoned on Senator Jesse Helms, who made it illegal for any U.S. aid to be spent on compensation for land reform. The problems that arose from this land-reform program have since grown beyond my modest warnings. Most land claims are under litigation, few land titles have been awarded. We are still paying the costs for this program in economic and political losses.

The Right took more than court action against the agrarian-reform program. Illegal evictions and violent attacks directly threatened those involved in the redistribution of the land. On the night of January 4, 1981, two gunmen killed Rodolfo Viera, the head of ISTA, and two American advisers to the land-reform program, Michael Hammer and Mark Pearlman. Viera was about to be replaced as president of ISTA by Morales Erlich, because a stronger administrator was needed. Viera had probably asked Hammer and Pearlman to come and discuss the changes planned.

Viera met Hammer and Pearlman for a late dinner at the Sheraton Hotel, where they were observed by Lieutenant Rodolfo Isidro López Sibrián and Captain Eduardo Avila. The officers were reported to have been socializing with two businessmen at the hotel. Someone proposed that Viera should be eliminated. The officers called two enlisted men from the parking lot and sent them into the hotel to gun down Viera and his dinner guests. It should be pointed out that Major Denís Morán, head of the Guard's intelligence unit, was present at the hotel the night of the crime, although his involvement was never established. I think the fact that after the shooting he, an officer of the law, made no attempt to initiate an investigation shows dereliction of duty, at the very least.

When the normal investigation took place, once again, as in the cases of Archbishop Romero and the nuns, there was little evidence and few witnesses. Anyone involved was afraid to testify. Only the most extraordinary judicial efforts, pursued by a determined investigator prodding the system along, would ever build a solid case. That is why I practically had to become the prosecutor myself in the cases of the nuns and Archbishop Romero. That is why since becoming president I have appointed a special investigating commission for the cases of Romero, Viera and others.

In the case of Viera, Hammer and Pearlman, we ran into major setbacks in the courts. AFL-CIO President Lane Kirkland and William Doherty, who heads their American Institute for Free Labor Development, were determined to see the killers of their colleagues brought to justice. Kirkland and Doherty worked closely with me and assigned a skilled investigator to help us here. The gunmen were arrested and confessed, telling how they had been ordered to kill the three men. But under Salvadoran law their word cannot be used in court against accomplices in the same crime.

Besides these technicalities of the law, those responsible for the crime had the protection of their status as officers and members of the elite. Our traditional legal system would bend over backward not to convict them. Also, the American impatience with judicial reluctance led to precipitate court action that we lost. Now, with more time and God's help, new evidence has begun to be uncovered. It seems that Captain Avila was arrested in Costa Rica for another crime. The gun in his possession may prove to be the same weapon used against Viera, Hammer and Pearlman. We have information that Captain Avila also confessed his role to American friends in Costa Rica, but it is their word against his in the courts.

Unfortunately, Lieutenant López Sibrián has used the legal

system to place himself beyond its reach. In November 1984, the Supreme Court ruled that the statute of limitations for introducing new evidence had expired in his case. All I could do as president was insist that he be cashiered from the armed forces. There are many people, particularly Americans, who think that if enough U.S. pressure is applied, El Salvador's society will live up to American standards. Yet not all the pressure the United States brought in the Hammer and Pearlman case could change the way our courts worked.*

U.S. pressure and U.S. aid, on a scale we had never imagined, began penetrating El Salvador within a month after Reagan's inauguration. When Secretary of State Alexander Haig decided to draw his line against international Communism right through El Salvador, our problems suddenly became the world's problem. The long, bloody struggle between the Salvadoran Right, the leftist guerrillas and the Christian Democrats was transformed into a metaphor for the East–West struggle. It became an issue between Republicans and Democrats, and a stage for anyone wanting to star in a morality drama.

The internationalization of our conflict in 1981, when an army of journalists invaded our small country, took most Salvadorans by surprise. We did not know how to react when the world suddenly began to examine El Salvador through the camera's eye. The leftists understood the importance of press coverage. They had daily bulletins that kept the press informed. They provided journalists with underground contacts and pointed reporters toward sensational stories. Their campaign worked well. The journalists became convinced the guerrilla triumph was inevitable. The only question was, "How soon will they take over?"

*As this book goes to press, Lopéz Sibrián is in prison, as one of the leaders of a kidnapping ring that has recently been broken.

The government started badly in the information battle. We fumbled and blamed the press for the wave of international criticism. The growing hostility toward the foreign press was rooted in a perceived bias. If the government provided information, it was ignored or greeted with skepticism, but any guerrilla source was considered newsworthy and factual. The armed forces resented the type of coverage orchestrated by the Left and made matters worse by treating journalists as their enemy.

Just when I had hoped to create a little space for free expression in the country, the Right launched a national campaign against the press. The local papers seemed to take delight in denouncing the foreign press. It was easy for them to shift the blame for our deteriorating international reputation onto the one powerful alien group, the cars and vans with the big letters "TV" taped on them.

Governments all over the world began to offer opinions about the problems in El Salvador. The guerrillas let it be known that they were willing to open negotiations with the government, changing the position they had taken prior to the failure of the final offensive. When the Church offered to mediate in October 1980, the junta accepted, but the FDR-FMLN rejected talks. The Reagan Administration's hard-line policy, however, produced a flurry of peacemaking efforts by European and Latin-American countries. By this time, the guerrillas were constantly proclaiming their willingness to negotiate.

The Socialist International offered to mediate between the FDR-FMLN and the junta, sending its envoy Hans-Jürgen Wischnewski traveling through Central America in April 1981. We showed him a captured guerrilla document, signed by Rubén Zamora, explaining that the call for negotiations was a tactic the guerrillas could use against the government. The document talked about all the intermediaries whom they planned to use, including the Pope. Wischnewski looked deflated after he read this cynical document. He asked if he could take it with him to verify its authenticity. We were later informed that he had shown the document to Fidel Castro, who confirmed that it came from the guerrillas. Castro then complained that these revolutionaries had turned into bureaucrats with all their paperwork!

Overall, we were being crushed under the avalanche of international press coverage. We had been totally unprepared for it. If there had been some structure to handle the press, some capacity to investigate charges and demonstrate what was true or false, we might have done better. Mixed together were lies and truths, omissions and exaggerations. The government became isolated. Other countries withdrew their ambassadors and closed down their embassies. The lowest point for the junta government came in August 1981 when France and Mexico gave diplomatic recognition to the FDR-FMLN as a representative political force.

The United States, meanwhile, debated the issue of aid to El Salvador. We had begun receiving military aid in February, and by March the number of military personnel attached to the embassy was proliferating. The idea of sending advisers came from Washington, without consulting me. In honor of the American Undersecretary of Defense's visit to El Salvador in June, U.S. Ambassador Hinton, invited Colonel Gutierrez, the Secretary and me to dinner to discuss the need for more U.S. advisers with a high-ranking Pentagon official. Several American officers made presentations about what was happening in the battalion where each one was stationed. Hinton told me the United States wanted to increase the aid and send more advisers.

"Look, before you send any more aid, I want to ask a favor," I replied. "I'd like some of the experts from the U.S. Joint Chiefs of Staff, with the rank of general if possible, to study the military situation here. Tell me exactly what they think we should do. All that your officers have told me tonight is anecdotes. Neither you nor I really can come to any conclusions at this moment about what is happening or where the military situation of the country as a whole stands." I had my own ideas and a general plan based on the information given to me by the Salvadoran Army Chief of Staff, but I wanted to compare notes.

The U.S. military study done at my request came back with three alternative plans: one for defeating the guerrillas in a short time period, the second to win over the longer term, and a third that would just enable us to survive by preventing a guerrilla victory. The first plan involved sophisticated American military equipment, spending $700 or $800 million a year, and increasing the ratio of soldiers to guerrillas to ten to one, with more U.S.-trained rapid-reaction battalions. At that time we had changed the internal and rigid concept of the army and we had just trained one rapid-reaction battalion, the Atlacatl, and they said we would need ten. (There are now seven.) The Pentagon wanted to send a large number of advisers, but I asked them to explain, one by one, exactly what each adviser would be doing. The ambassador and I discussed this until we came up with the number of fifty-five advisors, agreed upon by everyone, and that figure has been maintained up to this moment.

My objective was to reorganize the armed forces, bringing all the commands into a more disciplined and professional structure. Then our policies could actually be carried out. Gutierrez, though nominally commander in chief, had limited control because the Defense Minister, García, really managed the armed forces. Even García did not really try to control the regional commanders. García knew he would win more favor by allowing each commander to run his own show. I thought that by creating mobile battalions and placing the command structure for each theater of operations directly under the Joint Chiefs of Staff, we could break the static system of the locally entrenched, autonomous military commanders. Our whole military structure was geared for peacetime police duties, not for fighting a guerrilla war.

The armed forces rejected the theaters-of-operations plan. They alleged that it was too expensive. As a junta, we had no chance of reforming the military bureaucracy or making the lower levels responsive to our orders. Our decrees on controlling the abuses of authority were never even transmitted to the local commanders. Only Colonel Vides Casanova in the National Guard and Colonel Reynaldo López Nuila in the National Police made a personal effort to begin disciplining their men and weeding out the most abusive ones.

A few other commanders were ready for the changes, but the structure was not. Some commanders had to be forced out, even using U.S. pressure to get results. Defense Minister García was building up his power. His base was Colonel Morán in the Treasury Police, and gradually he convinced the Right to provide him the political support he needed. He was adept at blaming the junta for everything that went wrong, pretending he could do so much more if he had the means. We tried to oust him several times, but we never had enough support. My own position as president was getting weaker and weaker because the United States started dealing directly with García. When military aid was conditioned to human-rights improvements, the U.S. ambassador became more powerful than I was as president. My complaints were less important than the ambassador's, because he controlled the flow of money.

I tried to prevent this situation by talking directly to the U.S. Congress and the American people. This was my main objective when I traveled to Washington in September 1981.

Before leaving on that trip, I wanted the junta government to take one important step that could change our ebbing political tide. I wanted to schedule elections for the following March. The timing of elections was intended to bring the political initiative back to El Salvador. Internationally, we were being pushed and pulled by other countries proposing unacceptable peace negotiations. It even appeared that the U.S. government considered this alternative.

Shortly before my trip to the United States, we discussed holding elections at the weekly political-committee meeting of military and civilian leaders. These sessions usually ended up in a fight between García and me. By this time García could see the pressure building for negotiations with the guerrillas, and he was afraid of it. During our meeting, Ambassador Hinton appeared for some reason. All discussion stopped until he left, but we felt that some unilateral decision in the United States was brewing as a result of the French-Mexican pressure.

I told the committee the junta government was exhausted politically, but we still had one trump card to play. One of the guerrillas' documents we had captured said the guerrillas were at a disadvantage whenever the government took a political step that, in effect, rewrote the rules of the game. We had the power to take such a step by calling for elections. To focus maximum attention on the announcement, I proposed we issue the call on the eve of my trip to the United States. Everyone agreed.

During our Independence Day celebrations on September 15, I told the people they would be asked to go to the polls March 28, 1982. They would elect delegates to a Constituent Assembly that would write a constitution for our new democratic government.

The next day I left for the United States. Since I had not been officially invited by the American government, I had to make my own arrangements. As a matter of fact, I never have been officially invited. My greatest effort was concentrated on the television talk shows, the interviews in which I could present my views to the American people. On Capitol Hill, I walked from office to office, explaining the situation in my country. My reception was cool. The Democrats had their doubts about my liberal credentials as a military-appointed president. The conservatives had their own doubts, fanned by the Salvadoran Right, which once again sent a mission to work against me among the Republicans.

There were some congressmen who understood that I was trying to gain control over the decision-making process of the country, which was still in the hands of the military. They could see that by placing their own conditions on U.S. aid, they would undermine my authority. Unless the bill was rewritten so that I could be the judge of military improvement on human rights, the Army would not pay attention to my demands. They would work with whomever their U.S. military aid depended on.

Either I failed to convince enough congressmen or else they preferred a direct U.S. role as overseer on human rights. The vote went in favor of certification every six months by the State Department that El Salvador had made progress in controlling violence and achieving justice. The U.S. ambassador's role was strengthened. I lost.

While I could not sway the Congress, I found President Reagan willing to listen to what I had to say, despite his hostility to the junta government during his presidential campaign.

My White House entrance was not by the back door this time. But I was not given the front-door treatment either. This visit was treated as a private meeting. Not until May 1984, after I had been elected president, would I be publicly welcomed to the White House.

In 1981 I was ushered into a room with Ambassador Ernesto

Rivas Gallont and Fidel Chávez Mena to await President Reagan. There was a sense of formality, which was not as natural to Reagan as the informality in our later meetings. He asked questions, I answered. He always has a tiny card with the topics he wants to discuss written down. We discussed aid for El Salvador, and he assured me that everything was being done to get the aid I needed approved by the Congress. I thanked him and explained my strategy for leading El Salvador toward political dialogue and the electoral process. Then Reagan added something that surprised me.

"I have a message for you from my friend José López Portillo," he said. Reagan had met with the Mexican President recently. He explained that López Portillo wanted him to ask me if I would be willing to meet with the FDR-FMLN representatives in Mexico, and said López Portillo offered to make the arrangements.

"I thank you, Mr. President, for doing me the honor of bringing me this message," I answered. "But you have to understand that for us Mexico is not a neutral country. The joint Mexican-French declaration recognizing the guerrillas was an interventionist and partisan action. Therefore, we could hardly accept Mexico as a mediator."

Reagan changed the subject, and asked if I would talk at more length with Vice-President George Bush. I agreed. We shook hands, and Bush led me to another part of the White House. Bush took an active and personal interest in Latin America. He has been very friendly with me, and my son Alejandro has gotten to know his son John.

The next time I would see the Vice-President was in El Salvador in December 1983, when his mission was to demand that the death squads be brought under control. All the leaders of the political parties, including myself and d'Aubuisson, were invited to lunch with the American Vice-President. Bush spoke harshly, without any diplomatic cushioning, about the appalling number of killings. D'Aubuisson responded by saying he personally condemned death squads. If the problem could have been resolved by words, there would have been no more political assassinations after the Bush visit.

There was always a difference between what the United States thought could be done in El Salvador and the results when Washington applied its formulas. Both the Republicans and the Democrats wanted peace and democracy for El Salvador, but at that time they did not believe my plans could work. However, the electoral process was about to start in accordance with our democratization program.

8

Elections

NOTHING was simple about the call for elections. Months of haggling shaped our first attempt at bringing a democracy into being by electing the sixty-member Constituent Assembly. The junta chose not to hold presidential, municipal and legislative elections at that same time, deciding instead on different successive elections. But first the assembly would have to be formed and then write a constitution to determine how the presidential, legislative and local officials should be elected. The military command wanted our election plan to spell out exactly what the constitution would contain. We convinced the officers that strings could not be attached to the people's right to their own constitution. We proposed that the government submit a draft constitution later, thus influencing the process without appearing to dictate to the electorate.

After announcing the March 28, 1982, elections for the Constituent Assembly, we invited all parties to send their representatives to the forum that would draw up the procedure for electing the delegates. We wanted the Left to take part in the discussions. When they refused, we still legalized two parties, the MNR and the UDN, so that the Left would have a vehicle to come in later, if they changed their minds. There was a general impression that if the Left did not take part, the elections could not be held.

At this point, in late 1981, the guerrillas were getting ready for another military offensive and scorned the election call. With the Left unwilling to be involved, only the Right was hammering away at us, trying to shape the election format to favor themselves.

The election fit into d'Aubuisson's overall strategy for building an overt political organization. Meanwhile, he was operating underground because we had had a warrant out for his arrest since March. The charge was plotting a coup against the government. To bring the violent extremes into the political process, an amnesty had been arranged. We decreed that anyone could participate in the elections as long as the person publicly pledged to uphold democracy and renounce violence. D'Aubuisson appeared at a newspaper office, announcing his intention to join in the democratic process. It was a move Guillermo Ungo or anyone on the Left also could have made.

D'Aubuisson unveiled a new party, the Nationalist Republican Alliance, known as ARENA. It was financed by the oligarchy, conceived as a political antidote to the Christian Democratic Party. The old rightist party, the PCN, reformed its ranks and refused to cede to ARENA. After all, many peasants had been taught they were expected to vote for the PCN or risk dire consequences. Why confuse these sure votes? All the other small parties, each revolving around a single leader, clustered at the right of the political spectrum—with the possible exception of the Democratic Action (AD) Party founded by René Fortín Magaña to be an alternative between the Right and the Christian Democrats. It was all the parties against the Christian Democrats. I think voters became confused, thinking there was an actual choice between these parties, without realizing the Right could count on the natural alliance among them all against the Christian Democrats on any major reform issue.

The odds were against my party. The Christian Democratic Party had to be rebuilt. By 1980, we had been practically eliminated as a grass-roots organization. As the 1982 election drew near, it warmed my heart to see the old Christian Democrats coming forward in so many villages, willing to take all the risks again. However, the party had recovered to only about 50 percent of its organizational level by the March 1982 campaign.

Our party is organized by province. Each one holds its own convention to elect leaders, who must then be approved by the national committee. Internal fights over leadership are normal, but in 1982 there was a new phenomenon. Some of the best and the brightest—such as Fidel Chávez Mena and Pablo Mauricio Alvergue—did not want to be candidates for the Constituent Assembly. Those who did accept—such as Rey Prendes and Antonio Guevara—knew they faced major confrontations with the Right over the constitution. Other parties also had trouble finding candidates. The exception was ARENA, which projected the image of the winner and got whomever they wanted to run.

The Central Election Council was meant to be nonpartisan, but the Right was determined to control it. Later, when they wrote the constitution, they changed its nature from a professional agency to a party-coordinating committee. In the meantime, they could not touch the Central Election Council president we had chosen. Dr. Jorge Bustamante was well respected. But they did insist on removing two Council members accused of being Christian Democrats.

One of the thorniest decisions facing the Council was how to determine voter eligibility. The Christian Democrats wanted an electoral system that would allow broad participation by all Salvadorans. But the Right wanted a complicated system of voter registration and assignment to polling places. The Right was so used to fixing elections that they were sure that I intended to use my position as junta president to guarantee a Christian Democratic victory. That is why they kept insisting on controls. There was no way, however, to compile a realistic voter-registration list prior to this election. Five years of war had uprooted and dispersed about one-fourth the population. We simply agreed to allow each voter to present his identification card at any polling place, have it stamped, and a finger dipped in ink to prevent double voting.

For me, the election had two objectives: defining the people's commitment to the democratic process and choosing who would take part in the Constituent Assembly. My task was to ensure the commitment to democracy. I campaigned for a large turnout, urging people to cast their vote, whatever party they favored. I traveled and planned the publicity with the same enthusiasm as if I were running for an office. My real opponent was the Left, who campaigned against the election. They were telling people not to vote, to support the revolution by abstaining.

On election day, I cast my ballot, then went to man my post in the Presidential Palace, knowing there would be trouble. The complaints began coming in from poll workers, who reported that local commanders tried to interfere with the voting. I asked Colonel Gutierrez to take military steps to stop this, but much of it was beyond his control. Besides the intimidation and tricks of the Right, the Left tried to obstruct the voting. Guerrillas waged a battle in Usulatán, attacked San Francisco Gotera and fired on polling places north of San Salvador in Apopa and San Antonio Abad. Many voters bravely stood in line despite the gunfire.

When the votes were counted, the Christian Democrats had won a plurality with 40 percent of the votes, but had only twenty-four seats in the Constituent Assembly. ARENA and the PCN had thirty-three together. The Right was in control.

To think that more than a million Salvadorans would come to the polls was once considered only a crazy dream of mine. The norm is about 600,000 to 800,000. There is no doubt that more people voted in 1982, despite the gunfire and the threats, than in any other election before or since. Both the Left and the Right resorted to fear, while I had asked for trust. Some journalists have said people voted because they were afraid of what would happen to them if their identity card did not carry the stamp showing they participated. Voting has always been obligatory, but everyone knows that no fines have ever been imposed. I do not believe that people would have walked for miles, leaving the guerrilla strongholds, standing in line for hours, even under fire, only because they were more afraid of an unenforced law.

If fear had been the motivating factor, then the guerrilla threat to cut off the inked finger of those who voted should have kept more people away. Those journalists who asked the voters standing in lines why they had come heard the same answer over and over: "Because I want peace." This is what I told the voters. "Violence will not solve anything. Democracy is the way to peace. Do not let a small group of people with rifles in their hands run this country. Take charge of your own destiny by using the vote." From the sixties through the seventies and now in the eighties, my message has never changed.

To say that more than a million people did vote is not to say the election was entirely free of fraud. Nor could one election bring peace. The tally of 1.48 million votes cast has been challenged by a Jesuit university study. There probably was some ballot-box stuffing, but the Jesuit study misrepresents the problem. For instance, the study claimed it took three minutes for one person to cast a vote—from the time the identity card was checked and the ballot marked and deposited in the urn to the voter's departure with an inked finger. But the study does not take into account that, while one voter marks a ballot, another is already presenting his identity card and a third is leaving. The study fails to note that, in places where fraud was charged, such as Arcatao, ARENA got the challenged votes, not the Christian Democrats. For the first time in our history, the fraud was working against the president's party.

Despite our having "lost" the election, the day I left the junta, turning power over to a provisional president elected by the Constituent Assembly, was the proudest of my life. It was then that I kept a promise to myself and a promise made to Simón Bolívar in front of the other democratic presidents of Latin America.

In December 1980, on the 150th anniversary of Bolívar's death, the presidents of Venezuela, Colombia, Ecuador, Peru, Panama and the Dominican Republic had met together with the Prime Minister of Spain to commemorate the event in Santa Marta, Colombia. They included me in the ceremony at the time when I had just accepted the presidency of the junta, under siege from the Right and the Left. I faced the democratic Latin leaders in a private session, with only our foreign ministers present. They looked upon me as a bastard son. Ecuador's President Jaime Roldós made sure I knew it, condemning my role as a military-installed president. I swore to them in Santa Marta that I would bring democracy to El Salvador and then return to the tomb of the Liberator of the Americas to say, "Mission accomplished."

This was the theme of my speech at the inauguration of the

Provisional President, May 2, 1982. "El Salvador is a nation full of hope, that has shown its lofty spirit and the courage to meet the challenge of its destiny. For us, the revolutionary junta government, this milestone in our history has special significance because we can say to the people: mission accomplished." No sooner had I left the government than I boarded a plane for Venezuela to go to the pantheon of Bolívar, fulfilling my promise.

But the process of choosing a provisional president had been less lofty than Bolívar and I might have wished.

As soon as the votes for the Constituent Assembly delegates had been counted, d'Aubuisson made the astute move of calling all the parties together and confronting the junta with the elected power of the assembly. The junta's role was ended, they said. Within the junta, we debated whether the assembly was meant to take power from us or simply write the constitution. I thought that only the elected assembly had legitimate power—there was no longer justification for the junta. The armed forces also opposed any extension of the junta government. García intended to get rid of the junta so that he could rule as defense minister in the vacuum. The majority among the officer corps wanted a civilian president because they thought the junta government had been damaging to military prestige. The struggle then began over who would be the provisional president.

It was a horse race. Dozens of names were entered. The PCN trotted out Chachi Guerrero. D'Aubuisson had not planned to take the transition role of president, because he counted on being elected later, while controlling whoever was president during the interim. He first backed the conservative lawyer who had served in the 1961 junta, Antonio Rodríguez Porth. Then d'Aubuisson became worried that Gutierrez was mobilizing support among the military and countered by telling Colonel Carranza that he should be president. Carranza went to García and Gutierrez to announce he had a party coalition behind him, only to be vetoed by his military colleagues. There was no consensus around any military candidate among the officers.

The U.S. Embassy, hearing the rumors about Carranza and d'Aubuisson, was very worried. The Reagan Administration wanted a moderate civilian in the role of provisional president. The names that were said to have the U.S. ambassador's blessing included a Christian Democrat, Abraham Rodríguez, Dr. Bustamante of the Election Council, Fortín Magaña of the Democratic Action Party and a banker named Alvaro Magaña Borja, among others.

But d'Aubuisson, seeing the disagreement among the military, decided he should take the job himself. Since he had the votes in the Constituent Assembly, it was only a matter of gaining military acquiescence. D'Aubuisson's mistake was overconfidence, I learned. The cocky major went to Gutierrez to offer him the post of Salvadoran ambassador to Washington. Gutierrez kept his anger under control, quietly saying he would prefer to stay out. D'Aubuisson, who was drinking at the time, thought Gutierrez had accepted the job, so he regaled him with all his plans for his Cabinet. The more Gutierrez knew, the more reasons he had to convince the armed forces that they should not allow d'Aubuisson to take over.

The high command knew that the United States opposed d'Aubuisson. The embassy was so concerned about a d'Aubuisson presidency that Washington was asked to send reinforcements to help block this development. President Reagan dispatched General Vernon Walters, his trouble-shooting ambassador, who was then involved in trying to end the war between Argentina and Great Britain, which broke out five days after our elections. Walters, a direct man who speaks to Latin military leaders in their own language, works well as Reagan's envoy. But before General

Walters could arrive the high command decided that the issue of the provisional presidency had to be settled.

There was one unexpected visitor who was brought into the military conclave, the Honduran Army chief, General Gustavo Alvarez. The Honduran general was officially there to bring congratulations on the elections. But Gutierrez asked him how the Honduran military had gotten an acceptable president after its Constituent Assembly was elected the year before. Alvarez said they had formed a military committee whose decision was imposed on the parties. Gutierrez then proposed that the armed forces back Alvaro Magaña as president. Magaña was viewed as a friend by the military, politically neutral, acceptable to the U.S. Embassy—a good compromise. The entire officer corps was consulted and approved.

By the time Walters reached the meeting of the high command, their decision to impose Magaña's presidency had already been taken. The officers quickly accepted U.S. advice to do what they had already planned.

The high command called in the political parties, one by one, to let them know. Once the junta had been dismissed by the military, I had no political role. Our party's only power was our votes in the Constituent Assembly. We approved of Magaña as provisional president, because compared to d'Aubuisson or Carranza he was an angel. ARENA, of course, screamed foul. The PCN leaders saw the chance to bargain. They would back Magaña only if each party got a vice-presidential position and several ministries. The government was carved up. The armed forces claimed their right to certain Cabinet posts. García stayed on as defense minister.

Magaña's government was weak from the start. The Constituent Assembly was trying to undo the reforms of the junta, but the intense fight of the Christian Democratic delegates during the two years between the 1982 and 1984 elections kept the democratic process alive. Our strategy was to split the Right. We were helped by d'Aubuisson's character. Few people trusted him. His party finally split, and a bloc of legislators from the PCN formed the PAISA party. No one had a majority in the assembly, and d'Aubuisson was not adept at building coalitions. Military and police training does not hone the skills necessary for parliamentary politics.

The constitution drawn up by the Constituent Assembly contains the philosophy of the Christian Democrats, but it has clauses written by the Right to impede the application of our principles. The constitution guarantees human rights and the general welfare. But on every economic matter the rightist parties locked together. By law, further agrarian reform is limited. Furthermore, they made it almost impossible to amend the constitution. To do so requires passing an amendment by a two-thirds vote in the second consecutive legislative session after it is proposed. This means that any amendment would be held up until after the next legislative election took place.

While the constitution was being written, the war, violence and injustice were the day-to-day reality. The responsibility for El Salvador's dire situation fell on García. Provisional President Magaña had no political base, so he provided no buffer to the pressures. García's relationship to Magaña inverted the normal role of president and defense secretary. Magaña would go over to the Treasury Police headquarters to keep an appointment with García, instead of vice versa.

The clash for power squared off García against d'Aubuisson and his military group. It broke into the open in January 1983, when Lieutenant Colonel Sigifredo Ochoa, the field commander in Cabañas, declared a mutiny. He refused to obey an order from García which banished him to a diplomatic post. Ochoa identifies with the rightists, but he probably acted on his own. He sensed his power to rally elements of the military against García. He was right. Several high-ranking officers took Ochoa's side.

At the time of the crisis, I remember talking with Magaña and Vides Casanova. I told Magaña he should not stay aloof, because he was sacrificing the authority of a president. He regarded it as an internal matter of the armed forces. I warned Vides that it would be a mistake to support Ochoa against García, that García was not going to last. There was going to be a dangerous situation, and Vides should mediate.

My advice did not please them, but a compromise was worked out by Colonel Vides, Colonel Adolfo Blandón and Air Force Colonel Juan Bustillo. Ochoa would leave for a post in Washington with the understanding that the high command would remove García as defense minister after ninety days. Ochoa apparently felt triumphant about the delayed-reaction coup he had pulled off against García. Later, he would not hesitate to challenge my presidency.

The second crisis came after the ninety-day period had passed. Magaña did not not fire García. Colonel Bustillo demanded that Magaña uphold the agreement, because he felt the word of honor of the high command was at stake. At this juncture, Magaña made the only decision that could save his presidency. He named Vides Casanova to replace García. Magaña turned to the one natural leader of the armed forces, the man García knew he could not fight.

While Magaña sat in the Presidential Palace, in the eye of the military storm, I was only a private citizen. The day after I turned over the presidency, I placed an advertisement in the local papers. It said: "José Napoleón Duarte wishes to advise the Salvadoran people that he will continue to serve them in any way he can from his private office." It gave the hours and the address. From that day on, I talked with hundreds of people, who sometimes formed lines down the street in front of the walled two-story house that I used across from Christian Democratic Party headquarters.

They came from all parts of the country, with all kinds of problems. Some I could help them with, others I could not. I did not have a wealthy foundation behind me. I lived from my savings, but I sat behind a desk and was willing to listen. It would be hard to imagine any kind of problem that I did not hear about. Most people came about recommendations for jobs. Many others came because they had suffered from the violence; usually their son or daughter had disappeared. I would try to help them get information. Sometimes a person needed medical care, and I would ask my friends who were doctors to help.

During this period of my life, I also started up a radio station, specializing in news. I began a newspaper, which failed for lack of advertising. But gradually my attention turned to the 1984 presidential campaign. About eighteen months before the March 25 election, the Christian Democrats began to speculate about whether I would be a candidate. I was in for a shock.

The first hint came when I was in Venezuela talking with the former President, my friend Luis Herrera Campins. He asked me about the division in my party. When I denied knowing of any problem, Campins frowned and repeated that he had heard there was a split. I paid no attention until the subject arose again, while I was in West Germany. The Christian Democrats there specifically asked about the division between myself and Fidel Chávez Mena. I vehemently denied there was any truth to this rumor, explaining that except for my own sons no one was closer to me than Fidel. He was my friend and colleague from my first campaign for mayor, my contact at home while I was in exile, the foreign minister while I served on the junta.

When I returned to El Salvador from my trip abroad, however, a group of party leaders came to tell me Fidel was holding meetings at his home. The discussions centered on my political status, alleging that I was burned out, that my participation in the junta tainted me, that I was associated in people's minds with the violence that took forty thousand lives. The Christian Democrats must find a new leader, they said. Obviously, Fidel was ready to be that leader.

The Christian Democrats who came to see me wanted to know one thing: Did I still want to run for president? They had heard I was tired, unwilling to take the risks of being the Christian Democratic candidate any longer. The whole weight of the intrigue within the party struck me at once. But I was not left speechless. I told my colleagues that there was so much more I felt we had to do before El Salvador would be the country I envisioned leaving to my children. I was not ready to give up. The opportunity to win the presidency in a free election and to serve my people was the moment I had worked toward for twenty years. My willingness to go forward had not changed. I was ready to be their presidential candidate—if that was what the party wanted to know.

From that moment on, we began the equivalent of a primary campaign within the party, but not an open one. The group splitting the party did not propose Chávez Mena immediately. They advocated anyone other than Duarte. The campaign was only against me. Duarte is too old, they said, a liability to the party, blamed for everything the junta did or failed to do.

My own campaign began with small meetings all around the country, sounding out the party representatives. Many were undecided, including Rey Prendes and Morales. The rumors came thick and fast, saying the business sectors and even some opposition party members could accept Chávez Mena as a consensus candidate. The one Christian Democrat who supposedly alienated other voters was Duarte. The Right may have backed Chávez Mena in hopes of splitting the Christian Democratic Party. The rumors said the armed forces, the Church and the United States also preferred Chávez Mena.

To find out whether any of this was true, I met with each group separately. The head of the Army Chiefs of Staff told me Chávez Mena had spoken with him. The officer said the Army would have no problem accepting Chávez Mena as the Christian Democratic candidate, which was hardly an endorsement even though it was being interpreted as one. A similar response came from U.S. Ambassador Hinton, who said, "We respect democratic procedures, so the Christian Democratic Party has the right to select you or Chávez Mena. Whoever is chosen, we're satisfied." Next I went to see the Archbishop. Monsignor Rivera Damas said the Church hoped whoever was elected would be able to negotiate peace terms. He told Chávez Mena this. The Jesuits had taken up this line, saying Chávez Mena would be better as a peacemaker.

Within the Christian Democratic Party there was a reaction to these efforts to present Fidel as the choice of powerful groups. It seemed as though outsiders were trying to dictate to the party. Party members believed that Chávez Mena should have been seeking support within the party, not outside. The fight was getting more personal, bitterer and nastier.

In the Constituent Assembly, the debate was whether presidential, legislative and municipal elections should be held all at once. The Right hoped the internal struggle among the Christian Democrats would debilitate us. I advocated settling the presidential candidacy among ourselves as soon as possible in order to concentrate on the real battle with the Right. Chávez Mena's group wanted more time to build up support, but the party officers voted to hold a national convention immediately.

The day before the convention, Chávez Mena asked to see me. He came to my house to see if we couldn't personally come to an agreement on what was best for the party. I remember telling him, "Fidel, leadership can't be carried off, you have to earn it. Anyone who lets leadership be snatched away from him is not a real leader. Therefore, as long as I'm the leader of the party, I'll defend my leadership. If someone wants to be a leader, he must win the position. There are different ways to win. One way is by working with me." Then I asked him to become my vice-presidential candidate.

"If you accept, you will be the heir to my political leadership," I told him. "But you have never run for political office. You've never gone out there to convince people to vote for you. You have to win their confidence before you'll be a leader."

We talked a long time. Fidel agreed with me, but said he did not want to appear to be the loser. He asked for time to convince those who supported him that my way was best. I agreed to postpone the convention because we had an understanding. I told the convention that we had agreed to allow more time to find a solution without dividing the party. I left the meeting thinking Fidel and I had worked it all out, but I soon began to hear reports that he was out campaigning for himself. He made no effort to contact me again. I called a meeting of the political committee and laid out the problem. We had a violent argument over whether he had broken his promises. He charged that I insulted him to the degree that made compromise impossible.

On April 18, 1983, the Christian Democratic convention convened again to decide the matter. He had nearly eighty supporters, I had just less than the 120 I needed for a two-thirds majority. He believed that the convention would deadlock, then turn toward him because of outside pressures. When the convention voted not to have a secret ballot, Chávez Mena's forces lost the first round. They thought some of my supporters might vote for him if the voting were secret. Fidel was still sure I could not get more than 117 votes, so when his turn came to cast a vote he chose to make a noble gesture. He voted for me. When my turn came I voted for myself, explaining that I could not vote against my conviction that my country needed me. I won 121 votes, one more than I needed, and received the party's nomination for president.

We held another convention to decide on a vice-presidential candidate. Everyone expected Fidel would accept, to bring the party together. He refused; he could not immediately get over the emotional barrier of defeat. Fidel did, however, work for the party's victory in the 1984 elections, because he understood that it was essential for the party and for El Salvador.

The Right wanted to polarize the country, uniting all their parties to defeat my presidential candidacy. The Constituent Assembly set up the electoral law to require a runoff between the two leading presidential candidates. They calculated, based on past elections, that the Christian Democrats would get no more than 40 percent of the vote, while the Left accounted for 5 to 8 percent. They were sure the Right, when united, could take 50 percent or more.

The Left refused to take part in the elections. Unless they were already wielding power in a transition government, the guerrillas said, they could not safely participate in an election. "Give us power first, then we'll talk about elections," has been the guerrilla position. To them any election they choose to boycott is a "farce," one subject to disruption by attacks on the voting places, the electricity or the highways.

The election came down to a duel between the Christian Democrats, whom the Right tried to equate with the Left, and the parties of the Right. I have never believed in socialist ideological solutions, but my plans to reform the imbalances in the economy, making the government work for the people, infuriated the Right. I sought a social pact between managers and workers to promote our economic recovery, but my opponents promised to solve all

The 1980 junta members, from left to right: Duarte, Dr. Ramón
Avalos, Colonel Adolfo Majano, Colonel Jaime Abdul Gutierrez,
Antonio Morales Erlich.

The 1981 junta—Dr. Avalos, the recently promoted General Gutierrez, Duarte and Antonio Morales Erlich.

Pope John Paul II and the Duartes on their private visit to Rome in 1983.

Duarte's 1984 presidential election campaign.

Another moment in Duarte's 1984 presidential election campaign.

The Inauguration, June 1, 1984.

José Napoleón Duarte at his inauguration as president, June 1, 1984.

Duarte with President-elect Ronald Reagan in the Oval Office, May, 1984.

At the chapel in La Palma after the first peace talks with the FMLN guerrillas, October 15, 1984. To the right of Duarte, Julio Adolfo Rey Prendes, in the back at the right, General Carlos Eugenio Vides Casanova, and to the right, Monsignor Rivera Damas.

Inés Guadalupe Duarte, on October 24, 1985, when she was freed by guerrillas in a prisoner exchange. She hugs her father and her oldest son.

Inés Guadalupe Duarte hugged by her father after being released by guerrilla kidnappers.

The Duartes and their children, from the left: Napoleón, Maria Elena, Maria Eugenia, Mrs. Duarte, José Napoleón, Ana Lorena, Inés Guadalupe and Alejandro.

the country's problems by defending the supposedly infallible free private-enterprise system. I offered a dialogue for peace, while my opponents promised to win the peace by waging a harsher war.

The Right were ready to fight me, but they did not agree on a presidential champion. Those supporting ARENA thought d'Aubuisson had the pop-star looks and nationalist appeal to be packaged as the people's choice. D'Aubuisson projected the image of a strong man, the strength of machismo, the strength of a military officer. I knew I had to match his strength with my own—strength of character, strength of popular support.

Almost by accident, I found a way to symbolize this strength. After a rally downtown, the Christian Democrats had planned a dance in Cuscatlán Park, about six blocks away. The party leaders were milling around, waiting to walk, when I said, "Let's run."

Knowing I was being called an old man, burned out at fifty-eight, I decided to show some physical stamina. I set off jogging toward the park, counting on the energy that I had always channeled into sports before politics absorbed me. But my political colleagues could not keep up, dropping back one after another. And the women in their high-heeled shoes, including my wife, gave up. I decided that in future, to keep the party together, I should limit myself to walking rapidly. With just a rapid pace, we could get across the idea that the Christian Democrats had more vigor than ARENA.

ARENA had no past, so the party promised everything for the future. It used flashy ads, catchy tunes and beat-the-Communists cheers to whip up enthusiasm. ARENA was trying to leave behind as outmoded the traditional rightist party, the PCN. But the PCN politicians recognized the vulnerability of d'Aubuisson, who was tied in most people's minds with the death squads.

Preferring someone less controversial to lead the Right, the

PCN carefully chose their most experienced politician to run against me—Chachi Guerrero.

The three smaller parties on the Right also had their own candidates. Everyone was fighting for second place in the first election by arguing they could beat Duarte in the second round. Within the Christian Democratic Party, we hoped d'Aubuisson would emerge as the candidate to meet in the runoff. I felt he would frighten even some conservative voters, giving us a chance to obtain that 50 percent of the vote we needed.

Some U.S. officials were said to favor Chachi in the first round. In a runoff between myself and Chachi, whoever won would be acceptable in American eyes. Apart from Senator Jesse Helms, d'Aubuisson could not count on much sympathy from the U.S. Congress. If d'Aubuisson won the presidency, then El Salvador's economic and military aid would have a difficult passage in Congress.

Regardless of their desire for U.S. aid, several military officers supported d'Aubuisson. They were convinced that under no condition would the Reagan Administration ever abandon a Salvadoran government battling with the guerrillas. The officers had an old habit of meddling in election politics, so I was not surprised at the actions of Colonel Jorge Adalberto Cruz, one of d'Aubuisson's strongest allies and commander of the Morazán garrison. The day we planned a rally in his region, Colonel Cruz decided to do a little army recruiting.

For the past fifty years, the draft in El Salvador worked like this: the Army grabbed young men off the streets on certain days, then determined if they were eligible to serve. When Colonel Cruz began seizing the Christian Democratic youth coming to our rally, a panic started. Every man of draft age stayed home. At the end of this discouraging campaign tour, our party leaders gathered to wait for a flight home from San Miguel's airport, a dusty strip of pastureland with a hangar and some wooden benches. Cruz's men suddenly appeared all around us, their guns ready.

"Look out," I heard someone yell. "They're going to kill Mazier."

Mauricio Mazier Andino, one of our representatives in the National Assembly, stood not far from me. Soldiers had seized him, and the colonel took out his pistol, raising the butt to hit Mazier in the face. Mazier ducked away as I moved in quickly to stand between them.

"What's going on here?" I demanded.

"This man was armed," Cruz said.

"Well, he's a member of the assembly, it's his legal right," I replied.

Cruz pointed to another man. "He's armed and he doesn't have that right."

"Yes, he does. He's my bodyguard," I replied. But Cruz found a pretext for disarming the man.

Cruz still had us at gunpoint, saying he was only doing his duty, when I saw Colonel Domingo Monterrosa arrive at the airfield.

"Colonel Monterrosa, could you come here?" I asked. Monterrosa was the soldier's soldier—not spit and polish, but a man who went into battle at the front of his troops. He had led the first rapid-reaction battalion, the Atlacatl, to strike back at the guerrillas. Now he commanded the entire eastern region, and Cruz was his subordinate. I knew that Monterrosa fought for his country, not for any political party.

Not everyone in the Army was allied to d'Aubuisson. I had faith there were officers like Monterrosa, who would realize that democracy was best for their country. When I told Monterrosa what was happening, he said, "Leave Cruz to me. I'll speak to him." He and Cruz then left together in a military plane.

Cruz's men still sulked around us. Our plane bumped in, propellers grinding away as we boarded. Then, as we picked up speed, shots rang out. The soldiers were firing into the air, shouting, "Viva ARENA!"

From my experience in the campaign, the guerrillas seemed less hostile. When I headed for a region where we might encounter the guerrillas, I would leave my bodyguards behind. Anyone who accompanied me had to go unarmed. I did not want those who belonged to the security forces coming along, because the guerrillas might consider them the enemy and kill them. My best protection came from the journalists with me, not bodyguards, because the guerrillas would not harm me while the eyes of the world were watching. They cared about their image and knew the advantages they gained from favorable press coverage.

Usulatán province was one area where I knew we might run into the guerrillas as our campaign moved from village to village. One village, grandly going by the name of California, appeared to have been abandoned by all the powers that be. There was no National Guard detachment, no mayor, and yet no guerrillas either. The residents had gathered in front of the church as I began my campaign speech from the steps, when I saw a guerrilla column marching up the street. I kept on talking, the people continued to listen, and the guerrillas walked right through the town, passing two yards in front of me. To my amusement, one of the guerrillas, without breaking pace, pulled out a pocket flash camera and snapped my picture.

The guerrillas were hardly friendly on election day. They threatened to mine the roads, burned voters' ID cards and attacked several towns. But more dangerous politically were my military opponents. Colonel Denís Morán, the army commander of Zacatecoluca, called some two thousand officers and militia leaders under him, ordering them to work for the victory of ARENA. In some conflict zones where the Army carried out the town's ballot boxes, such as Arcatao, we did not get one single vote!

Despite these problems, the 1984 elections suffered less from fraud than any previous election. During the 1982 elections, the Christian Democrats lacked party observers at most polling places. By 1984 our party was less intimidated, and more poll watchers appeared. The system also worked better because the various parties of the Right were competing with one another; they all wanted a fair count. Five different parties were represented on the Central Election Council, keeping any one faction from overruling the other.

The Right could not believe that the Christian Democrats had really won even 42 percent of the vote in 1982 without cheating. So this time they insisted on a ponderous system of voter registration, using American-financed computer technology. The result was utter confusion. Many people did not know where their names appeared on a list. Many stood in the wrong line for hours. Sometimes lists or ballots failed to arrive. The Right did not care whether voters got discouraged or gave up, because a lower turnout was supposed to favor them, especially in San Salvador.

I spent election day, March 25, 1984, at our party headquarters. I fielded the complaints about interference, intimidation and legal violations called in from one polling place or another. We were in permanent contact with the Army headquarters, because the military high command had taken on the responsibility for enforcing the election rules that local commanders were flouting. General Vides Casanova stated publicly, "The armed forces reiterate their pledge that nobody, absolutely nobody, will sway the free choice of the ballot box."

Imperfect, but not impaired, the election results came in from around the country. My son Napoleón ran the party computer, analyzing the reports we received from our party observers at each ballot count. Both my sons and my daughters, their husbands and wives, worked for my candidacy in the party. By 11 P.M. we had our first projection, but only by 1 A.M. could we be fairly sure of the results. We knew that the Christian Democrats had won 45 percent, not quite a majority. D'Aubuisson was second with 29 percent, Chachi third with 16 percent. When the official results were counted, they gave us a bit less than our count: 43.4 percent of the vote.

In the next round, between myself and d'Aubuisson on May 6, we had to receive more than 50 percent if I were to become president. The Right could stop me if the votes for Chachi and the other rightist parties went to d'Aubuisson. The critical difference would be made by the undecided voters who had not cast their ballots for me or d'Aubuisson the first time.

Our strategy was to talk with the local leaders of the smaller parties and seek out those voters who abstained during the first round. Instead of rallies and mass-media saturation, the second round of campaigning was quiet, personal, door-to-door canvassing.

Chachi told us his party would not make a deal with d'Aubuisson. He told PCN members to vote according to their individual consciences, but the local leaders went for d'Aubuisson. D'Aubuisson charged into his campaign, raging for a total confrontation with me. There is no denying he built up an anti-Duarte, anti–Christian Democrat hatred. They wanted an emotional campaign, but we refused to match their hysteria. Our campaign was reasoned and calm, to avoid inciting violent clashes between ARENA and the Christian Democrats.

D'Aubuisson played on nationalism, saying the Christian Democrats were internationally controlled. The press called me the American candidate, while the Far Right in the United States, led by Senator Jesse Helms, told d'Aubuisson the Christian Democrats were getting money from the CIA. We did not receive CIA funds. I know because we worked very hard and went into debt for our money. The party had saved some money that went to the Institutes for Christian Democratic Studies, supported by foundations and donations. For years we donated the proceeds from our lectures. For our campaign, we took out bank loans that are still being paid off with contributions from individuals. The government also provided funds to parties based on their percentage of the vote. I do not think money or external influence made any difference in this election.

On the second election day, in May, I stayed at home with my vice-presidential running mate, Rodolfo "Chele" Castillo. Chele and I spent the day watching old movies on television, drinking coffee, pacing back and forth, while the party structure managed the process. Because I was afraid of what such fervid d'Aubuisson allies as Colonels Cruz and Morán could do, I asked the military high command and the international observer missions to go to their areas, Morazán and Zacatecoluca, on election day. As one U.S. senator after another came into Morazán, with journalists and high-ranking officers too, Cruz realized what was happening and took off into the mountains with his men. Morán was neutralized, too. Except for a few small towns where it is easy for the Right to intimidate people, the observers and the press did help to keep the elections honest.

Election morning, the guerrillas launched a major attack on San Miguel. They even fired on the observers' helicopter, but within hours the guerrillas had fled and the people were back in lines at the polling places. The guerrilla threats never discouraged most Salvadorans from voting.

Compared to the first presidential round, the number voting increased because the elections were better organized. People had learned the first time exactly where they were assigned to vote.

They did not have to search from table to table for their names. This time the choice was simple—only two candidates—and those running the polling places had become more efficient.

All that night I kept phoning the party election center, where my son Alejandro was handling the computer projection. He would not tell me the results. He kept saying it was too early, which convinced me he was keeping the bad news from me. I went down to the party headquarters personally, but even then Alejandro said, "Please wait until I finish this projection." The Spanish International Network (SIN) television pollsters projected us as the winner, sending the party workers into euphoria, but I trusted results only. The copies of the ballot-box counts from La Unión province had not come in at all. That worried me, because La Unión was the place where the government changed the vote count in 1972, denying us the presidential victory we won then. This time our delegates took no chances. They personally picked up every voting tally in La Unión, taking all night to do it, and that is why the results were late.

By midnight, Alejandro came to me with his first projection. "You've won the election," he said simply. "Fifty-four percent of the vote." He had wanted to be absolutely sure before he told me, because he knew what it would mean to me. I had been elected president by the people of El Salvador despite, or because of, all that had happened in the past—the stolen elections, seven years in exile, my role as a junta member and figurehead president in the bloodiest times.

When Alejandro told me I had won, I could not feel it emotionally. That moment came when I was sworn in. On election night, I thought only intellectually about what the results meant.

I had not taken any votes from the Right. Town by town, ARENA's votes were the sum of those cast for other rightist presidential candidates the first time. The votes that made the difference came from those who had not voted in the previous round. I won because we had a better turnout.

Our largest share of the vote came in the cities, not the countryside. D'Aubuisson used these statistics to say he won ten out of fourteen provinces. Just after the election, he launched another campaign publicizing his complaints, trying to erase the fact that he had lost. D'Aubuisson is not the type of man to tolerate being beaten fairly. With false figures and wild denunciations, he claimed he really won the election. Only hours before the Central Election Council was to formally present to me the official certificate saying I had won the presidency, D'Aubuisson demanded that the election be annulled. We also uncovered a plot to kill me that day.

Military intelligence sources heard that the assassination plot was to be carried out on May 16, the day I was to receive the certificate designating me as president in a small ceremony at the National Theater. The American Embassy also learned of the plot, which included the assassination of U.S. Ambassador Thomas Pickering as well. The information from the embassy coincided with ours on several points. First, the assassins planned to use a high-powered rifle with a telescopic sight, shooting when I entered or left the theater. Therefore I entered from a side door, while army sharpshooters were posted on the roofs of all surrounding buildings. The assassins expected another opportunity if I went into the streets to greet my followers after becoming president. We had to cancel any victory celebrations where I would join with people in the streets.

President Reagan took the plot seriously enough to send General Vernon Walters, now his envoy to the United Nations, to San Salvador to have a talk with d'Aubuisson. Walters paid a call on me, but the threat was mentioned only in passing. There is a diplomatic understanding on these intelligence matters to reveal only the minimum information required. Whatever the United States said to d'Aubuisson was private.

D'Aubuisson's behavior after he lost the election seemed to me that of an anxious character. His first gesture had been surprisingly friendly. He sought an informal meeting with me. D'Aubuisson said it was time to erase the past and start over with a clean slate. He seemed extremely nervous as he spoke, and asked for a drink. Rey Prendes did not want to serve him one, saying we should talk seriously first. Rey Prendes could not bear to see d'Aubuisson fidgeting, however, so he served him the whiskey.

D'Aubuisson offered to help me in my presidency. He still controlled a large bloc of votes in the National Assembly and the Christian Democrats lacked a majority. There was only one condition that he brought up. He wanted me to stop creating problems for him by always bringing up the issue of the death squads and the murder of Archbishop Romero.

"As president, I want to work with other political groups in harmony, but I cannot forget my promises to the people nor ignore facts," I told him. "There will be no unfounded accusations, but any information that can be found will have to be investigated. If false accusations have bothered you, then bringing to light all the truth will be a relief." I told him that I did not hold any grudge against him. He, as a Salvadoran citizen, had a place in the democratic system. But I explained that I was not the kind of politician who made deals for convenience. My ideology dictated what I must do as president.

He did not seem to like what I was saying. He was anxious to leave. After this meeting, he sought to annul the elections. Then the plot against my life was uncovered.

The day I went to receive the official notification of my election as president was more tense than joyful. When I left the theater with Vice-President Chele Castillo, I suggested we go to the Metropolitan Cathedral, where Archbishop Romero is buried. The Cathedral, on the main square, Plaza Barrios, stands unfinished, a hulk of reinforced concrete. It remains a symbol of the Church's commitment to help the poor before spending more on the house of the Lord. The nave to the right of the altar holds the plain marble tomb of Archbishop Romero, his portrait on the wall above, plaques and tributes to him all around. Castillo and I walked into the cavernous shade of the Cathedral. He was trembling as I took his hand and we knelt to pray silently before the tomb.

"Monsignor Romero," I prayed, "I am conscious that all the suffering, all the thousands killed, and your own death, were part of the process that led to my becoming president of the Republic. I've become president to see if we can find peace by way of democracy. I'm going to investigate your murder, but not for the sake of revenge. I know you don't want that. But those responsible must be brought to justice for the sake of your people, for their health. Your death wounded them, and to recover the value of life in our society, justice must be done. God help me."

Before I could even begin my presidency, I had the task of choosing a Cabinet. Every president faces a difficult period when he names his Cabinet, because, if my experience is any example, you are attacked from all sides by your friends! Rumors start appearing in the newspapers every day that you have selected So-and-so. Five other people besiege you, pointing out all that person's faults.

What astonished me most was that women can be their own worst enemies. I wanted to appoint women to as many high-level positions as I could, recognizing their professional capability and their important role in the party. But every time a woman's name was mentioned for a post, other women would feel it their duty to give me information that amounted to little more than gossip about the lady in question.

The women concentrated on the morals of their sisters to the exclusion of all else. Out of nine women I considered for high-level appointments, I was able to get agreement on only five. None made the Cabinet, because no woman had sufficient experience. This will change as women hold senior posts in government and advance. I was pleased that nine out of our fourteen Christian Democratic candidates for governors of the provinces were women.

The first Cabinet member I selected was the Defense Minister, General Vides Casanova. Rey Prendes, Alejandro and I had prepared a twenty-seven-point program on how the armed forces should function. I had consulted four officers on my plans. If Vides accepted my offer to be defense minister on the basis of the twenty-seven-point plan, then he was the logical choice. He had led the armed forces to conduct fair elections, he had the support of the officers corps. His presence in the government would inspire confidence within the armed forces.

When I asked him to be my defense minister, Vides responded, "I want to tell you that I've never felt a duty to you, only to the armed forces. But you've offered me the Defense Ministry and I will accept it to carry out faithfully the twenty-seven-point plan." He has repeated this to the officers when there have been accusations that I try to manipulate the armed forces. Vides stressed his loyalty to the democratic program, not to me.

The most important part of this program was controlling the death squads and stopping the abuses of officers. Some of them had to be removed, disciplined or investigated internally. I was determined to pursue by every legal means those responsible for crimes such as the Viera-Hammer-Pearlman murders. We agreed that when there was solid evidence of involvement, we would take action no matter who was accused. Finally we talked about the military structure, and although it was not popular, I decided to separate army and police functions into two subsecretaries of the Defense Ministry. My choice of Colonel López Nuila to head the police forces had to overcome resistance because it placed him on an equal status with higher-ranking officers. López Nuila became the undersecretary for public security, managing the National Police, the National Guard and the Treasury Police. Since their intelligence services had been identified with the death squads, one of the first things I did was to abolish the intelligence section of the Treasury Police.

In selecting the rest of my Cabinet, I asked the party's political committee to help me. We each drew up a Cabinet list, with two names for each post, then compared our choices and gave reasons for them. I took the lists and made my own decision, sometimes reaching beyond the persons suggested there. I talked with other parties, hoping to bring them into my administration, but the PCN made so many demands for influential posts that nothing could be worked out with them. Afterward they made a pact with ARENA to divide between their parties the positions on the Supreme Court, which is appointed by the National Assembly. This hurt us.

It is almost unbelievable how much was at stake in the selection of the Cabinet. We were trying for a social pact to bring as many different groups into the government as possible. The private-enterprise sector was brought into the economic ministries. In order not to weaken the Christian Democratic presence in the National Assembly, I planned not to draw on any legislators, but a delegation of the party wore me out with their arguments.

My decision to offer Fidel Chávez Mena the Planning Ministry caused an uproar in the party. My supporters did not think he or his allies should be included in the government. But I wanted a government of reconciliation, tolerance and peace for the nation. The best place to start was within my own party. He was reluctant at first, then accepted.

The conflicts and pettiness involved in choosing my Cabinet caused me much personal stress. My oil painting, which I use to relax, reflected the tension. A painting of sunset among the trees turned into an image of a raging forest fire during that period. My blood pressure soared to 180/120. My daughter Inés Guadalupe called the doctor, but she misunderstood the dosage of the pills he prescribed. Instead of giving me one every two days, she began giving me two a day. My blood pressure dropped so far I nearly fainted away. Those days, when I should have been looking forward to becoming president, I remember as one more difficult period.

Once I had chosen the officials of my Administration, there had to be a clear understanding of what I expected from them. I spoke to each one individually, and all of them together. I laid out my plan for our government and the five goals: humanization, pacification, democratization, participation and economic reactivation.

The way we worked toward these goals is the story of what has happened since I became president. When I first met with the Cabinet, my intent was to define a style of government. First, no corruption would be permitted. Not only would anyone found guilty be removed from office, but there would be legal prosecution for any such acts. Going even further, I said that certain practices, while not illegal, were not honorable. I expected those appointed to the government to be concerned with their reputation for honesty and fairness. Second, there would be equal treatment for all citizens. The humblest man in a straw hat was to be treated the same as the man in a suit and tie.

Once when I was campaigning for president in a shantytown,

speaking to a crowd of several hundred, one shabby man raised his hand and asked to speak.

"Look, you're probably going to become president," the man said, "and as soon as someone's elected he forgets all about the poor. When you need to see the person in the government, you can't. They send you from ministry to ministry and require impossible things from you. I'd ask you, Engineer Duarte, to remember the poor."

"I promise you," I replied, "that I will name a representative for the poor, with an office in the Presidential Palace, whose only job will be to receive you and make the bureaucracy respond where it should." This office is working now.

I told my Cabinet that we would face the greatest economic problems without the budget we needed. I warned that great pressures would be placed on us and that the Left would try to destabilize our government.

Finally, I spoke about bringing peace to the country. I told the Cabinet there would be a dialogue with everyone, even the guerrillas. When I became president, "dialogue" was considered a bad word by many powerful people. But we would play that card.

9

Peace Talks

"B LESSED are the peacemakers: for they shall be called the children of God."

Pope John Paul II preached the words of Christ in San Salvador on March 6, 1983. He instructed us, "All of you, each one, businessmen and workers, teachers and students, all have the duty to be peacemakers."

His words stayed with me, for he defined what a true dialogue should be. I felt that a responsibility had been placed on me. At that time, I was out of office. The Magaña government did not include me in any of the functions planned during the Pope's visit, an omission the Holy Father noticed. He wrote me a kind letter.

During my 1984 campaign for president, I promised I would find a way to talk with those who had taken up arms to fight for a revolution against the injustices in our country. I made the distinction between a sincere dialogue and a tactical dialogue. The latter is used only to achieve temporary advantages in order to triumph in the long run. This definition of the kinds of dialogue was the Pope's, not mine. "The dialogue that the Church asks is not a tactical truce, used to fortify positions in order to proceed with the struggle," he said, "but a sincere effort to find an agreement that responds to the anguish, the pain and the exhaustion of so many who desire peace."

My plan was to open the dialogue once I had been in office for about a year. My first year as president would be spent building the right conditions for peace talks. Before we talked to the guerrillas, the human-rights abuses had to be brought under control. The economic situation had to improve. Our political power must be consolidated, and a better international image created. Public opinion had to form behind such a dialogue.

Creating the right conditions for talks with the guerrillas depended on how effective I was as a president. The support of the armed forces was essential. I also hoped that the legislative elections, coming ten months after I took office, would come within the "honeymoon" period of the government and give my party a legislative majority. During that first year, each month I took stock of how close I was to reaching these goals, grading myself with percentages. After the first month, for instance, based on my observations during a trip abroad, I rated our international standing at 80 percent of what I hoped to achieve.

When I returned from my South American trip in September 1984, a little after my first quarter in office, I shut myself away with my pencil and paper, going over my goals. That evaluation convinced me that the minimal conditions for the dialogue with the guerrillas were going to be in place sooner than I had expected—probably in February 1985. I was receiving excellent cooperation from the armed forces. The government's relations with the private sector had started off well. The death-squad crimes had decreased significantly. On human rights, I have always found a good barometer in the International Committee of the Red Cross, who are always present on the front lines, in the jails and the barracks. The ICRC reports to me directly each month, and I trust them completely.

I considered the timetable. If I had waited until February, the month before legislative elections, to begin talks with the guerrillas, any offer I made would be treated as nothing more than a campaign ploy. Either I took the initiative immediately or I would have to postpone it until spring. I decided to make the invitation to the guerrillas as soon as possible. The place I chose was the United Nations General Assembly, and the time October.

I made that decision alone, and it surprised many people. Only a week before my U.N. appearance, I took Rey Prendes and Alejandro into my confidence to help me write the speech. My private secretary, Carmen, who has served me loyally since my days as mayor, was entrusted with typing it.

When Ambassador Pickering stopped by my home three days before I left, I mentioned that I was thinking about the dialogue, but the hint did not catch his attention. The same thing happened with Generals Vides Casanova and Blandón, who told me later, "From the way you said it, I didn't think you were serious." The only person to whom I revealed everything was Vice President Castillo. He had to be ready here in El Salvador for whatever happened as a result of my peace initiative. We could not discount that those opposed to a dialogue with the guerrillas might attempt a coup, especially since I would be away in New York.

Standing at the podium of the world in the great hall of the United Nations, I aimed my words toward the remote mountains of my country, to those Salvadorans killing and dying, not those dispatching messages from the comfort of Managua or Havana.

"I refer to the *comandantes* in the mountains of my country, weathering the elements, able to see the real position of the Salvadoran people when they attack villages," I said. "To those waiting in vain to be received as liberators each time they subjugate the people, to the *comandantes* whose ideals conflict with this reality, who made a mistake about the people and now confront the truth; to the *comandantes* who feel the historic error they are committing."

I acknowledged that these revolutionaries may have had good reason for taking up arms when there was no hope of economic reform, social justice or free elections under the tyranny of the oligarchy allied with the armed forces. El Salvador, however, had changed over the last five years. "I am here to declare and proclaim that as president of the republic and commander general of the armed forces, I can uphold, under a constitutional government, the means to permit you to abandon a stand that runs counter to the history of the political evolution of the Salvadoran people."

With this premise, I asked the guerrilla leaders from the mountains to meet me, unarmed, in the village of La Palma, Chalatenango province, at 10 A.M. on October 15. It was the anniversary of the 1979 coup that turned El Salvador toward a new path. For that day, we would establish a demilitarized zone in a ten-kilometer radius around the mountain village.

I chose La Palma for two reasons. First, I was thinking of the Pope's call for peacemakers, artisans of peace. La Palma, whose artisans paint brightly colored, naïve designs on wood and leather, was symbolic. I also remembered how this artwork adorned Archbishop Hickey's chapel in Washington in juxtaposition with the faces of our martyred Archbishop Romero and the American women. La Palma reminded me of the joy and sorrow my countrymen shared. The other reason for going to La Palma was the reputation of the FPL guerrilla group that operates in Chalatenango. Of the five FMLN groups, this one treated civilians most humanely. I had the feeling I would find there guerrilla leaders with more human understanding, rather than the pathologically violent ones. I was not interested in the globe-traveling FDR-FMLN leaders who were only seeking power.

The motivation for these talks had to be humanitarian. Our purposes should not be selfish. My government was not out to gain anything, nor would we give anything up. There was little hope for agreement on what each side visualized as the political future of El Salvador. Instead, I thought we should ask ourselves: What do the people want? Do the people want to be able to travel the roads without fear of a mine exploding or their bus being burned? Do they want to live without fear of being bombed or strafed? That is what should be worked on, even if I did not have any concrete idea how we were going to achieve these objectives. The important thing was to try talking.

Democracy is a way of life, not just a way of gaining power. Democracy is the peaceful resolution of conflict. It accepts that human beings do not think alike, but we ought to be able to show charity and respect to one another. Leaders need to be democrats and Christians at heart. They can be Jews or Muslims—the religion is not as important as the ethical point of view guiding us. The democratic instrument of peace is participation, working together to resolve problems, not seeking a victory. If one goes into talks only to count up gains and losses—so much for you, so much for me—the purpose of the sincere dialogue is lost.

Once my invitation for peace talks was made, my control over the event was gone. The guerrillas decided to send in the political leaders. They wanted to enlarge the delegations, to change the date. I said no to changing the day. To begin by making concessions would have weakened the initiative and lost the momentum gained in the week following my U.N. speech. The

Salvadoran government would send five representatives into the talks. The FMLN would send two former colleagues of mine, Ungo and Zamora from abroad, plus two *comandantes* and two "observers" from different guerrilla groups. The only others present would be the Archbishop and Church dignitaries, who would preside.

The guerrillas spread their diplomatic wings and had the presidents of Mexico, Venezuela and Colombia call me to ask if their ambassadors could accompany the guerrilla leaders to the talks. I told them the best protection for the guerrilla leaders would come from the Red Cross. They later recognized that this was true—all the ambassadors waving their flags would not have matched the respected efficiency of the Red Cross. Crowd control was assigned to the Boy Scouts, and we ultimately had to rely for safety on the moral authority of the Church and the vigilance of the international press that bore witness to our peaceful endeavor.

The presentation we would make to the guerrillas was hammered out in a meeting of the political committee joined by Generals Vides and Blandón, Colonels Flores Lima and López Nuila. To accompany me into the talks, I chose the first and second alternate vice-presidents: Abraham Rodríguez, one of the founders of the Christian Democrats, and René Fortín Magaña, head of the Democratic Action Party, the one center-right party allied with us. I asked the Minister of the Presidency, Rey Prendes, and the Defense Minister, Vides, to come as well.

It was a hard decision for the general to make. I know what it cost him to agree, but Vides decided to go because he said it was the duty of the Defense Minister when the President requested him to go. I was also approached by Chachi Guerrero, who had run against me for president on the PCN ticket, and who had been appointed chief justice of the Supreme Court by the rightist majority of the assembly.

"I think I should go with you to La Palma," Chachi said. "You're running the risk that the Right will accuse you of acting unconstitutionally in consorting with criminals. After you meet the guerrillas, they may call for your impeachment. I'm offering to accompany you to show that I would resign as head of the Supreme Court if they try this." Chachi rode with me in the car to La Palma.

The greatest problem was the military situation. Our intelligence showed that large groups of guerrilla forces were moving into the area around La Palma that was supposed to be demilitarized. We realized later that Comandante Fermán Cienfuegos, on his way to the talks, marched nearly one hundred miles up from the San Pedro Mountains to La Palma, mobilizing about three thousand combatants who moved with him.

Because the guerrillas occupied La Palma itself, I sent Colonel Ochoa, who was now commander of the Fourth Brigade of Chalatenango, to take the town. As usually happens, the guerrillas filtered into the hills before the troops arrived. Then my Minister of Agriculture, Carlos Duarte (no relation), who was known to the townspeople because his family has a home there, made a speech. He explained to the La Palma residents that no military forces would come within ten kilometers of the town until after the talks. Colonel Ochoa then withdrew his men. The guerrillas, however, never respected the demilitarized zone, stashing arms in the La Palma school and camping in the nearby hills at Miramundo.

Moving down from La Palma, some of Ochoa's troops clashed with a guerrilla patrol, capturing papers that showed a guerrilla plan to surround and take La Palma. There was also an order to kill the Christian Democratic mayor of a nearby village, Dulce Nombre de María. The guerrillas had decided this was an opportune moment to get rid of the mayor and blame his death on the rightist security forces. I immediately called the mayor to San Salvador, warning him and suggesting he stay away from the village for a while. The mayor said the plan to kill him did not surprise him. He told me that many guerrillas had been moving through his town in the last few days.

The Army's first reaction to these intelligence reports was that I should cancel my plan and not go to La Palma. They regarded it as sheer folly to have me and most of the Cabinet practically hand ourselves over as hostages to the guerrillas. On the other hand, the guerrillas must have felt they were taking the greatest risk by placing their leaders in one place where the security forces could trap them. Whether the guerrillas' fears motivated their extensive military operation or not, the whole peace plan was being endangered.

There was no way I would reconsider my decision to go, but I asked the high command to draw up the military plan for a rapid response if we were attacked in La Palma. They were to concentrate as many troops as necessary outside the demilitarized zone, encircling the guerrillas' circle of La Palma. Helicopters would be standing by at El Paraiso army base in the foothills. Vice-President Castillo would be at the Presidential Palace while I was in the mountains, with my instructions to try to rescue us with helicopters, then order the Army to counterattack.

On the eve of the talks, Joaquín Villalobos, the senior military commander of the guerrillas, sent word that he would not be able to get to La Palma in time. He wanted us to provide a military helicopter for him. Villalobos heads the ERP, operating in the eastern provinces as a ruthless military machine, reflecting the character of its leader. Villalobos is reputed to be the executioner of the noted Marxist poet Roque Dalton, killed during a power struggle among the guerrillas in 1975.

When Villalobos audaciously asked for an army helicopter, I

was not willing to take the risk of being blamed for his death if anything went wrong with the helicopter. I thought the only solution would be to get a private helicopter or one from another country, but time ran out before these arrangements could be made. The day before the talks, Ungo and Zamora arrived with their flock of ambassadors in the airplane provided by Colombia. They entered the Red Cross vehicles, speeding directly to La Palma rather than spending the night in San Salvador as expected. Ungo's family had a summer home in La Palma, from which they slipped off to the guerrilla encampment in Miramundo to confer with the *comandantes*.

At 5 A.M. on October 15, my party prepared to leave in a caravan of a hundred cars from the presidential residence. The Cabinet, the Christian Democratic leaders, everyone seemed to be going with me, all of us unarmed. Soldiers lined the highway to prevent any attack by the Right that could abort the peace talks, but the Army's protection ended at the last bridge, just before the two-lane road turns up toward the mountains surrounding La Palma. It touched me when General Blandón and Colonel Ochoa bid us farewell from the last army post, saying, "God bless you, we hope you're able to bring peace."

People lined the road, waving white flags, crying, "Peace!" Just outside La Palma, we stopped at Carlos Duarte's mountain villa to have breakfast and pass the remaining two hours before we were to walk down to the chapel in the town square where the meeting with the guerrillas would take place.

My nerves were in a bad state. I could not sit still, so I walked around the pine forests with Carlos. The local priest and mayor came to tell us everything was ready. We left the cars at the edge of town, but before starting to walk down the winding street my friends and co-workers gathered around me.

"Well, gentlemen, from this point on, as you know, we'll be

surrounded by guerrillas," I told them. "We may die, but we'll be dying for peace. It's worth the attempt for the sake of our country. Let's go."

The Christian Democrats, who formed a human chain around me, had all been given a colored scarf to wear, with orders that anyone not wearing the scarf should not be allowed into the circle around me. Chachi and Abraham walked on either side of me, General Vides just behind. I looked at the Christian Democrats there, some of whom I had known all my life. Some were ordinary people, like the hefty lady who lost her shoe but kept striding along beside me anyway. They sweated from tension and exertion, but they looked so proud it sent chills through me.

When I reached the steps of the chapel, the Boy Scout in charge gave me the Scout salute and I returned his handshake. The Archbishop and three other monsignors waited in the arched doorway and led us into the modest concrete chapel.

The pews had been pushed back. A long table was set in the middle of the chapel with six chairs facing one another. There was another table at the end for the clergymen who would preside. We took the seats facing the altar. No protocol greeting had been planned, but when the FMLN leaders filed in they came to shake hands with every one of us.

Once seated, Archbishop Rivera Damas prayed, then said, "Since it was Engineer Duarte who called us together, let's have him speak first."

I started by saying that, as president of the Republic, I had sworn to uphold the constitution. With the same faithfulness with which I had taken that oath, I would look for a solution to our problems within the constitution. I gave a copy of the document to everyone across the table. Then I read the plan for peace we had drafted. It suggested the creation of a special commission: six members selected by the President, six by the guerrillas, led by a moderator designated by the Church. This commission would discuss the ways to end the violence, to bring full political participation and democratic rights to everyone in El Salvador, permitting the guerrillas to return to peaceful lives. The most important thing was for us not to leave this chapel without providing people with a reason to hope. That, I concluded, was needed more than anything else.

Ungo spoke next, saying it was necessary to find the way to peace. He took issue with several points in my United Nations speech—the history as I outlined it and the implication that there was a discrepancy between the reality perceived by guerrillas in the country and the ideals of those working abroad. He said the conditions in the country had not changed since 1979. The FDR-FMLN was indivisible and had constantly sought peace through negotiations.

Zamora seconded Ungo's analysis, talking about the whole political and social structure that had to be changed. He said we at the table represented the military power of both the guerrillas and the armed forces, the political power both of the Left and of the Christian Democrats which formed a majority of the country. Therefore it was up to us to change the society. He was all for eliminating the rightist sectors, but I told him that his theory was totalitarian, because I believe that the Right should also be incorporated into the democratic process. Besides, societies cannot be transformed overnight by an agreement. Wouldn't it be more practical to perfect the country through a democratic process and not through destruction?

Cienfuegos spoke longer than anyone else, nearly two hours. He talked about the guerrillas' military achievements. "We never studied it at school, but we've learned how to wage war," he said. He began painting a picture of the country in the harshest terms, highlighting the areas where the guerrillas saw no improvement.

But toward the end he admitted there had been changes. The most obvious change was the fact that we were sitting here talking, he said. At one point, realizing he had talked for quite a while, the *comandante* wondered aloud if he should stop.

"Please continue," Abraham Rodríguez spoke up. "I know fairly well what everyone else at this table thinks"—he looked at his former colleagues Ungo and Zamora as he said it—"but I'm deeply interested in what you have to say."

Cienfuegos continued, and then Facundo Guardado, the other guerrilla commander, spoke briefly about the need for peace.

When General Vides' turn came, he declined to speak, saying he could not agree with the guerrillas' military analysis, but we had come to talk about peace, not contradict one another. He added that he supported the peace plan I had presented.

One thing that must have bothered Vides, even more than the rest of us, was Guardado's wearing the uniform of a dead army lieutenant. The name badge had been torn off the dirty uniform, but at the peace table the guerrillas should not have flaunted the fact that they killed one of our men.

This was the only discordant note at La Palma. Otherwise we shared a sense of commitment to peace and to our country, the feeling of being one family. Cienfuegos made a point of chatting with Vides, catching the general as he came out of the bathroom. Cienfuegos also spoke privately to me, asking about his parents, who have been my friends for years. Eduardo Sancho Castaneda (Cienfuegos' real name) is the son of a Costa Rican chemist who settled in El Salvador. I had known the *comandante* as a little boy. During the day of the peace talks many families held brief reunions in La Palma, where relatives came looking for brothers, sons or daughters they knew were fighting with the guerrillas.

When the time for lunch came, Monsignor Gregorio Rosa Chávez asked us if we wanted to take a break, but we decided to continue talking. Zamora then asked, "Monsignor, why don't you just spread the food buffet style on a table and we'll help ourselves?" He obviously expected a more luxurious meal than what was planned. The priest smiled as he said, "There's only fried chicken in cartons." I quickly gave up on the rubber chicken and the soggy french fries, and noticed that other people put theirs aside after a few bites, with the exception of the four guerrilla fighters. They ate all the chicken and fries, including the leftovers, and put the little sweet cakes offered for dessert into their knapsacks for later.

Our time for talking was limited. There were air-travel plans and logistics problems, so we set a deadline. A joint document had to be prepared, and Ungo repeated my phrase about not leaving without producing something to answer the people's need for hope. Rey Prendes and Zamora had the task of writing the agreement statement.

We decided to form a commission, with only four representatives from each side, that would study the proposals for peace, find ways to humanize the conflict, develop procedures to incorporate all groups into the peace process, and do whatever necessary to bring peace as soon as possible. The FDR-FMLN wanted to set a date for the commission to meet, but I advised we work the date out through contacts with the Church. There were too many factors to resolve now. Our joint communiqué said the meeting would be held in the second half of November. We left unwritten two agreements about the exchange of prisoners and the Torola bridge. Both Ungo and I had received petitions from villagers in Morazán, asking us to agree to let the bridge over the Torola River be reconstructed. The bridge, linking the villages north of the river with the rest of the country, had been blown up twice by guerrillas. We rebuilt the bridge in November, but Villalobos' men destroyed it again despite the La Palma agreement.

I had watched the interaction among the guerrilla delegation with interest to see how it reflected their division of power. During the talks, Ungo took charge, but Cienfuegos spoke with more authority. At the end, I watched Ungo turn to Guardado, half apologizing for the lack of progress. Ungo pointed to the bright side by saying, "At least there'll be a second meeting in San Salvador."

Cienfuegos spoke about organizing the people to demand peace, which seemed to be the guerrillas' main interest—using the cause of peace for their own political organizing. This could work against them in the end. The overwhelming desire to end the years of war could turn people against the guerrillas—if they see the hope of peace sacrificed in the name of Marxist dogma. In La Palma, though, everyone felt we were part of a historic moment. Peace seemed not only possible, but imperative. The meeting had gone well, thank God.

We each made a brief statement outside the chapel. The guerrillas then returned through the church to leave by the back door. I said my few words, then followed them, picking up the rest of my colleagues as we headed for the cars. By my car radio, I followed the progress of Ungo and Zamora's vehicle, asking the security forces to keep me informed of their position. Their safety was my responsibility. I could not rest until they were safely out of the country. It would have been so easy for a rightist assassin or any lunatic to have woven through the throng of people in La Palma or along the road and totally ended the chance of peace with one shot, at them or me.

Driving down from the mountains, Chachi pulled out a whiskey bottle. I felt this was one day I was going to have a drink. Ever since an encounter with tequila and mescal in Tijuana over thirty years ago, when I became so sick my wife had to call a doctor, my stomach takes punitive action if I have a drink. Nevertheless, I welcomed the glass Chachi offered me. I was tremendously tense. We lost track of Ungo and Zamora for a few hours while they apparently visited with family members, and it was late evening before I knew they had reached the airport safely.

The next question was, How would everyone react to the prospect of peace? I organized meetings with the private sector, the unions and the military officers. With the high command, we concluded that the guerrillas would make a show of strength to prove they were not going into the talks because they were losing. The first guerrilla attack came the day after La Palma and confirmed my suspicions that Villalobos intended to exert his influence, scorning Cienfuegos' "weakness" in talking to us. The Army stepped up their own operations throughout the country.

One week after the La Palma talks, the Army suffered a devastating blow. We lost Colonel Domingo Monterrosa, the military commander for the entire eastern region, along with two of the Army's best combat officers, when their helicopter went down in Morazán. The guerrilla radio immediately claimed they had killed Monterrosa. Until a thorough investigation was made, we could not be sure whether the helicopter crashed due to a mechanical failure or a bomb or a surface-to-air rocket.

When the pieces of the helicopter were brought back for analysis, I went to look at them. As an engineer, I still do not rule out structural failure or metal fatigue as the possible cause of the crash. But the American experts seemed convinced that a bomb had been planted on board, among the passengers in the center. The bomb could have been inside the captured guerrilla radio transmitter being carried on board, or it could have been planted by someone. The priest of the San Miguel barracks, who had gone to say Mass in the village and died with the officers, had taken two altar boys with him. One disappeared just before the fatal flight back. The missing altar boy might have planted a bomb in the priest's satchel.

In preparation for the second session of the peace talks, I formed a working group to discuss proposals with each interested sector: the political parties, the Church and the armed forces. We wanted to propose a Christmas truce, a complete cease-fire. The Church approved. With the military, I suggested that the officers discuss the proposal among themselves without my presence. The officers' discussion was inconclusive. They felt inhibited, unwilling to approve or disapprove the truce.

"Well, then it's my turn to talk," I told the commanders. For eight hours, the military officers and I went over the plan in which I laid out my political and strategic analysis of what the truce would mean.

Finally, one of the commanders spoke up. "The President has proposed a strategy and we are meant to respond yes, no or maybe. I feel we should recognize that so far everything that he has proposed to us has been successful. Therefore, I think we should follow his lead and support his decision in this."

The other officers agreed to back my judgment in the second round of peace talks. I took this as a mandate to make a decision, but with prudence. I had to be sure of the outcome.

To see how the guerrillas were thinking, I took advantage of a forum in Los Angeles provided by an academic group that wanted to stage a debate between the government and the guerrillas. I decided to send Rey Prendes and a team with instructions to raise certain points in the debate and see how the FMLN representatives reacted. Afterward, we analyzed their responses carefully. We found that the guerrillas had more interest in a truce as a propaganda device than as a serious step toward a solution. We realized they would not seriously consider a cease-fire, so we reduced our next proposal. We would ask for a limited Christmas truce and humanitarian measures.

The problem of where to hold the second round of peace talks led to more delays. The guerrillas wanted to hold them in San Salvador itself. They hoped to organize impressive demonstrations and create the image of widespread sympathy for their position. They wanted the talks to be held in the glare of maximum public exposure, which rarely helps opposing sides to find grounds for compromise.

My greatest concern was their security. I could not take again the risks we had run in La Palma. The easiest place to protect the guerrillas would have been the international airport at Comalapa, where they could fly in from abroad or from small mountain airstrips. It was less dangerous than these caravans of cars on roads, but they rejected the airport plan. We settled on Ayagualo, a former seminary on a hilltop, run by the Church as a retreat, close to San Salvador and the airport.

This time, instead of guerrillas surrounding the meeting place, they had to rely on the armed forces for protection. The hilltop was under the jurisdiction of the Red Cross, the road below was controlled by the National Police, and three of the Army's rapid-reaction battalions patrolled the neighboring hills. Although we would have preferred not to involve foreign governments, the FDR-FMLN brought several ambassadors with them.

Because the second round was meant to be a working session, it didn't seem appropriate for me as president to go. We assumed that my presence would be needed later, after some concrete agreements were prepared. Still, I sent the highest-level delegation I could. It included the Minister of the Presidency, Rey Prendes; the Undersecretary of Defense, Colonel López Nuila; the Planning Minister, Chávez Mena; and the first alternate Vice-President, Abraham Rodríguez. The guerrillas sent Rubén

Zamora, seconded only by low-level representatives of the FMLN.

The guerrillas arrived at Ayagualo on November 29, 1984, with their own proposal. It consisted of a three-stage peace plan practically unchanged from the one they circulated in 1979. They wanted an end to American military aid in the first stage, guerrilla participation in the government and a cease-fire in the second, and by the third stage guerrilla forces to be welded into the "reorganized" armed forces. Then they would call for elections. It was as if they wanted the clock turned back, as if the people's effort in the 1982 and 1984 elections meant nothing, as if the armed forces had not changed at all, as if a Christian Democratic government did not exist, as if everything we had said in La Palma were erased!

They had gone back to the hardest line, which is the same tactic used by Marxists in labor negotiations: ask for every conceivable concession so that you can appear to give in on some while actually achieving exactly what you planned. Had our La Palma plan been my bargaining position, I would have started with demands like the removal of Villalobos from their military high command or reparations to be paid to those whose property was destroyed by the guerrillas. Instead, the guerrillas ignored my effort to be realistic and sincere and to work for the benefit of all. They refused to discuss humanization, discarded our cease-fire proposal and rejected even the Church's truce proposal.

After twelve hours of nearly futile discussion, the Ayagualo communiqué announced an agreement to "facilitate free movement on the roads for civilians from December 22 to January 3," and to continue the dialogue. The announcement was anticlimactic, but the speeches following Archbishop Rivera Damas' reading of the meager communiqué reached a crescendo. Zamora gave a political diatribe that would have caused consternation by itself, and Comandante Guardado followed him with what sounded like a guerrilla recruitment pitch. This was all being carried live on national television. I think Zamora and Guardado directed their remarks to their guerrilla comrades rather than the Salvadoran people. They were sending the guerrillas a message of how tough they could be.

No one missed the guerrilla message or its threat to the peace process. It was so obvious that, in the mansions of the Right, they uncorked the champagne to celebrate the demise of my peace initiative. Everyone in the country felt the surge of frustration and anger. There were those in the armed forces who thought Ayagualo meant the end of any compromise, leaving only a military solution. As my delegation reported back to me, I knew that if I did not do something to counteract the impact of the guerrillas' provocation, we would soon face a crisis and possibly a coup.

There was no time to wait. I went on television to respond in kind to the guerrillas. Weakness on my part would have meant the end of the dialogue, and I couldn't let down the people who had supported my effort. There are moments to be magnanimous and moments to hold the line.

"Here, before the people," I said, "I state that I'm willing to continue the search for peace, willing to continue the dialogue. But I cannot accept—I categorically reject—any position that is fundamentally unconstitutional. For this reason, I ask those who have taken up arms to rethink their proposal and come up with one in accordance with the spirit of the Salvadoran people."

After Ayagualo, the peace talks stalled. The guerrillas continued to seek more one-day stands, with access to all the media, but I refused. I could not see how progress can be made unless we sit down privately over a period of time, united by some greater principle than a need to share the public platform.

In the search for peace, there have been many attempts in other parts of the world. Some have succeeded and some have disintegrated. Everyone has a model they want the Salvadorans to try. Rubén Zamora says I am trying to follow the Venezuelan precedent. He is wrong. In the early sixties, when the Venezuelan imitators of Fidel Castro tried to launch their revolution, the dialogue was begun by the President with guerrilla leaders held in jail. The guerrillas were negotiating their way out of prison, obviously not the case in El Salvador. This meant a totally different balance between the Venezuelan government and the guerrillas.

Zamora wanted us to imitate the pattern of Colombia, where President Belisario Betancur negotiated a truce with several leftist guerrilla groups. He would prefer that model because Betancur permitted the guerrillas to keep their arms and maintain a military presence while they are organizing politically to come into the democratic process. This peace plan began to unravel when the M-19 guerrilla group decided to break the truce. In November 1985, guerrillas stormed the Palace of Justice in Bogotá, seizing the Supreme Court justices as hostages. The guerrillas' treachery and attack on the very legal basis of the government left Betancur no choice but to order the Army to retake the palace, at the cost of more than a hundred lives. No one mentions Colombia as a model for peace negotiations anymore.

From the beginning, Betancur's situation was very different from the Salvadoran context. Colombia's guerrillas have been fighting for over twenty years. Their numbers are small, relative to the total population, and the areas where guerrillas persist are insignificant. Colombia had not suffered the extent of economic damage from the guerrillas that El Salvador has. It is also worth noting that Colombia's guerrilla groups are divided, not united. Betancur could negotiate a separate agreement with each group. Colombia also has the advantage of a process of democratization which has gone on for twenty years, strengthening the civilian government in relation to the military powers.

El Salvador is no more Colombia than Vietnam or Lebanon. Our history is our own, and the way to peace must be uniquely Salvadoran.

Shortly after the Ayagualo fiasco, Archbishop Rivera Damas came to consult with me. He was about to leave on a trip abroad and expected to be in contact with the FMLN. He wanted to know if there was any way I could suggest to continue the dialogue. I told him that the political space in which I could move was very small. The Left would have to understand the effort I would be making, because with the Right up in arms about the guerrilla stand at Ayagualo, my policy of pacification would now become an issue in the March 31 legislative elections. I thought the elections could serve to create greater support for the peace process, but this would depend partly on the Left. The actions the guerrillas took before the election could influence the outcome. The composition of the new National Assembly would determine my ability to take further steps toward peace.

Unfortunately the guerrilla response was the exact opposite of what I had hoped. Their attacks on highway traffic, on towns and on economic targets increased. Instead of promoting peace, the climate of tension and discouragement increased before the elections.

10

Turning Point

FOR the fourth time in four years, I watched anxiously as the Salvadoran people went to cast their votes March 31, 1985. Somehow it had not gotten any easier, this fragile act of faith in the democratic process. Riding the Army's Huey helicopter, doors open, I cruised over Cuscatlán Park, where San Salvador's polling places were strung out like carnival stands. I asked the pilot to circle once more. The voters clustered below would choose the next National Legislative Assembly and 260 mayors.

I was pessimistic about our chances. The Christian Democratic Party was stronger now, but it would take a landslide for us to win the thirty-one seats needed for a majority in the assembly. I expected us to fall two or three seats short. I had resigned myself to three more years battering against a hostile legislature determined to stop me on every major issue. The assembly had already stacked the election deck against the Christian Democrats by designing an electoral law to handicap us.

But as I looked down from the chopper, the vote count was not the only concern I had. Intelligence reports warned that a car bomb full of dynamite might explode in one or two voting sites. The extreme Right planned the bombing to scare away voters in San Salvador, where the Christian Democrats are strongest. Vaguer threats came from the leftist guerrillas, who once again pretended that the elections were a meaningless contest between U.S. puppets and were forcing anyone who wanted to cast a ballot to run the risk of guerrilla attacks.

The gratification I felt from observing large numbers of voters in the park was mixed with my concern that a high turnout might mean more casualties. Each car I saw below seemed suspicious, and I tried to locate where the soldiers stood, wondering if they had searched the area thoroughly enough. There was nothing more I could do, so I signaled the pilot to go on. The helicopter leaned away from the park, gaining speed for the flight east to San Miguel.

Less than an hour later, the dust billowed up from the landing field at the army barracks there. Colonel Monterrosa's successor, Colonel Miguel Méndez, was waiting for me. Beside him, I saw Miguel Charlaix, a Christian Democratic colleague who had been appointed as commissioner for the eastern region. Charlaix could hardly control his enthusiasm.

"The voting is practically normal," he shouted as we got away from the noise of the helicopter. "Normal! Nobody's bothering us."

Normal elections had never been the norm in this region. Last year in the presidential election, the Right had been instructing voters how to cast ballots with threats, while the guerrillas had launched a military assault on San Miguel. The absence of violence and harassment was unprecedented for the Christian Democrats here. Colonel Méndez reported only one incident that marred the morning: a young priest, on his way to say Mass in a village, had been killed by guerrillas, apparently for violating their ban on election-day travel.

Violence could detract from the elections and discourage voters, but whatever happened, the ballots would still determine the way power in El Salvador was exercised over the next three years. Since 1982, the rightist parties had controlled the legislative power, and through it the judicial branch as well. As long as they retained this control, they could block much of our Christian Democratic program for economic reforms and an effective judicial system. That is why the Right had insisted upon its tricky electoral law. The assembly had written the law to permit parties to appear separately on the ballot but form a coalition behind one candidate. Voters without education often recognized parties by their symbols: the fish for the Christian Democrats, the clasped hands of the PCN and the cross of ARENA. The PCN and ARENA wanted to combine forces, but they did not want to lose those votes of the peons who learned over the years which symbol their landlords expected them to mark on the ballot.

With four rightist parties, minority representation was a must, built into the system. Seats in the assembly were based on a system of proportional representation: one seat would go to the party winning a plurality, the next to the runner-up, and the third seat depended on the margin of votes between the competing parties. If the front-runner had significantly more, his party took the extra seat.

The rightist parties also believed that a lower turnout would favor them. Consequently, more confusion and complications were introduced into the 1985 voting plan. The locations of all the polling places were changed. In 1982, voters had been allowed to vote at any polling place with their identity cards. In the 1984 election, computerized registration lists had complicated the system, but persistent voters had still been able to find their assigned place. Special tables had also been set up for those displaced by the war and unable to return to their hometown. But this time, everyone had to vote in the town where his identity card was issued. This rule practically disenfranchised all the refugees from war zones. Hundreds of thousands of displaced families would be unable to travel back to their homes. The rightists assumed that the destitute war victims probably leaned toward the Christian Democrats.

To undercut us in the capital, the electoral law prohibited relatives of the standing President from running for office. Because Alejandro was gaining support for his work as appointed mayor of San Salvador, the Right wanted to prevent him from winning the voters' approval. The Right howled about nepotism, but politically they feared another Duarte for the next generation of voters.

And just to be sure that any protests about the conduct of the election would be settled their way, the rightist parties set up the Central Election Council with a two-to-one majority in their favor.

Faced with this biased electoral law, but under the pressure of time moving us toward elections, I vetoed only two parts of the law: the disqualification-of-blood-relatives clause and the hidden-coalition clause. The Right challenged the constitutionality of this line-item veto. Of course the Supreme Court justices were all selected by the Right, including the Chief Justice, Chachi Guerrero. There was talk that a Supreme Court ruling charging me with violating the constitution would give the assembly a basis for impeaching me. But Chachi and the other justices did show some caution, invalidating my veto, but without ruling that I had violated the constitution.

By election day, ARENA and PCN were overconfident about

their power to the point of boredom. "The ARENA people have sent their servants to stand in for them as poll watchers," Charlaix observed to me in San Miguel. "Most of the PCN officials didn't even bother to show up."

Charlaix, other party members and I walked among the voters lining the main street of San Miguel, with Colonel Méndez and his men around us. Surprised to see their President striding by, people clapped and followed us. The March sun beat down on the men and women gathered around the tables with voter-registration lists and ballot boxes. The Election Council, in its rightist wisdom, had organized polling places outside, in the open air, rather than in schools or public buildings. Leaving voters without even the minimal protection from the weather or terrorist attacks was another way to try to discourage voter turnout.

The turnout in 1985 was significantly below the three previous elections, but in San Miguel I began to feel that the rightist plan to control these elections might fail. We had calculated on losing in the eastern provinces, just as the Christian Democrats had lost there in the previous elections. But I sensed that a change in the conditions in San Miguel boded well, and I headed back to the helicopter more optimistic.

The presidential helicopter eased down into the walled courtyard of the Sixth Battalion barracks in Usulatán shortly after noon. Colonel Miguel Vasconcellos, the commander, took me down to the streets where the voting continued. There was no lack of ARENA and PCN poll watchers here, and I heard very little applause as we walked down the almost silent street.

"Any trouble?" I asked Vasconcellos.

"We encountered guerrillas in Jucuarán this morning when we took the ballot boxes in," the colonel said. "A firefight, nothing significant."

"How slowly the hours are going by today," I commented.

"I feel the same way," responded the colonel. "My men are spread too thinly trying to protect the polling places. We're really vulnerable to guerrilla attacks today."

The outward empathy between the colonel and me made me want to smile. Colonel Vasconcellos was, after all, a classmate of d'Aubuisson's at the Military Academy. Class ties had often proved the strongest bond among the military officers. But whatever his own political views, Vasconcellos' behavior this election day seemed above reproach.

I had no doubts whatever about the political conviction of the other officer who greeted me there, Colonel Manuel Antonio Nuñez. This was the same man who had laid his life and career on the line to stop the election fraud that rigged the 1972 presidential election against me. Back on active duty, he was now on the front lines in this embattled province of Usulatán, guarding the democratic process.

After lunch in the officers' mess, I was heading for my helicopter when two more choppers swept into the barracks enclosure. One of the ubiquitous U.S. congressional delegations observing the elections had arrived. The congressmen recognized me with surprise and ran over to shake hands.

"Everything looks good, Mr. President, we're sure going to do our best to see you get the aid you need," one said.

There had been some doubt about the U.S. preferences in this election. Unlike the last round, when the Right claimed that the Christian Democrats were being favored and funded by the United States, the rumors this time said the embassy sympathized with the Right. U.S. diplomats allegedly worried that the rightists would have no stake in the democratic process if they lost control of the assembly, according to the press, so they feared a Christian Democratic victory. Losing their legal powers might tempt the rightists to go back to their illegal means of exercising influence, the diplomats warned, a throwback to the days of terror and military coups. Whatever the Americans thought, I did not feel the election results would be influenced by them.

Flying back to the capital after seeing San Miguel and Usulatán, I added up again the provinces where I thought we would win seats. I concluded that we still lacked a majority in the assembly. Back at the presidential residence, my grandchildren came bouncing down the stairs from the television room. "We're winning," they chanted. My wife was in charge of all the grandchildren while our sons and daughters worked at the polling places. The first phone call I took from Vice-President Castillo explained where the children had gotten their optimistic election prognosis. "The SIN television network's exit poll predicts we're going to win a majority," he said.

"That's just a poll," I replied.

By the fourth call, Castillo was beginning to change my mind, but my attention was elsewhere. The Army informed me that 230 soldiers were caught in a guerrilla trap in San Fernando, deep in the northern mountains of Chalatenango province. The guerrillas attacked the town on all sides, backing the Army up against the Sumpul River that separates El Salvador from Honduras. The last helicopter, before the guerrillas closed in, carried away the ballot box. Then clouds settled down over the mountain battleground. The clouds made it impossible to evacuate the men or send in any reinforcements or air cover.

I placed a call to the Honduran President, Roberto Suazo Córdova. To ask the Hondurans for permission to cross their border was a touchy matter. Here we were, fourteen years after the Salvadoran armed forces invaded Honduras, having no choice but to ask the Honduras government to permit Salvadoran troops to cross the border.

Suazo Córdova listened to my plea. After warning that communication links to the border were tenuous, he said that he would alert his troops to receive the retreating soldiers. The besieged Salvadorans were to forge the river and surrender to the Hondurans, who would load them into trucks to be driven to a safe border crossing. The symbolic surrender was needed to soothe Honduran feelings, just as it would be necessary for both governments to deny the next day that a Salvadoran invasion had ever taken place.

Because of the tense military situation, I was not able to be at the Christian Democratic headquarters as the election results began to come in. I headed for the Chiefs of Staff war room and discussed with the commanders my conversation with Suazo Córdova; at that time there was nothing more we could do until we heard from the men fighting out of San Fernando. When I arrived at the party election center just after 11 P.M., I looked at Alejandro's computer projections based on 7 percent of the votes. The first results from San Salvador showed a narrow margin of victory, instead of the usual two-to-one advantage.

"We're weaker than I thought," I told Alejandro.

"That's what I've been agonizing over for the past two hours," Alejandro confessed. "All the results I've seen are like this."

But an hour later, with more returns from the countryside, we reached the point where the Christian Democrats could be sure of at least thirty seats. By 1 A.M., we had what I refused to believe was possible: at least a two-seat majority in the National Assembly.

Despite the euphoria throbbing through the old building and warehouse where the Christian Democrats had survived, had been held hostage, sweated and celebrated, I could not feel the joy of this crucial victory. I tried to sleep later and failed. By 5 A.M., I was up to prepare for an early-morning meeting with Colombia's President Belisario Betancur. He was stopping over briefly at the airport on his trip to the United States via Central America.

Betancur was fresh, animated and keen. I tried hard to cover up the fact that I was distracted, tired and worried because there was no news of what had happened at San Fernando. I learned only after Betancur left that the men were safe.

Even with that load lifted from my mind, the election victory did not seem real to me. My uneasiness proved correct. By the next day, I learned that the Right had not resigned itself to allowing Christian Democratic control of the assembly. This election had not gone the way ARENA and the PCN had planned, so they fell back on the alternative strategy: use the Central Election Council. Both parties charged fraud and irregularities, demanding that new elections be held. Their scorn for the election was so great that even the Army was chastized for allowing the alleged fraud while its men were guarding the polls.

At the presidential residence, my closest advisers appeared almost immediately: Alejandro, Castillo, Rey Prendes, Chávez Mena and the others. They looked calmer than I felt after two nights without sleep.

I was ready to play the card I had never used before.

"If necessary, we'll call the people out into the streets to defend this election," I said. "I'm not going to let them steal this one from us."

We considered what that could lead to, and what our alternatives were. After all these years when we demanded that the law be observed, the Right could now frustrate us by acting legally. They controlled the Central Election Council, which had the power to enforce their false claims about the election. We were faced with a choice of letting the Christian Democratic majority be stolen with due process or abandoning the legalities to use whatever power we had to force a confrontation.

How would the military forces respond? Did the rightist parties have tacit support among certain commanders to extract the election results they wanted? It was unclear whether the antidemocratic thinking of the Right still found enough response among certain officers to undermine the government. Was this an attempted coup with legal maneuvering?

I called General Vides. The Minister of Defense agreed that the armed forces must make their position clear publicly and immediately. The Right had gone so far as to charge regional commanders and Colonel Bustillo of the Air Force with being involved in electoral fraud. The armed forces' mission had been to defend the electoral process from outside attacks. Now the officers were being asked whether the military commitment extended to defending the results from internal threats.

Vides scheduled a televised press conference the next day, Holy Wednesday, the last working day before the Easter holidays.

That afternoon, Alejandro's nine-year-old son found me in the garden of the presidential residence, a house on the slope of San Salvador's volcano. "Grandpa, come quickly, the generals are on television," he said.

Upstairs, in the family's living room, Alejandro, my grandson and I each took an armchair and watched the large screen where Vides frowned down on us. The television camera then pulled back to show the men seated on either side and behind him. There they were: every officer of the high command, service chiefs and battalion commanders—two rows of stern-faced men in combat uniforms.

The general read his statement, weighing each word with unrelenting emphasis. The armed forces' mission was to guarantee the election process. They had paid a high price to ensure that the greatest number of Salvadorans could vote. In the Army's five-week campaign to prepare for the election in as broad an area as possible, seventy-one soldiers died, 146 were wounded. The officers' faces showed that they did not take these casualties lightly.

"The elections are not a card game to be replayed at will," Vides said.

The Army had remained totally neutral in these elections, and those finding fault with the process should present proof that the armed forces acted incorrectly in any way, the general challenged. He brought up the specific examples the Right had mentioned, mocking their triviality. Had a gun gone off accidentally at a polling place? Was a minor allowed inside the voting area? Treating the Right's charges ponderously, the general made them look ridiculous.

Then Vides Casanova took questions from the journalists.

Would the armed forces accept whatever decision the Election Council took regarding the complaints, even if they called for new elections? The armed forces would abide by the decision of the legally constituted authorities, Vides insisted.

Alejandro looked at me, wincing.

"But all political forces must act honestly to consolidate democracy," Vides Casanova warned sternly. He made it clear he had no sympathy with the attempts to rearrange the results to fit the Right's strategy. The very presence of all the officers surrounding him showed a collective decision of the armed forces. Vides Casanova spoke for the armed forces. His message went to the heart of El Salvador's privileged conservative class, the ones who had used the military rule in the past, who had financed ARENA and d'Aubuisson's campaign. The old allegiances had changed.

The armed forces supported the electoral process and the choice made by a majority. The Right cannot turn back the clock to 1972, or 1932. The armed forces are giving their lives to stop a guerrilla movement. They want a popularly elected government to defend, one that has the support of more than the moneyed class.

No sooner had the general's image faded from the screen than the television anchorman announced that the PCN had withdrawn their complaints about the election, disauthorizing their leader who had lodged the protest. The Right had no intention of going against the armed forces.

Without a word, I picked up the phone and asked for General Vides. "You cornered them with democratic concepts, General," I said.

Alejandro, smiling, caught my eye as I finished my call to my Defense Minister. We had won the election, and something even more unprecedented had taken place. The armed forces had backed the democratic process.

Now we could begin to put the Christian Democratic philosophy to work on the problems of the country.

11

Bad News

THE messengers of bad news are familiar to me. They have come so often during my life. But nothing had prepared me for the news that Captains Gilbert Henriquez and Mauricio Chávez Cáceres brought me one September day in 1985.

The Cabinet members working on the next budget had been arguing all morning and into the afternoon as we sat around the iron table under the thatched pavilion in the garden of the presidential residence. When Captain Henriquez, the army officer in charge of presidential security, quietly called me away from my budget session, I knew he was one of those messengers.

"Inés Guadalupe has been kidnapped," he said.

There was no doubt, no possible mistake. Before telling me, the captains and the guards had raced to the university, the site of the frantic radio message "Gunfire at Forty-ninth Street! They've taken Carnation!"

"Carnation" was the code name for Inés Guadalupe, my first

child, born thirty-five years before. My first thought was, How will I tell my wife? But I could not let my feelings take over. I began reeling off what had to be done. I told the captain to summon my three other daughters here to the residence for safety. My two sons were abroad. We had to contact them. I was already phoning General Vides Casanova, to alert the armed forces to search for the kidnappers. But the security forces already were mobilized.

We later reconstructed what had happened just after 3 P.M. on September 10, outside a private university on one of San Salvador's busiest streets. Inés Guadalupe had borrowed her mother's car because her own needed repairs. She liked to drive herself, so the two bodyguards assigned to her (as to each of my children) months earlier, after we learned of kidnap threats, drove a separate van. That day Inés was giving a lift to her classmate Ana Cecilia Villeda.

Inés Guadalupe was always helping someone like that. Ever since she was a child, she had been more concerned about the people around her than about herself. She is thoughtful, giving, patient. She is love. There is some of each parent in a child, but I have a communion with Inés. She inherited the better part of me. In every human being, along with the good and the bad in us, there is some degree of nobleness. Whatever nobleness I have, whatever concern for the poor and unfortunate, she has intensified, surpassing me. She also inherited her mother's character, so she absorbs pain without letting it show. I knew how she was reacting to the terror of being kidnapped. Wherever she was, she would turn inward, keeping her suffering to herself.

There were eighteen guerrillas waiting in the vicinity of the university. About 130 altogether participated in some way, stealing the four cars the kidnappers used, acting as lookouts or jailers at different points. On Forty-ninth Street, the men lingered along the sidewalk in the crowd, some dressed in suits, some in jeans or work clothes. As Inés' bodyguards parked their van by the curb, with Inés pulling in behind, the guerrillas emerged from among passersby in synchronized motion. Seven men closed in to the sides of the cars. The others moved vehicles into position at opposite ends of the block.

Both bodyguards were shot immediately at close range, one still in the van, the other on the sidewalk as he went to open the passenger door for Ana Cecilia. One man was grabbing Ana Cecilia while another reached for Inés. In those few seconds, the kidnappers apparently were unsure which woman was my daughter. Their leader yelled, "Take both."

In the next instant, they would have known which was my daughter, because Inés fought back. Ana Cecilia did not resist the man pulling her toward the waiting truck. Inés would not be pulled away until the man grabbed her by the hair. Her instinct to fight had been reinforced three days earlier. Worried about her brother Alejandro, she had asked him to be careful. She had a feeling he was going to be kidnapped. Alejandro told her that he would fight as hard as he could against the kidnappers because he assumed that, once taken, he was doomed. All my children took for granted that, as president of the country, I could not make bargains for their release.

Inés' resistance turned to desperation when she saw the blood of her bodyguard flowing across the pavement. "Why?" Inés yelled helplessly at her kidnappers. "Why are you doing this?"

"We've come for Daddy's little princess," the leader said, then cursed Inés in more insulting terms.

"Don't kill me. I have children," Inés pleaded as they threw her down in the back of a closed van and began blindfolding her.

"If we'd wanted to kill you, we'd already have blown your brains out," the man replied.

One of her bodyguards, left for dead by the kidnappers, rolled himself off the sidewalk and down into a ravine. He managed to send the radio message heard by the presidential security team. They reacted immediately, contacting a lieutenant who was already driving in the direction of the university.

Captain Henriquez took a van with his men and reached the scene within ten minutes. A retired colonel who happened to be taking classes there had picked up the weapons and the radio of the dead bodyguard. He then found the wounded man and drove him to the military hospital. From the radio communication center, the presidential security officers had notified the police to start setting up roadblocks on the highways leading out of the city. We had the city sealed twenty minutes after the kidnapping.

The kidnappers, however, operated with speed and precision. Within ten minutes they had changed Inés and Ana Cecilia to another vehicle, abandoning the van that witnesses would describe. Within fifteen minutes, they were outside the city limits on the northern highway. They turned onto a dirt side road. Within an hour, there was no more road, and Inés was forced to begin a walk up the mountainside that would last all night.

Once I knew the armed forces were taking action, I had to go to my wife. She was at her office, running the program she had started to help needy children. She had not been well, and our doctor met me there. When I had called to say there was bad news, she thought I was referring to her brother, who was being operated on in the United States.

"It's worse," I told her.

When I said they had kidnapped our daughter Inés Guadalupe, she said firmly, "No, that's not possible." But the moment she saw my face, the truth sank in. She cried, and the doctor gave her a tranquilizer.

"Let's go home," I said. I had given orders that all our children and grandchildren were to be brought to the presidential residence. I knew that my sons, Alejandro and Napoleón, would be here on the first flights available.

When I first learned that Inés Guadalupe had been kidnapped, I did not speculate about the possible motives. I took action. Because the best kidnap plans are always subject to unforeseen flaws, we had to try to take advantage of any mistake the kidnappers might make. In the first few hours, there is still a chance to find the victim. That is why it was so important to mobilize all the security forces, to control traffic and search everywhere. Only later did I sit down to face all the dread possibilities and the political ramifications.

The first lesson one learns about kidnappings is that the family goes through unbearable emotion. Relatives and friends come running to offer their sympathy, but their pity and fear often make it worse for the family members. They come bringing psychics who claim to know where the victim is. But all their bewildering words do little to alleviate the tension of waiting day by day for news that does not come. The emotional strain hinders any calm, clear analysis of what has to be done to resolve the kidnapping. I knew that the first thing one had to do was select a mediator to take charge of the case. While the armed forces started their search, I named a committee to manage the crisis. They would work out the choices to be made and recommend a decision to me.

I chose my son Alejandro to be on the negotiating committee, for three reasons: his analytical capacity, his experience in dealing with kidnappers—gaining the safe release of his brother-in-law several years ago—and his role as the representative of the family. Similarly, I chose General Vides for his ability, for his experience in the kidnapping of his brother and as the voice of the other interested party, the armed forces. I also needed someone who would understand both the family and the armed forces, but be able to synthesize their views. The third man was Abraham Rodríguez, with whom I had founded the Christian Democratic Party, the lawyer who also serves as first alternate vice-president of the nation.

Rodríguez, Vides and Alejandro actually managed the negotiations, but others joined the coordinating committee in specific roles. Rey Prendes, my minister of communication, served as the sole spokesman throughout the crisis. Chávez Mena took part in the diplomatic end of the negotiations. The Deputy Defense Minister for Public Security, Colonel López Nuila, who had professionalized the security forces, headed the investigation of the crime.

I never took a decision until the committee had presented their analysis and recommendation to me. Many times I had my own point of view, but I relied on the committee to handle the day-to-day progress toward a resolution of the kidnapping crisis.

When my Cabinet was called together the morning after the kidnapping, I told them that, except for those assigned to the special commissions dealing with the kidnapping, we were all going to carry on normally. I would carry out my duties as president and be briefed by the committee at the end of the day. The government must not be paralyzed by the crisis, because surely that was the objective of the kidnappers, whoever they were. But who had taken my daughter?

I knew that both the violent Right and Left wanted to destroy me. I have always been willing to give my life to the cause of democracy, and my wife, my sons and my daughters all encouraged me in this struggle. They were fully aware of the risks we took. Even so, the violence against Inés Guadalupe still seemed incomprehensible. It is so hard to understand that human beings can be like wolves, preying off one another. Even worse, they attack an innocent woman, not me. They want to use our love for our children to wound us. How dehumanized have we become?

One of the basic objectives for my government is humanization. To humanize El Salvador means to regain the basic moral values we have somehow lost. Humanization means respect for each woman and each man. It means placing the welfare of El Salvador's children above our quarrels. I think we can find ways to agree on this, step by step. That is why I made humanization of conflict the basis for peace talks with the leftist guerrillas.

The first days after Inés Guadalupe was taken, I still was not sure that the guerrillas were responsible. We worked hard to identify those involved. Twenty-four hours after the crime, the police had drawn composite portraits of the kidnappers from witnesses' descriptions. They had found two abandoned cars used by the kidnappers, but the operation had been so professional that the only fingerprints left were those of the hostages. The overall pattern was identical to earlier kidnappings carried out by leftist guerrillas. Those stealing the cars which had been used identified themselves as members of the Farabundo Martí National Liberation Front.

But the FMLN did not claim responsibility for the kidnapping. Its Radio Venceremos said nothing. The civilian allies of the FMLN, known as the Revolutionary Democratic Front, denied any link to the kidnappers. We could not rule out the possibility that a dissident group among the guerrillas might have kidnapped Inés Guadalupe on their own. There was also a possibility that the Far Right could be responsible. Our analysis left us with the agonizing conclusion that we could only work on the police leads and hope that the kidnappers would reveal more by trying to contact us. The security forces, using every lead they had, raided thirteen suspected guerrilla hideouts in the city, arresting around thirty people. We hoped our pressure would bring some response.

The second day after the kidnapping, my personal secretary, Carmen Vallejos, answered the telephone.

"Mrs. Duarte, we have your daughter," a man said. He thought he was talking to my wife, and Carmen was trying to draw out more information. But he said only that we were to tune in a certain military-radio frequency the next day at noon.

My son Alejandro followed the instructions, sending out a message on the military frequency. But there was no response. Later, an army radio operator with a patrol, code-named Jupiter, received a message saying that the President could talk with those who held his daughter on that same frequency. The voice gave his code name as Liberty, and said I must respond as Jupiter.

We had decided against my being personally involved in the negotiations. But now we reconsidered because perhaps it was the only way to establish contact with the kidnappers. I sat in front of the transmitter until we picked up the signal. Every nerve taut, I felt I was shaking.

"This is Napoleón Duarte. To whom am I speaking? Over."

"You know what this is about?" crackled a man's voice.

"You're the ones who know. Duarte here. This is Jupiter. Who are you?"

"Listen, I'm going to give you a message from your daughter."

"Fine, I'm listening."

Then I heard a tape recording of her voice. "Friday, the thirteenth. Papa, I'm okay. Ana Cecilia is with me and she's well. I miss you very much. Please do whatever they ask. Tell Mama and the children that I miss them and love them."

Her voice stopped. The man said, "Inés Guadalupe Duarte Durán is in good health."

I interrupted him. "She needs the following medicines," I said, reading off the prescription for her migraine headaches. She would suffer them several times during her captivity. The voice replied that it had all been taken care of. He then began dictating in the most derogatory and insulting terms a list of demands:

NUMBER 1: There must be direct and personal communication between us and Napoleón Duarte.

NUMBER 2: All communication must be kept secret, without any intermediaries, without the press.

NUMBER 3: The agreement must be secret.

NUMBER 4: To continue the conversation you must prepare three MX 100 radio transmitters [no such model exists] to be given to the International Red Cross to hand over to us at a time and place that will be specified later.

NUMBER 5: If Napoleón Duarte follows these instructions, he will know what the conditions are for the freedom of Inés Guadalupe.

NUMBER 6: The search is useless. She's out of your reach, so every attempt to find her merely jeopardizes any resolution of this case.

NUMBER 7: It depends on Napoleón Duarte whether or not there is a favorable outcome.

NUMBER 8: Comply with these demands and don't ruin things. We'll find you later. Over and out.

"Who is this? Over." There was only silence.

Being unable to identify the kidnappers frustrated me. But the next day, five days after Inés Guadalupe was taken, the radio message began: "The Pedro Pablo Castillo guerrilla commandos of the Farabundo Martí National Liberation Front . . ."

They demanded we suspend all military operations, ground the Air Force and withdraw troops from the fronts. They were demanding that we surrender the country!

Not since the Greeks set out for Troy had so much been asked of an army for the sake of one woman. As much as I loved my daughter, I would never hand El Salvador over to the guerrilla forces. I told the armed forces to continue their normal operations, except in the area where we thought Inés Guadalupe was being held, in the eastern mountains of Chalatenango province.

I was wrong in my guess about her location. But we had good reasons for believing she must be a prisoner in Chalatenango. First, the route of the kidnappers, as far as the police had been able to track them, headed north. Second, the area was known to be a guerrilla stronghold, with scattered hideouts that were hard for the armed forces to reach, near to the porous Honduran border. Third, the week after my daughter was kidnapped, nine mayors from towns in Chalatenango were taken off by guerrillas.

This tactic of kidnapping municipal officials began in the eastern region of the country after the election March 31, 1985, but the guerrillas in Chalatenango had not yet used it. All summer, we had been conducting secret negotiations for the mayors' release, but the FMLN made impossible demands. They wanted the Christian Democratic government to admit responsibility for certain guerrillas they claimed had disappeared after arrest. We could not confess to crimes we had no basis for acknowledging. There was little point in kidnapping more mayors except to sow terror or to prevent them from reporting back to me that Inés Guadalupe had been seen in their area. We did hear reports from peasants who said that two women had been walking with the guerrillas in Chalatenango.

Given all these indications, I ordered the military commander of the region, Colonel Sigifredo Ochoa, not to launch any offensives in a forty-square-kilometer area in those mountains. The guerrillas could mistake an army sweep for a rescue attempt and kill their hostages. Ochoa resented the restraints placed on his men. The Right would take advantage of his discontent later.

Despite the logic of our deductions, the place where Inés Guadalupe was held was not Chalatenango, but the slopes of the Guazapa volcano, within sight of San Salvador. Thus she was not spared the war. Our intelligence revealed two large concentrations of guerrilla combatants in the Guazapa area. Before approving the attack on their positions, I wondered if my daughter might not be there. But it seemed unlikely that they would hide her in a place where so many people would know her whereabouts. From a strictly military standpoint, we had to engage the guerrillas gathering in Guazapa, so our soldiers forged into the area with air support and artillery fire. Later I learned that this was one of the worst moments for Inés Guadalupe, forced to hide with her captors as the war once again swept through the battle-scarred hills.

The third radio communiqué from the guerrillas rejected "all gestures from abroad." It was their response to international condemnation of their action and to the efforts by world leaders to obtain her release. I was thankful for the overwhelming expressions of sympathy reaching us from around the world.

I sent my own message back to the kidnappers. I told them the International Red Cross had agreed to drop off new radio transmitters they requested in the designated area. (These apparently never worked, because the guerrillas continued to use other frequencies, even opting for short-wave radio, on which it seemed the entire press corps was listening.)

In return for the radios, I wanted the Red Cross representatives to be able to see Inés Guadalupe and Ana Cecilia to ensure that they were being treated well. This was never allowed. I also challenged the kidnappers' assertion that they were from the FMLN, citing the denials given abroad by their spokesmen. Finally, I sent a message to my daughter saying, "Your children, your sisters and brothers, your mother and I are all well. We love you and we are with you."

The reply on the next radio contact was the first set of demands: the freedom of thirty-three guerrillas. Another name was added to the list later. There were precedents for an exchange of prisoners—even the Israelis have done this. In El Salvador, a deputy defense minister held by guerrillas for more than two years was finally released in an exchange. So was General Vides' brother. But many factors had to be weighed in coming to such an agreement. There are possible and impossible demands. Their demands were designed to be rejected and to cause friction between me and the armed forces. In the case of the mayors, the FMLN so far had insisted on the impossible. Now they had my daughter and Ana Cecilia as well.

We had to construct a consensus for any agreement that we might decide to offer the kidnappers. Our strategy included consultations with all branches of the government, with representatives of the parties, the private sector, unions, the media directors, the Church and the U.S. ambassador.

Even Major d'Aubuisson initially laid aside his hatred for me and offered his support in the moment of crisis. Later, he had second thoughts. The Right was tempted to take advantage of the kidnap negotiations to create divisions among the armed forces. D'Aubuisson's ARENA party abstained when the National Legislative Assembly voted on an amnesty for one of the prisoners on the kidnappers' list, a Costa Rican convicted of arms smuggling.

Also on the list of prisoners to be exchanged were two leaders of the Communist Party arrested in August, Mauro Américo Araujo and Hector Acevedo. We knew that the plans to kidnap one of my children had been developing for some time, but I believe the capture of these two leaders was the primary motiva-

tion for taking my daughter. The guerrillas suffered several setbacks in 1985, and the efficiency of our armed forces kept
increasing. In April, one of the FMLN's key political strategists,
Castellanos, defected to us. It was a moral blow to them, but far
worse was the loss that same month of a complete archive of
guerrilla documents, captured along with Comandante Nidia
Diaz.

Hers was another name on the kidnappers' list. An army helicopter had spotted a guerrilla column marching along a hillside.
The soldiers on board fired on the guerrillas until all were hit. A
second helicopter which landed to pick up survivors, a woman and
a child, found knapsacks full of papers and files as well. On the
flight back, the woman tried to throw herself out of the helicopter. When I was shown a photograph of the disheveled woman I
could hardly recognize her, but it was clearly Nidia Diaz. She
had sat across the table from me during the peace talks in La
Palma.

She had been wounded and was in poor health, suffering from
malnutrition, parasites and lice. (My daughter ended up with
some of the same problems, which are endemic to guerrilla life.)
The Red Cross visited Nidia Diaz as soon as she was captured, and
their doctors recommended delaying the delicate operation needed
on her leg until she was in better health. There were protests
from abroad by an association of doctors charging she did not
receive adequate treatment, but her care was exceptional. Micro-
surgery was performed on her leg after special arrangements at
one of our best private hospitals. I also received a letter from her
mother, which I personally answered. Nidia's mother was concerned about her daughter's medical care, but she also told me
that she had received threatening phone calls and that shots had
been fired at her house. I ordered the police to provide her with
protection.

Nidia Diaz refused to answer any questions. She would say only, "You know all about me. You have the documents."

Among the captured documents were plans for the kidnapping of each one of my children. Each of the five guerrilla groups was allotted one target. We increased the protection surrounding my family, and my youngest daughter, Ana Lorena, escaped one kidnapping attempt. Perhaps complete protection was impossible over a long period of time. I have a large family, all with their own lives to carry on.

Anyway, the guerrillas seemed to have chosen other targets for a while. They assassinated four U.S. Marines and seven civilians who happened to be sitting in a sidewalk café. One of the killers was wounded. He died on the operating table, but his identity led to other suspects. Some escaped by leaving the country, but our investigation succeeded in dismantling a guerrilla network. The number of prisoners we had, especially the two Communist leaders, precipitated the kidnapping of Inés Guadalupe by the Communist Party's guerrilla wing, known as the FAL (Armed Forces of Liberation). We learned this through our investigation, but the FMLN was still refusing to take responsibility for Inés Guadalupe and Ana Cecilia, even though most of the thirty-four on the kidnappers' list were FMLN leaders.

The problem with the list of thirty-four was that we had no record of any arrest for nine of them. We investigated each name on the list. As a gesture of goodwill, I immediately ordered the release of two persons on the list, along with the wife of one of them. There were no formal charges against these three as yet, so their release was not difficult. To free the other twenty-two would require a political act, circumventing the legal process. This undercut one of my basic objectives—to create a fair and viable judicial system in El Salvador. We are still far from achieving the ideal legal society, and in times of war saving lives takes precedence over due process.

Our efforts to find everyone on the kidnappers' list took me into jails and barracks where they claimed clandestine cells existed. The radio message from Inés' captors would say, "You claim you can't find So-and-so, but you haven't looked in the basement of the National Guard." Off I would go to look. There would be nothing there.

One of those unaccounted for was Mario Aguiñada García, the son of the Communist leader Mario Aguiñada. We discovered that the FMLN's radio broadcast of April 19 reported that he had died "heroically" in combat. The Army found false identification papers on the body of a guerrilla combatant that day. His photo matched exactly with those of Mario Aguiñada. We therefore reported he was dead, but the kidnappers kept demanding we produce him alive.

The radio messages insisted we must find all thirty-four persons on their list, while denying that the mayors' release was even on the negotiating table. All along, we insisted that any deal must include both the mayors and my daughter. Publicly, the kidnappers would claim to be only the Pedro Pablo Castillo Commandos, but privately we now had confirmation that the FMLN was behind them.

President Betancur of Colombia called me to say that Mario Aguiñada had admitted to a Colombian diplomat that the FMLN was behind the kidnapping. I received similar calls from Mexico, France, Venezuela, Panama and Costa Rica, each with confirmation from their own sources.

Unknown to us, Willy Brandt, president of the Socialist International, sent his own emissary to discover who was behind the kidnapping. Hans-Jürgen Wischnewski, Brandt's envoy, went first to see Fidel Castro in Cuba, then on to Nicaragua before coming here to report. We knew Wischnewski from his previous peace missions to Central America. His contacts within the FMLN this time assured him that they could free my daughter and the mayors if a reasonable number of concessions were made. We thanked Wischnewski for his effort, but since another negotiating channel already was opened through the Church, we thought it better to rely on Archbishop Arturo Rivera Damas. I believe in solving Salvadoran problems among Salvadorans.

By this time, Inés Guadalupe had been a captive for three weeks. The kidnappers sent a photograph in response to our pleas that someone be allowed to check on her physical state. She and Ana Cecilia stood before the camera, dressed like guerrillas, looking down at a current newspaper. By radio, her recorded voice gave the required plea for us to give in to the demands, then she added a personal message: "Tell the children to keep on studying, especially Patricio, who must work hard to get good grades on his finals. This will be the best present he can give to me when I get home."

Patricio, then fourteen, is the eldest of her children. She asked her eleven-year-old daughter Lucrecia to look after the youngest, Alfredo, who was six. The children had gone to stay with their father, from whom Inés Guadalupe had been divorced a year earlier.

As negotiations over the prisoner exchange dragged on, our political unity began to crack. The emotional empathy of the first moments after the kidnapping drained away and opportunism seeped in. Voices on the Right began to say that I wanted to save my daughter no matter what it cost the country. Other voices, trying to split the Christian Democratic Party, said I would abandon the mayors in order to free Inés Guadalupe. One newspaper published a story from the Spanish Civil War of a mayor who let his son be killed rather than give in to enemy demands. The article practically suggested I let the kidnappers murder Inés Guadalupe.

Colonel Ochoa smelled a chance to weaken my influence within the armed forces. He had cultivated the image of a tough, uncompromising guerrilla-fighter. Ochoa had led a mutiny against Defense Minister García in 1983, and been transferred to Washington. When I became president, Generals Blandón and Bustillo argued that they needed Colonel Ochoa to take command in Chalatenango, where the guerrillas had been hitting hard, even seizing the army base there in El Paraiso. The generals said Ochoa had learned that political maneuvering was no longer acceptable in the armed forces. Colonel Ochoa himself gave me his word that his only ambition was to serve as military combatant. He promised unswerving loyalty to the democratic government.

Yet, one year after aggressively taking charge of the army troops in Chalatenango, Colonel Ochoa called in his officers to consider whether or not they approved of my policies. Combat-weary officers who had seen their comrades die in the struggle with guerrillas were asked if they approved of my freeing the prisoners they had captured. In this way, Ochoa manipulated his junior officers including cadets at El Paraiso into signing a declaration rejecting any concessions to the guerrillas.

The document that circulated among the armed forces was tantamount to a call to rebellion. It said that, with due respect to the feelings of a father, national security should come first. "The price is too high and unjust for the freedom of one citizen." The arguments in the document were identical to some petitions that some rightist organizations were promoting. After I had studied Ochoa's declaration, I sounded out other army commanders to learn their thoughts. Their support reassured me, and General

Vides gave me shrewd advice on how best to nullify Ochoa's insubordination.

"Let me manage this," the general said. "I would rather treat this declaration as an expression of concern, not incitement to rebel. Instead of making it a matter for discipline, I would present it to all the commanders for discussion." Vides explained that in this way we would bring all the officers to a well-understood consensus. Ochoa's ploy would be openly rejected by his colleagues.

Over the weekend, Vides consulted the officers individually. On Monday, he presented the matter to the assembled commanders. He pointed out that the guerrillas' hope for a revolution in El Salvador had been diminishing ever since the armed forces united with the elected democratic government. The guerrilla demands in the kidnapping were intended to cause dissension, to split the officers from the President. If the Army limited the President's power to negotiate or withdrew its confidence from me, then the FMLN would have its greatest victory.

What was the value of a few prisoners compared to the power to undermine the democratic government? he asked. That, not the release of the prisoners, was the guerrillas' ultimate objective. As the general finished his argument, Ochoa began to look as if he were a dupe of the guerrillas.

After eight hours of discussion, the matter was put to a vote. Did the armed forces have confidence in the President's ability to conduct these negotiations in the best interest of the country? The officers voted in my favor. Seeing the overwhelming support of the officer corps, Ochoa raised his hand to make the vote unanimous.

Within three months, Ochoa's continued political posturing would exhaust the patience of the high command. He was ordered off to a diplomatic post.

Vides' intuition about the armed forces' reaction had been correct again. As happened in the past, his leadership was able to keep the armed forces united. Instead of creating resentment, his handling of the Ochoa challenge brought the officers together on the issue.

Another aspect of the Ochoa incident was the supposed intervention by the American ambassador. The day before the military officers met to discuss the Ochoa declaration, U.S. Ambassador Edwin Corr appeared on television expressing strong support for me. The ambassador's words would not have influenced the outcome of the military debate, because by the time he spoke General Vides had already determined that the majority would back us. Later, Ambassador Corr called to let me know that the question had come up in the interview. His reply made clear that the United States had full confidence in my presidency. Despite rumors that the U.S. government did not approve of negotiations with kidnappers, Ambassador Corr never pressured me in any way. He was kept informed and was always ready to help.

His kindness, in fact, led to a political blunder on our part. More than a month after the kidnapping, the family's nerves were ready to snap. If there was no progress in the negotiations for Inés Guadalupe and the mayors, it seemed that the guerrillas might take another member of the family to increase the pressure. This had happened in another kidnapping case. My wife was distraught any time one of her daughters or grandchildren was away from her side, but we could not all remain prisoners in the executive mansion.

We decided that some of us should spend alternate periods in the United States, with two daughters and their children going for a couple of weeks. Alejandro was making these arrangements when Ambassador Corr graciously offered places on an American military plane for the women and children. He said the plane

259

would be stopping here on its way to Miami, and why not let the family all go together? Alejandro thought this would be a comfort to everyone and accepted.

It was a mistake. The October 14 departure appeared to be a panicky evacuation of family members. In the public eye, we created more tension, not less. But for my wife and me there was a great sense of relief.

My wife had found peace through prayer. She and a few close friends kept a vigil one night, praying until morning. Then she felt calm, certain that God was with us. I told her to pray for me, for the negotiators and for support in any decision they would have to take.

I asked Archbishop Rivera Damas to take upon himself the responsibility for finding a solution to our plight with his contacts with the guerrillas. On October 15, Monsignor Rivera went to a meeting place near the Guazapa volcano to talk the rebel leaders into accepting a formula for release of all hostages. He took with him a letter to Inés Guadalupe from her mother, along with a rosary and a Bible. My wife wrote, "Tell your kidnappers that I have forgiven them, and I ask God to forgive them because they cannot know the pain they have caused me."

The six guerrilla leaders, two from the Communist Party and one representative from each of the FMLN groups, met with the Archbishop and Father Ignacio Ellacuria, head of the Jesuit Central American University. The Archbishop made his proposal to the guerrillas, after which they withdrew to consider it. The Archbishop's plan was to begin with the freedom of Inés Guadalupe and Ana Cecilia, in exchange for the release of the twenty-two prisoners from the list whom we held. The Church then would take the responsibility for getting the government to allow the transfer of ninety-six wounded guerrillas to foreign hospitals, with the understanding that the captured mayors would be freed.

Father Ellacuria argued strongly that time was running out for a reasonable political solution. The consensus to release even the twenty-two prisoners would not hold up much longer. He said some agreement had to be reached, even if the mayors were not included, or all would be lost. But the guerrillas had come up with a list of another twenty-nine prisoners. These were not combatants, but persons assigned to infiltrate unions, provide intelligence or buy goods for the guerrillas. This next group of twenty-nine would be exchanged for the mayors, the *comandantes* said. The prelates said that such an exchange was not feasible, but that the Church would use its good offices to speed up the legal process in these cases.

The guerrillas agreed to the Archbishop's plan. To us, it seemed that Monsignor Rivera had promised far more than we were able to offer. The Archbishop assumed we would accept the transfer of so many wounded because he knew that the humanitarian argument would win me over. I was inclined to trust his fairness, and certainly we could not refuse to honor the Archbishop's commitments without undermining the basis of all our peace negotiations.

Finally, an agreement seemed to be within reach. In order to work out the logistics of how the exchange would take place, two delegates from the FMLN and two sent by me were to meet in Panama City. For the first time in five weeks, I began to think Inés Guadalupe might be coming home within a few days. But on Friday, October 18, the guerrillas' radio message crushed our hopes.

"Liberty calling Jupiter. Eighth message from the Pedro Pablo Castillo Commandos for Napoleón Duarte: We announce for October 22 the following operation: the simultaneous exchange of Inés Guadalupe and Ana Cecilia for the twenty-two FMLN comrade prisoners on the list, and the prisoners of the FMLN in exchange for the evacuation of ninety-six wounded and, at the same time, the freedom of the imprisoned union organizers."

The radio message went on to say I must formally promise to investigate the disappearance of the nine guerrillas unaccounted for, and make all the arrangements for international supervision of the exchange.

The agreement they were proclaiming was *not* the one the Archbishop had presented to us in writing. Monsignor Rivera told us he had been tricked. He had not committed us to freeing the FMLN's twenty-nine second-rung activists. He knew I would have a hard task convincing the other political forces to accept even the Church proposal, let alone this guerrilla manifesto.

Alejandro, General Vides and Abraham Rodríguez came to me for the final decision. But their conclusion was that the government could not accept. The negotiations had failed. They had been scuttled by the guerrillas. There was nothing to do but accept the possibility that Inés Guadalupe would remain a prisoner. The chances of any rescue operation were very poor. The odds were against getting her back alive.

I was left alone with the reality that all was lost. All along, my political intuition told me that the guerrillas had set their demands excessively high in order to make a solution impossible. They wanted to destroy me. They wanted to incapacitate the Christian Democratic government. Despite my intuitive pessimism, however, I had to exhaust every possibility before giving up. I wanted to be sure there was not a single door they had left open before I accepted that negotiation was futile. Then I saw the door. Panama!

We would go to Panama. They had called the meeting to "finalize'' their plan, but we would go there to negotiate further. There was nothing to lose, and it would be the first face-to-face contact between the guerrillas and the government since the kidnapping. I told Monsignor Rivera I was sending Rodríguez and Rey Prendes. My first thought was that Alejandro would not be able to sit calmly across the table from his sister's kidnappers. Then I realized that I wanted him in Panama to make decisions on the spot.

As we sat together in the back seat of the armored presidential car, speeding home through the night from the Presidential Palace, I suddenly turned to Alejandro. "You and Fidel Chávez Mena will go to Panama as well," I said. "The two who are in the room negotiating will need to have you outside. Then they can go out for consultations at difficult moments."

The Archbishop presided over the Panama session. He was angered by the guerrillas' manipulation of his effort, but he never gave up insisting that an agreement could be reached. The guerrillas designated as their two representatives Mario Aguiñada and Salvador Samayoa. As education minister during the first junta after the 1979 coup, Samayoa had decided to resign and join the guerrillas. He had forgotten that when he was captured a few months later, I convinced the Army to let him go, and he flew to Mexico.

Sitting together in Panama, Aguiñada, Samayoa, Rodríguez and Rey Prendes went over the ground that forty days of negotiation had laid. The first session lasted twelve hours. After a few hours' sleep, they started again. The second session lasted twenty hours. At one point, when the FMLN was insisting on the twenty-nine extra prisoners, Rey Prendes walked out, saying no agreement was possible. He consulted Alejandro, who told him the only thing left to do was try to get Monsignor Rivera in to see Inés Guadalupe so that she would know the truth about our efforts and to give her Communion.

But the Archbishop would not let the talks end. He kept the delegates in the room. By dawn, there was an agreement. Alejandro called me and General Vides around 4:30 A.M. to get our approval. The solution was the same one that the Archbishop had proposed to the guerrillas at Guazapa. There was also an understanding that in the future no one's family members would be used as hostages.

As the mechanics of the agreement were being worked out, the Panamanian Army chief, General Manuel Noriega, came into the room to inquire about the progress. The Archbishop explained the arrangements, then Aguiñada expounded further, implying that the guerrillas' proposal had been accepted. Rey Prendes was furious. He said Aguiñada could rectify his mistake or they could all leave now. In front of Noriega, the terms were then established: the release of twenty-two prisoners and the transfer of wounded in exchange for the two women and twenty-five municipal officials. This operation would take place in two days' time, on October 24.

That day I went to Army headquarters to be able to monitor all aspects of the exchange by radio. Despite my faith in the efficiency of the Red Cross, I worried that some tiny cog could stop the whole clockwork movement of hostages, prisoners, medical evacuees and escorts. What if someone wanted to sabotage the deal? It would take only one false shot in some remote area to destroy the good faith of everyone involved.

Archbishop Rivera and the ambassadors from Mexico, France and West Germany were to go to the deserted town of Tenancingo to meet the guerrillas bringing Inés Guadalupe and Ana Cecilia. The prisoners who wished to rejoin the guerrillas would be driven to Tenancingo. We chose Captain Gilbert Henriquez to go with Monsignor Rivera to get Inés Guadalupe. I would not risk sending another family member into guerrilla hands. In case something went wrong, I wanted the person there to be capable of quick, sound decisions. I also wanted someone Inés Guadalupe would be glad to see. Kind, capable Captain Henriquez had won the affection of my whole family while protecting me. He was the man.

From the moment the Red Cross vehicles arrived in Tenancingo, Henriquez held the radio and narrated what was happening. Tenancingo has been a ghost town of roofless houses since a fierce battle was fought there in 1983. Many of the refugee families from Tenancingo live just a dozen miles down the winding dirt road, in the village of Santa Cruz Michapa, where Alejandro and an army escort awaited the arrival of my daughter. The villagers and refugees gathered excitedly in the town square to wait with them. Two helicopters stood in a nearby field, ready to fly the freed hostages home.

The appointed hour of the exchange came and went. Minute by minute I looked at the silent radio, waiting for word from Henriquez. He reported that there was a delay. Then he said the Archbishop had been informed that Inés Guadalupe was twenty minutes away. There was no more emotional moment for me that day than the instant I heard Henriquez say, "I can see Inés Guadalupe. She's coming. She's okay."

He kept on describing the scene, telling us she was hugging the Archbishop, the ambassadors, and "now we're hugging each other." But the guerrillas were not yet through. They told Henriquez there would be a ceremony. Inés Guadalupe and Ana Cecilia could not leave yet. The guerrilla commander asked to use Henriquez' radio to speak to Comandante Américo Araujo at the prison where he and the others were waiting to leave. I felt the emotion in their voices as the *comandantes* greeted each other by radio.

There was a discussion of whether or not the prisoners' Red Cross vehicles should have an army escort on the road. The guerrillas said no. Finally the truckload of prisoners ground into motion, and Inés Guadalupe, along with Ana Cecilia, climbed into the Red Cross car. Then the commander told Inés Guadalupe that the guerrillas who had been assigned to guard her wanted to bid her farewell. They were children, barely in their teens. As the endless hours of her days on the mountain went by, she had taught them a little math and grammar. With sorrow in her heart for the tragedy of their lives, she got out and went to hug each one of them. Their presence had been a reminder of the possibility of humane feelings among us, in stark contrast to the one masked guard who had always been in the room. He was the guerrilla assigned to be her executioner should any escape or rescue attempt be made.

Once the car was driving down the winding mountain road toward Santa Cruz Michapa, we lost radio contact with Captain Henriquez. Intermittently we heard something. I felt another wave of relief when Henriquez said they were coming into the town. Alejandro and Inés Guadalupe saw each other from a distance. She got out of the car and ran, crying, to him. The people applauded, and cheered, "Viva Duarte!"

Alejandro had asked the nun in charge of the local school to lend him a room where he could take Inés Guadalupe and Ana Cecilia to rest and be seen by our doctor. Both were barely able to walk. They had been marching with the guerrillas for three days; they trembled and their leg muscles cramped. The doctor gave them pills for the pain, a little water and a cola. Inés Guadalupe would not let go of Alejandro's hand.

An unexpected problem came up. Inés Guadalupe said she was not going in the helicopter. She associated the helicopter with the bombing, and the sound caused her too much fear. I told Alejandro to do whatever he thought best. He sent away the military helicopter, keeping the civilian one. Then he explained to his sister that the released prisoners were moving up the road below them. The wounded were going to be transported down. They would not expect to see any other cars. Since there was no protection along the road, he did not want to risk driving down with her until it was all over. When Inés faced the prospect of several hours' delay, her desire to see her children and parents overcame her fear.

"You decide what's best," she told Alejandro.

"Come on, we're going by helicopter," he said.

Over the radio I heard Alejandro's satisfied voice. "We are about to enter the helicopter. Inés Guadalupe is fine, she's with me. Don't worry any longer."

"Thanks be to God," I answered. "I entrust her to you just until this journey is over."

The helicopter landed on the athletic field of the Military Academy in the pouring rain. The television cameras watched us. They watched Inés Guadalupe run to her mother, her children and me. We all hugged each other, and she reached over to bring Ana Cecilia into our circle. Ana Cecilia's mother lives in Los Angeles, so only her aunt and uncle were there. It was just like Inés Guadalupe to be thinking about including Ana Cecilia in this moment of reunion with her family.

Of course I was happy to have my daughter safe, but I worried about the mayors, the other parts of the exchange that day. I also knew there would be long-term consequences. There was a political cost to pay for this momentary happy ending. Everything in this world has its cost. I had to consider how the other political parties would use this against me. I also knew that all the energy spent in negotiating could have been applied to trying to find peace, to trying to rebuild the economy, to reuniting our people in a participatory society. The suffering my family and I had been through was no different from the pain many other Salvadorans have felt. My only hope was that as president I could change El Salvador and lessen the suffering.

12

Looking Forward

WHEN I finish my term as president, I hope to write a sequel to this book. First, I would like to write how we made peace. I would like to write how the structure of the economy changed from a rigid, lopsided, dependent economic system to a dynamic, evenly distributive, self-sustaining one; how the political structures became vibrantly democratic; how the social structure became multifaceted, representing everyone with dignity. Finally, I would like to describe how our values changed. Respect for each individual is the foundation of a nonviolent, tolerant and mutually beneficial society. When the structures and values of Salvadoran society exemplify a democratic system, then the revolution I have worked for will have taken place. This is my dream.

Revolution is a process, not the act of taking power. The process of the revolution may begin with a change of government, but the revolution takes place only when there has been a transformation of the economy, the social patterns, the armed forces, the education and culture of a country. To carry out a revolution, the leadership must have an ideology and the political, economic and social strategies to apply it. These strategies affect all sectors of society and the international factors as well. They must respond to the conditions at any given moment.

The conditions in El Salvador are very different in 1986 from the ones I faced in 1980. They will continue to change. I have begun the democratic revolutionary process by setting short-term, medium-term and long-term goals, using five policies to achieve them: humanization, pacification, democratization, participation and reactivation of the economy. The method that I use to carry out my policies depends on the political space available at any time.

This political space is determined by the action and interaction of the Right, the guerrillas, public opinion and international influences. I am always working to expand my political maneuvering room by obtaining positive responses from different sectors of society. Sometimes the space that I have is not large enough for the programs I want to implement. Then I have to adjust my plan and choose priorities. Once I decide to go ahead, it is not enough to say, "This is what we must do." I have to convince the people. An autocrat can give orders; I must give the reasons why.

Beginning with the most practical of my policies, economic reactivation, my plan has to take into account both the objective and subjective problems. Objectively, El Salvador's economic panorama was bleak when I became president. Due to the guerrilla warfare, many parts of the country lie in ruin. With 400,000 displaced persons, families have been unable to plant even their subsistence plots. Besides the lost crops, the direct costs of guerrilla sabotage amount to over $200 million a year. Capital has flown the country and no one has wanted to invest in El Salvador.

Subjectively, the attitude of businessmen was pessimistic. The agrarian and banking reforms promoted by the Christian Democrats led the private sector to take an antagonistic attitude toward our government. They wrongly believe that we are against the free-enterprise system. In fact, our aim is to increase the private sector by allowing more people to participate. Let there be thousands of entrepreneurs! We are not antibusiness, only opposed to monopolies and cartels.

The economy has to be democratized, too. The concentration of power in the hands of any one sector is dangerous. Why should a handful of bankers hold the power of decision over all applicants for credit? The banking reforms were necessary to guarantee credit for a wider range of people. If any small group has the power to control just one link in the economy—whether credit or transportation or marketing—that group will take advantage of everyone else involved in production. The solution is not to give the government total control over the chain of production. State capitalism has failed repeatedly. The Christian Democrats believe that the just median can be found between too much government intervention and too little.

The role of the government should be to direct the orchestra of the economy. The government sets the pace and corrects the mistakes of individual players. Harmony can be created when the government is sensitive to the social needs of the country and knows how all the instruments can work together.

Traditional economists see the economy governing the universe. By studying its variations, they tell us how we should fit into the free-market scheme. Social benefits are meant to be a by-product of the unrestrained pursuit of profit. Marxist economists, on the other side, interpret the economic science to tell us how only state control can benefit the people. The benefits to the state and the people are one, in their view. The Christian Democratic view is that the free-market economy must serve the needs of human beings. We start from the premise of what the economy should do for society, then we find ways to adjust the economy, not adjust people. This we call "Economia Social de Mercado" (Social Free Market Economy).

In January 1986, I found the political space for an economic plan designed to alleviate the crisis without making the poor bear the brunt of an austerity program. The depreciating value of our currency, the debt and the budget deficit, the unemployment and inflation, all required urgent measures on the part of the government. The economic experts, including those at the U.S. Embassy, were pressing me to take drastic measures to rationalize the economy without taking into consideration the effect on the poorest Salvadorans. I knew that their economic package would not fit into the existing political space—where I was walled in by the Left and the Right.

After listening to the president of the Central Bank, I said, "I'm sorry, but I cannot accept this program. After twenty-five years of fighting for the poor, I am not going to make a decision to sacrifice them to an economic theory."

Instead, I proposed adjustments to their economic plan. Rather than a simple devaluation, there had to be monetary reforms. I added a social dimension to the plan, making sure the measures would have less impact on the poor than on the rich. For instance, the new exchange rate for the dollar would double our cost of oil, but because the world price was falling, we had a cushion for the impact of the devaluation. We structured the impact so that petroleum products used by the poor—diesel for buses, propane gas for cooking, kerosene for lighting—would rise by only a small percentage. The price of gasoline—a luxury here—was raised higher.

Because we knew that the devaluation would inflate the costs of imported food and medicine, we raised the minimum wage and gave a salary increase to public servants—except those at the top in the Cabinet, the courts and the legislature. A social gain was made because, for the first time, the minimum wage for men and women was equal. Up until now, women were paid less than men when they did the same work, side by side, in the fields. In this country, women have been second-class citizens. From now on, they will have the same rights as men.

Trying to close the budget deficit is a problem even President Reagan shares with me. The government spends more than it collects in revenue. While we are fighting guerrillas, there is no way to economize on defense. In the midst of poverty, the social services must not be cut back. Given the miserable living standard of most Salvadorans, the government should be spending more on education, health and the infrastructure. Without being able to cut expenditures, I had to increase our revenue.

Fortunately, we were aided by an outside force—the price of coffee. Although the prices of our export products had fallen for years, in 1985 a drought in Brazil sent the price of coffee upward. We placed a one-year 15 percent tax surcharge on coffee exports. The coffee growers were going to have to share their windfall profits with the people of El Salvador. The extra tax on coffee sales would help balance the 1986 budget.

I view the economy as an engineer looking at a hydraulic system. The water keeps flowing from one area to another: prices affect the economy as do interest rates, savings, exports, credit. The government policies are the valves on the system, which can be opened or tightened. While we cannot control all the factors, we can use the valves to compensate. The best system is when all the values are open and the system is self-balanced.

This is a structural change because the old economy did not permit the government to regulate the valves. Taxation is a valve that can be adjusted. There are wealthy lawyers and doctors who paid no taxes, so we decided that professionals will be taxed for their services just as salaried employees are. Revenue can be increased by cracking down on tax evasion. Our economic plan included a 50 percent bounty for anyone who exposes smuggling operations. We also banned the importation of luxury items to ensure that dollars earned by exports would not be wasted on foreign cars, electronic toys or whiskey. Austerity is not just for the government in times like these.

The economic measures I have taken reflect our values in protecting the poor. They will restructure the economy by diversifying production and stimulating the informal sector. They also will work in our favor in the war. Every program from the agrarian reform to credit for microenterprises counteracts the guerrillas' claim that only a violent revolution will create a government that helps the underprivileged.

The guerrilla claims are inconsistent with their actions. They have shown little humanity. Terrorism is inhumane because its proponents assert that their political end justifies any means, no matter how many innocent people suffer. The fear created is meant to bring change, but terror will only engender more violence. Humanitarian concern must come first before any bridges can be built over the political differences dividing us.

Humanization is one of my fundamental policies. The concept obviously affects our values, but also works on the structure of society. Eventually, humanization can change El Salvador from a totally disorganized society to one with intermediary organizations for every sector. Without guarantees of human rights, attempts to organize are risky. When people feel they have the freedom and the right to organize to defend their interests, then they will begin changing the social structure.

The basic human rights are our most precious possession.

Without human rights, nothing we value is safe—not our lives, our liberty, our right to justice under the law, our right to worship, our right to express our opinions. The basis of our rights is respect for the individual. Human life is sacred. Tolerance must replace hatred. Differences among us must be settled within the legal framework, not by violence.

In the present conflict, guarantees of human rights and controls over the abuses of authority are vital. If I can ensure that the security forces and the government work without abuses, then the people will come to our side in the prolonged war that the Marxist guerrillas are planning. Both the guerrillas and the government are trying to win over the Salvadoran people and show the world who is right. The people will decide between Marxist revolution and democratic revolution.

The military strategy of both sides is to take on the role of protector of the people, or, as the Left says, "vanguard" of the people. In the past, the armed forces were not protecting humble Salvadorans. There have been improvements in the armed forces, but when abuses do take place, there must be punishment. My first task as president was to work with the officers to change the methods of operation and the attitudes.

Within the mind of an officer, there can be two clashing mentalities—one to repress ruthlessly the threat he perceives to democracy, the other to uphold the legal process essential to a democracy. When I hear that someone reportedly has been arrested, I call the head of the police or the National Guard. I ask for an explanation. These days the response is usually that the person was investigated, detained and charged by a judge. A few years ago, those picked up on suspicion of subversion routinely disappeared or their dead bodies were found. The routine now is to investigate, capture and bring charges against the prisoner where warranted. When this does not happen, I investigate, and I can count on many officers who share my determination to guarantee human rights. The rapprochement between the people and the armed forces is essential to bringing peace to our country.

The armed forces have learned that this war cannot be won with guns and helicopters alone. This is why we designed the National Plan, which includes civic-action programs, renewed government services for those abandoned in war zones, and organization of the inhabitants to defend themselves. The old system of civil defense was nothing more than a group of bullies who went around extorting money for "protection." The new system of self-defense is truly controlled by the community, which elects leaders and assigns duties to volunteers.

There have been some charges that the Army carries out scorched-earth tactics in conflict zones. This is the opposite of our policy. It makes no sense to burn crops and houses of the people the armed forces are serving. Our whole policy is to increase production and improve conditions for the poor. Anyone who raises a crop, even though the guerrillas take their share, is trying to keep from going hungry. Unfortunately, fires get started in battles, but this is not our strategy.

The guerrillas, however, do use the strategy of economic destruction, without regard to who suffers. They blow up bridges, destroy power lines, burn buses and trucks. The poor are the ones left in the dark and stranded without transportation, while the rich live in Miami. The guerrillas plant mines in roads and footpaths. Many children and farmworkers have been killed or crippled by these mines, as have soldiers. The guerrillas have even planted mines in the public park in Santa Tecla, just because the police cadets would exercise in the park some mornings. The risk to the hundreds of children who played in the same park did not concern the terrorists. Their object is to inspire fear in everyone.

Salvadorans are tired of living in fear. Pacification is another of the basic policies of my government. In order to bring peace, I proposed a sincere dialogue. The moment came when I felt that I had the political space necessary to take the initiative, asking the guerrillas to meet me in La Palma. The guerrillas then responded with the defiance of the Ayagualo meeting, causing the political space to close in on me. After the 1985 legislative and municipal elections, I tried to work with Archbishop Rivera Damas and Monsignor Rosa Chávez to pry open enough space to reopen the dialogue. I decided that gestures of goodwill on the part of the government were the best way to revive hope for peace talks. Therefore, I quietly arranged for the release of some prisoners and helped some guerrillas to leave the country.

My premise is that anyone who wants to quit fighting and prefers to leave the country should find goodwill on the part of my government. There has been a continual policy of amnesty, and thousands have taken advantage of it individually. In 1985, two large guerrilla groups asked, through the intervention of the Church, for help in leaving the country. It was hard to confirm what was really happening. Although the departing guerrillas said they would leave their arms behind, we went to the place indicated and found nothing.

Another day Monsignor Rosa Chávez brought a woman *comandante* to see me. She did not strike me as the kind of woman who would rise to a command position, but we talked for a long time. She told how she had been recruited to join the guerrillas by Jesuit priests in Aguilares, how she then recruited others in her township, how she was sent to take part in Monsignor Romero's funeral, how she fought in battles. By 1985, discontent developed among her contingent and there was a consensus to leave the country in small groups. Then a mutiny occurred because everyone wanted to leave at once. In the confrontation, she was disarmed and a new commander took over. Half the group left, but the others—about five hundred—were stranded in the mountains near the Guatemalan border, starving. They wanted my help. I told Monsignor Rosa Chávez I would support his humanitarian effort to aid this group.

There has been a change in the guerrilla strategy during my presidency. The series of free elections has influenced the people's attitude toward the government, undermining the guerrillas' call for violent revolution. The greatest setback to the FMLN, according to defectors, was the peace talks in La Palma. The popular response to my call for peace was overwhelming. The FMLN saw that they were being pushed to a bargaining table where they did not have the advantage.

This was why their military strategist, Villalobos, criticized Cienfuegos after the talks. This is why in Ayagualo they took a hard line—all or nothing, with emphasis on our differences. Villalobos has taken the FMLN back to the strategy of Cayetano Carpio—Prolonged People's War. The guerrillas will avoid direct clashes, work on building cadres for the next five or ten years, and use terrorism in the cities to destabilize the government.

Their tactics have been designed to reduce the space for dialogue, but publicly they must continue to call for negotiations. The concept of peace talks has too much support in El Salvador and abroad for the guerrillas to reject them openly. Their actions—such as the kidnapping of my daughter and the mayors—simply sabotage the chances for talks.

Before Inés Guadalupe was kidnapped, the Church had asked the FMLN to respond to our gestures of goodwill. The document they sent back was full of contradictions and excuses for not pursuing the dialogue. For instance, the guerrillas blamed the United States for exerting too much influence over the armed forces, deluding them into thinking the war could be won. What the guerrillas were saying was that army morale was high. Their charges against the United States were meant to justify gunning down four off-duty Marines and seven civilians in a sidewalk café. The guerrillas blame the United States for blocking peace talks, but every time I go to the United States I find only enthusiastic support for my peace initiative.

The FMLN proposed that peace talks be continued in a public session in what remains of the mountain village of Perquín, the center of guerrilla activity in Morazán province where Villalobos operates. They told us foreign witnesses had to be present because the Church was untrustworthy. The FMLN publicly criticized the Church, then apologized to Monsignor Rosa Chávez.

The guerrillas sometimes charge that the armed forces keep me from continuing the peace talks. If I could call for talks in La Palma, if I could negotiate the release of twenty-five captured guerrillas in exchange for my daughter and the mayors, then obviously I would not be deterred from going to Perquín if that would advance the peace process. Nothing would be easier for me than to stage a show of peace talks for tactical reasons. I could go with great publicity and make my case. The mere fact that we can sit down at the same table means nothing in itself. But each time we sit down and clash, achieving nothing, the people will feel deceived. Those who oppose the dialogue will point to its futility. Therefore, before meeting again, there has to be some indication of a will to reach some resolution to benefit the people.

There is no point in further airing of our differences. I do not expect the guerrillas to become Christian Democrats. They are welcome to their own political philosophy. But why can't we discuss points of concordance if, as we say, we both seek the welfare of the Salvadoran people? All I propose is that we concentrate on human concerns, not on dividing up power. When we have found some common ground, then it will be time to publicly show the people that the dialogue brings results.

There will be no common ground as long as the guerrillas believe violence is the only way they can gain power. There are opportunities for all political beliefs within the democratic system. The working class can organize to gain power within a democracy. But the guerrillas, who claim to represent the workers, seem more interested in attacking Christian Democrats than trying to change the unjust structure of our society. During the negotiations in Panama for the release of my daughter and the mayors, the FMLN leader Mario Aguiñada told my representatives outright, "We cannot permit the democratic process to be a success in El Salvador."

Why? If the Christian Democrats demonstrate in El Salvador that a democratic system can bring about structural changes peacefully, then the polarized choice between domination by the rightist oligarchy and violent revolution by the Left will no longer be valid. The new option for Central America and other countries would be the democratic revolution. El Salvador is creating this model, while Nicaragua represents the leftist choice.

The Marxist leaders of Nicaragua based their revolutionary process on the force of arms. The Sandinistas' first priority after overthrowing Somoza was to control all the security forces, turning them into instruments of the party. Their revolution was bitterly divisive, alienating former allies within Nicaragua and abroad. The peaceful means of expressing dissent are repressed, but the Sandinistas justify their actions by blaming the United States for inciting violent opposition to the revolution.

When we, the other Central American countries, have tried to work out a regional peace plan through the forum offered by the Contadora nations, the Nicaraguan government has insisted that peace depends on a separate agreement with the United States. But we have not demanded that Cuba or the Soviet Union give us guarantees similar to those Nicaragua wants from Washington.

An agreement supported by the Contadora nations—Colombia, Mexico, Panama and Venezuela—which are backed by other Latin-American countries and the European community, should be sufficient. I think peace depends on our own will, the will of the people of Central America, not solely on the will of the United States. I told this to Nicaragua's President Daniel Ortega, when we first met at the inauguration of Guatemalan President Vinicio Cerezo in January 1986.

While we were waiting for the ceremony to begin, Ortega began talking to the Honduran President-elect, José Azcona, and me. Ortega raised the subject of the Church, accusing the Pope of interfering in Nicaragua's internal affairs. Azcona reacted, saying, "You are attacking the Church and I don't think that is right."

Ortega said the Americans were to blame for using Cardinal Miguel Obando y Bravo as their voice. I tried to explain to Ortega that the Church, by itself, has the duty to call attention to actions by the state that harm the people. It has been painful even to me at times.

"The Church has criticized my government very strongly in the Sunday sermon from the Cathedral, which is broadcast live all over the country," I told Ortega. "You should be more tolerant. Censorship is wrong."

Colombian President Belisario Betancur joined our discussion. He said that while some enemies are considered invincible, such as the United States, one could always find examples where they had been vanquished. "All except the Church," Betancur warned Ortega. "The Church is never defeated."

Ortega turned the subject back to his fear of the United States. I thought how U.S. thinking has been marked by the Vietnam syndrome, and how Nicaraguans had their own political ghosts.

"You have a Marine-invasion syndrome," I said to Ortega.

"You excuse all your internal repression because of this syndrome. The only cure for you, the only guarantee of stability, is the political force that comes from your own people, from respecting their democratic rights and respecting the right of other countries to self-determination."

Nicaragua complains about the countries that allow anti-Sandinista rebels to move across their borders, even though Nicaragua aids leftist guerrilla movements throughout the hemisphere. The Salvadoran guerrillas have their headquarters in Managua. The leaders reside there, combatants train there and in Cuba. Without Nicaragua as a sanctuary, a source of aid and supplies, the FMLN would not be able to maintain the same level of warfare. Nicaragua cannot continue to export revolution while demanding protection against the counterrevolutionaries simultaneously.

The Contadora document's twenty-one points would establish a reciprocal agreement to stop the flow of arms across borders, to halt the escalation in armament, to end the presence of foreign military forces and to promote democratic pluralism in the region. This plan should lead to pacification in Central America.

Our policy for democratization in El Salvador, moving from the short term to the long term, should help end the war, restructure society and change our way of thinking. Democracy cannot be conjured up in a country by the mere fact of free elections—even though elections are fundamental. Democracy cannot exist without elections, but there are often elections without democracy.

To become a democracy, the way we think about our differences must be democratic. When disagreements arise, the opponents must resort to public expression of opinion, to political organization around their cause, and to the courts when challenging interpretation of the law. A democracy cannot function without the intermediary structures such as a free press, political parties and a fair judicial system. Existing institutions may not be democratic, requiring a process that transforms them into instruments of democracy. This cannot be done overnight in El Salvador. One institution that has been in the process of transformation from an instrument of dictatorship into one that upholds democracy is the armed forces. The process involves gradual changes in philosophy, attitudes and leadership.

Not everyone adapts easily to the democratic way of thinking. Old prejudices remain. Since I became president, there have been several strikes by public employees which threatened the basic services to our citizens. During these crises I would be asked, "How can you go on permitting strikes that are obviously going to destabilize the country?" I explain that strikes are part of the democratic process. Not all strikes are tolerable within a democracy, even in the United States. There are labor tactics that can threaten national security or violate the law, forcing the government to act. The best solution, however, is to find points of national interest that both sides can agree upon. Both union leaders and the government want to improve conditions for workers in El Salvador. Both the government and the businessmen want to increase productivity and growth in the Salvadoran economy.

Each sector must learn to understand the other points of view, and nonviolent, constructive tactics must become routine. By searching for points of coincidence, we can supersede the destructive enmity that has plagued El Salvador. Unification of my compatriots is one of the hardest tasks I face.

In order to make any progress, there must be participation. This is the fifth policy of my government. Democratization is not to be confused with the concept of participation by all members of society. We have to go beyond the casting of votes and acceptance of constitutional rules. Participation means looking for ways to improve our society, assuming responsibility and organizing ourselves to act with solidarity in reaching the objective. This concept is rooted in my Boy Scout days, my Red Cross and service-club experiences. Every one of us—man, woman or child—can serve our fellow countrymen in some way.

In the jobs that we perform every day, there is frequently a special contribution to be made in improving our country. For instance, when the annual Secretary's Day comes around and the usual roses are being passed out, I remind all secretaries of the enormous power they hold. When any administrator tries to cheat a little, the secretary is likely to know. If the secretaries want to stop corruption, they can. It takes initiative, organization and participation, but, first and foremost, they can become a moral force. They can also serve as intermediaries between management and labor, because good human relations are essential to good management. Secretaries, who control channels of communication, can change their companies.

Everyone who takes part in a school committee, a neighborhood group, a cooperative or professional organization, has a chance to lead us toward a better society. The worst attitude is one that assumes that an individual is helpless and everyone else is to blame for our problems. If I can inspire more Salvadorans to participate, then there is hope for this country. I have always said it would take a miracle to resolve our problems. I believe in that miracle because I trust my people. If each of the five million Salvadorans decides to do what he or she can, the miracle will take place.

It should be apparent that all of these policies are interrelated; none works alone. Each policy has aspects that are political, social, economic and international in their projection. The programs of my government derive from these policies. I shape the program according to the political space I perceive at any given moment. The attacks and sabotage from Right and Left can reduce my political space in the center. Yet the center holds. The space I created was not there five, ten, twenty-five years ago.

Sometimes when I see the mountain in front of me, I feel that my shovel is useless. But I force myself to keep digging because we will level that mountain. The daily struggle cannot defeat me, because I look so far ahead and I have faith. I can see the democratic revolution, the changes in structures and values.

Although I realize the process may not be completed in my presidency, I know what I must try to accomplish. The only certainty I have is my Christian faith. Christ taught us to love the poor. I have dedicated my life to serving my people as I believe God wishes. I have found comfort in His words, the Forty-first Psalm, which begins, "Blessed is he who considers the poor."